THE TEXAS WATER SAFARI HAS A POLECAT IN IT

THE TEXAS WATER SAFARI HAS A POLECAT IN IT

A Story of Faith, Perseverance & Competing in the "World's Toughest Boat Race"

WILLIAM (POLECAT) STAFFORD

Floodplain Ranch

CONTENTS

CHAPTER 1

Introduction

THE TEXAS WATER SAFARI HAS A POLECAT IN IT
A Story of Faith; Perseverance; and competing in "The World's Toughest Boat Race"

"The Texas Water Safari is "The World's Toughest Boat Race." The challenges include a 262 mile race course down two Texas Rivers, white-water rapids, multiple portages, and the scorching south Texas summer time heat. Competitors have four days and four hours to paddle from central Texas to the Gulf Coast. There is no prize money for the winners; just Texas-size bragging rights for the finishers."

The Texas Water Safari is an annual canoe race that starts in the college town of San Marcos and ends in the shrimping village of Seadrift on the Texas coastline. The first official race was held in 1963 and the safari will be celebrating the 60th anniversary race in 2023.

The primary requirement is a boat powered only by human muscle. Racers must take all equipment needed with them, receiving only water, ice and food along the way."

My name is Bill "Polecat" Stafford and I have had the honor and privilege of competing in this race 30 times. The very unique and interesting stories that I have personally experienced during this race motivated me to write this book. The first two chapters are primarily focused on how this passion for paddling started for me and how that passion eventually turned into a long history of competing in "The World's Toughest Boat Race". The rules and the characters involved in the race were a lot different back in the 1980's and 1990's and that is when most of the interesting stories happened to me. Full names are only used when documented facts are mentioned and I tried very hard to write everything in a positive and funny way and only use first names or nicknames in order to protect the innocent from embarrassment. All of the stories are true, but I will admit that some of the minor details and the exact timing may be a little off because of the many years that have passed since that time. Thank you for your interest in this unique story and I hope you enjoy reading the book as much as I enjoyed writing it. Take care and God Bless.

How it All Started

The interest and fascination with "The World's Toughest Boat Race" first started for Bill back in 1972 when he was a 16 year old sophomore at Victoria High School. High School friends were calling Bill by a new nickname during this crazy time period because he had developed a reputation as a street racer and partier. The racing started with off road motorcycles when he was fifteen and then slowly evolved into car racing on the streets around town. The partying attitude was just getting started and it would get a lot worse over the next several years. Wild Bill was his new nickname and it seemed to fit him perfectly. The general consensus among his friends was that he would not make it very far into adulthood because of his reckless lifestyle. River fishing was still very important to him because he had spent a lot of quality time with his dad fishing for catfish on the lower Guadalupe river when he was younger. Hunting and fishing is what he had in common with his friend Steve and they would get together occasionally and put lines out in the Guadalupe river near Victoria.

Wild Bill and Steve launched their flat bottom aluminum boat at the Riverside park boat ramp and started stringing out trot lines several miles upstream. They suddenly spotted something very unusual in the fast current ahead of them. A very long and strange looking wood strip canoe was broke in half around a large tree limb that had fallen into the river. The tree limb had broken away from a cypress tree and was just barely above the water line. It was blocking most of the river.

They had never seen a canoe like this before and it immediately caught their attention. Steve turned the outboard motor and they headed for the shoreline. Wild Bill carefully climbed out on the unstable tree limb and tried to dislodge the canoe with no success. It was very swift through this section of the river so they decided to continue on with the primary objective of setting out trot lines. They would bring back some tools the next day to help with the boat rescue.

Wild Bill brought a sharp hand saw with him the next morning when they headed back up river to run the lines. Several large flat head catfish were pulled into the boat. They decided to give the canoe rescue another shot before going back to the boat ramp. Wild Bill carefully crawled out on the broken tree limb with his hand saw and was able to saw the damaged wood strip canoe completely in half. Steve was patiently waiting downstream to try and retrieve the two sections.

Steve secured the floating sections with a rope and was able to pull the two canoe halves over to the nearest river bank. They didn't have a plan and were trying to figure out how they were going to get the two long sections back to the Riverside Park boat ramp. The wood strip canoe was over twenty feet long and each section ended up being close to ten feet long.

The only thing they could do was load one section at a time into the limited space available in the flat bottom fishing boat. Two round trips to the boat ramp would be required because they were determined to try and salvage this interesting canoe and repair it. Steve had his old rusted out 1950 Ford pickup parked at the boat ramp. They were able to carefully stack one section of the wood strip canoe on top of the other in the bed of the truck before heading out to Steve's grandparents ranch.

Steve's grandparents owned a large cattle ranch that was located a few miles out of town and they had a man made fishing pond on their place. Steve and Wild Bill figured that would be a good location to test out the strange looking canoe if they were successful in piecing it back together.

Steve's cigar chewing, storytelling grandpa just shook his head in disbelief when they drove up and unloaded the damaged canoe next to his workshop. Mr. Albrecht was a very unique character and he would usually entertain them with his rambling stories about his interesting life experiences. Wild Bill always enjoyed listening to his unbelievable stories. Steve and Wild Bill would often spend a lot of their limited free time at his grandparents ranch during the dove and deer hunting seasons.

Steve also had extended family members that owned a business in Port O' Conner and that connection gave them the opportunity to go spend time there during the duck hunting season. Port O' Conner was also a great place to catch large red fish in the bay that surrounded the area.

Mr. Albrecht had a very nice work shop and he was good at fixing things, so they were hoping that he would offer to help them with the canoe repair. "What are y'all going to do with that junk", was his sarcastic comment after looking over the broke in half canoe. Mr. Albrecht could not see anything positive in trying to piece together this badly damaged canoe but he finally agreed to let them use his shop and tools to try and fix it. Mr. Albrecht agreed to supervise the repair because he could tell that they were very interested and determined to piece it back together.

The repair job ended up taking several days of hard work. It was a very slow process trying to re-attach this odd looking canoe back together. Mr. Albrecht was standing close by to offer his help and supervision. They were finally able to piece it back together by installing new supports on the inside of the canoe along the damaged area and then adding a new coat of fiberglass to the exterior.

They were proud of themselves when they finally had the opportunity to launch the repaired canoe into the pond. It floated and did not sink but it leaked some and the hull moved back and forth in the damaged area. Steve and Wild Bill were very excited when they finally had the opportunity to sit in the leaking canoe for a test run.

This odd looking canoe had been set up for rowing and was rigged out with two sliding seats that the rowers would sit in with their backs to the bow while they oared down river.

Steve and Wild Bill excitedly paddled the pieced together canoe around the pond with single blade paddles. They tried to maneuver the long and narrow row boat around the pond but eventually got bored and lost interest. They pulled the leaking boat back up on to the shoreline. Mr. Albrecht was enthusiastically watching the comedy show and was enjoying the entertainment.

Mr. Albrecht was having a good time and was constantly encouraging them to keep paddling. The wood strip canoe eventually became a permanent fixture on the shoreline of the fishing pond. Mr. Albrecht turned it upside down and made it into a sitting bench.

Wild Bill started bragging about the canoe rescue to other friends. The comment was made that it was probably involved in the marathon canoe race that came through the Victoria area a few weeks earlier. Wild Bill remembered reading about this race because it was front page news in the local newspaper. The article said that the Texas Water Safari started in downtown San Marcos on the San Marcos river and the race course eventually merged into the Guadalupe river near Gonzales and finished next to a fishing pier in San Antonio bay at Seadrift.

The canoe rescue and attempted repair ended up being his first exposure to the Texas Water Safari and that is when he started paying attention to the "World's Toughest Boat Race". The wood strip racing canoe probably belonged to one of the Seadrift rowing teams. There were a couple of local rowing teams from the Seadrift area entered in the water safari that year.

Wild Bill never tried to track down the owner of the canoe even after becoming good friends with some of the rowing legends from Seadrift a few years later. The negative thoughts that they might want their canoe back worried him. The pieced together wood strip row boat was probably still being used as a bench seat and was decorating the shoreline at Steve's grandparents pond. That was a secret that needed to be kept stored away under the cowboy hat and never talked about again.

CHAPTER 3

Passion for Paddling

Canoeing was not a passion for Wild Bill until 1976. That is when he started hanging out with a group of characters who liked to paddle the Guadalupe river above New Braunfels and occasionally do overnight trips on the San Marcos river below Martindale. The Guadalupe river at New Braunfels was mostly a canoeing and rafting river back then. The normal flow rate below Canyon dam was usually high enough for whitewater canoeing and rafting and had way to much flow for tubing.

The San Marcos river below Martindale was also a canoeing river with very little human activity below Martindale. It was common for paddlers to do overnight trips from Martindale to Luling. They would camp out on the river bank with no interaction or push back from the land owners. This area was covered with large ranches and was populated with cows and wildlife instead of people.

Wild Bill and his canoeing friends started doing weekend trips on the San Marcos river and they became friends with Tom Goynes. Tom owned a canoe rental and campground at Martindale and his property was a good place to start the trip down river. Wild Bill was a regular customer. Tom liked to tell interesting stories about his experiences in the Texas Water Safari. Tom won the water safari a couple of times with Pat Oxsheer and they were one of the first teams to use a rudder and double blade paddles. Tom has a funny sense of humor and can tell a pretty good story. Wild Bill and his friend Shane really enjoyed listening to the crazy water safari stories that Tom liked to talk about.

Wild Bill started taking his young girlfriend with him on some of these canoeing trips in 1979. They would do weekend trips on the Guadalupe river below Canyon lake and she seemed to really enjoy the adventure. Wild Bill would try very hard to keep the canoe upright through all of the turbulent rapids because he wanted to impress his new girlfriend. Darla would paddle for a while and then she would put the paddle down and start sunbathing. Wild Bill would then have to struggle to keep the boat upright through the class three rapids by himself with very little help from his sunbathing partner.

They were approaching the takeout spot when Darla said, "The rapids have not been that bad today". The comment irritated Wild Bill and the boat suddenly flipped over in the turbulent rapid just above the boat ramp. Darla had to swim through the large standing waves and over to the shoreline while he tried to pull the submerged canoe into shallow water. Darla excitedly yelled out, "What happened"? Wild Bill sarcastically answered, "that rapid was a lot rougher than what I was expecting". "Did you enjoy the swim"? It was amazing how that rollover happened so quickly and without any warning. The sudden wipeout at the Gruene crossing still remains a mystery today.

The weekend canoe trips along with Wild Bill's very different and outdoor focused personality helped convince her to accept his marriage proposal in October of 1979. Darla and Wild Bill were married on ground hog day in 1980 and Darla would have a lot of positive influence on him.

Wild Bill started another canoeing adventure in 1979. Several canoeing friends talked him into teaming up with them and doing a week long canoe trip that went through a very isolated section of the Rio Grande river just below Big Bend national park.

Joe, Steve, Shane and Wild Bill decided to load the boats up and head out there in March of 1979. They piled into Wild Bill's truck and started driving towards the Big Bend area on Friday afternoon. There was a party atmosphere going on inside the truck when Wild Bill was suddenly pulled over for speeding by a sheriff deputy in a small community between San Antonio and Del Rio. The sheriff deputy could smell alcohol inside the vehicle and asked, "Have you been drinking". Wild Bill respectfully answered, "No Sir". "Either you have been drinking or your buddies have been pouring beer all over you", was the deputies angry response. Wild Bill passed the roadside sobriety test and was issued a warning ticket for excessive speed. The only thing the deputy demanded was that someone else would have to drive. The Rio Grande river adventure was getting off to a bad start.

It was very difficult to find a shuttle driver and get important river information. W. E. Ten Eyck operated the Dryden Post Office and Mercantile store. He was the only person that could set up shuttle drivers and get your vehicle to the take out spot on a private ranch below Dryden.

Mr. Ten Eyck was a very interesting character with a dry sense of humor. Everyone always enjoyed listening to his stories about how challenging it was for him and his family to live in Dryden and manage the store there. Dryden is located in the Chihuahaun desert and is surrounded by sheep and cattle ranches. The area has a fascinating history and the only water source is a natural spring located nearby. That is where many conflicts between the native American Indian tribes, settlers and soldiers from Fort Davis took place in the late 1800's. Mr. Ten Eyck liked to talk about the history of the area and could tell amazing stories if you had the time to buy a cold drink and stay for a while.

There was a critter infested and partially burned down hotel building located next door to the Mercantile store. That would soon become the overnight camp spot for everyone after the week long canoe trip down the lower canyons was over. Wild Bill was the self appointed leader of the group and he would ask Mr. Ten Eyck if they could spend the night in the burned out building after they got out of the river and his answer was always the same, "I can stand it if you can".

There were a lot of terrible planning mistakes made on that first trip but the worst decision was to drive to the La Linda, Mexico put in spot first. There was a single lane international bridge located there at the time. La Linda was a busy mining town located on the Rio Grande river in Mexico.

Wild Bill drove up onto the bridge and handed the Mexican border guard that was stationed there a nice tip. The border guard smiled and waved them on through. Shane and Wild Bill left the canoe's and their partner's on the Mexican side of the river under the bridge and headed back towards Dryden to try and find a shuttle driver.

Mr. Ten Eyck gave them the bad news that it would be difficult to find a shuttle driver on such a short notice. The only other option would be to hitch hike the 167 miles back to La Linda. The truck could be delivered to the private ranch takeout spot on the river in a few days but they were on their own trying to find a way back to La Linda.

Mr. Ten Eyck made them a nice card board sign that had La Linda written on it in bold letters. Shane and Wild Bill stood on the side of highway 90 trying to get one of the passing truck drivers to feel sorry for them and give them a ride. No one would even slow down when they passed by.

The futile attempt to hitch a ride dragged on for a while before an opportunity finally presented itself when they noticed a young couple in a van pull into the gas pump area at the Mercantile store.

Wild Bill slowly ventured over to the young man at the gas pump and started a conversation. The young man was friendly and explained that they were on vacation and were planning on a few days of camping in Big Bend national park. Wild Bill started telling him about how beautiful the La Linda, Mexico area was and that he would be happy to show them how to get there.

The enthusiastic sales pitch he was giving them seemed to be working. The young man eventually warmed up to the idea of heading in that direction and he agreed to give them a ride if they were willing to sit in the back of the van with their large dogs. Shane and Wild Bill sat on the floor of the van with their two dogs and were finally heading back in the right direction.

The young couple did not seem to be very impressed with the flat land scape and cactus infested desert scenery around them. Wild Bill could not help but think that they would probably change their minds and end up dumping them somewhere along the highway. The sales pitch describing the beautiful area they were headed towards helped to convince them that they needed to continue.

The highlight of the drive ended up being when they stopped at the Stillwell store to let everyone take a short break. Hattie Stillwell owned the large ranch and store that was located on the Texas side of the river near La Linda. Hattie was a very famous book writer and rancher and she could tell very interesting stories about life in the Big Bend area if you had the time to buy a cold drink and stay for a while. Wild Bill did not know he was talking to a local legend on that first trip.

The sun was starting to make its glorious disappearance on the western horizon when they finally arrived back at La Linda. Joe and Steve seemed to be very irritated with the all day wait. Shane and Wild Bill thanked their new friends for the lift and they quickly loaded into the canoes and started heading down river. The young couple watched them paddle out of sight and then they loaded their dogs back into the van and continued on their journey towards Big Bend national park.

It was time to get this adventure down the Rio Grande started because they needed to get a few miles down river before darkness set in. It did not matter if you camped out on the Mexican side or the U.S. side of the river back in those days. The stars were shining very brightly on the clear night. Wild Bill laid on top of his sleeping bag on the open ground next to the campfire and stared into the sky. The beautiful star lit skyline in front of him was one of the most amazing things he had ever seen. Wild Bill had been told several interesting stories about this area. It was the best star gazing place in Texas because of being out in the middle of nowhere and no city lights were located close by to obstruct the view. The unbelievable sight had him mesmerized and he was focused in on the show.

The long day of shuttle driving and hitchhiking was slowly catching up to him and it was time to get some rest. They would have to get up early and start the adventure through the lower canyons.

The sun started making it's glorious appearance early the next morning and they loaded back into the canoe's for the first full day on the river. Beautiful mountains and canyons covered with all types of cactus were surrounding them and he was captivated by the beautiful sunrise and the sight of tall mountains and narrow canyons in the distance.

The first couple of days were full of excitement while they struggled to stay upright through the rock infested class three rapids. Both canoes were upside down after a violent wipeout and swim at hot springs rapid. They quickly dumped the water out of the boats and headed down river because they did not realize where they were. The hot springs are located on the Mexican side of the river and that is a great place to set up camp and relax in the warm springs. They did not have any experience in the area and they did not know where they were so they just kept paddling down river.

The upper and lower Madison rapids were next in line and everyone ended up swimming through the upper rapid after banging into several large rocks and capsizing. Wild Bill's previous whitewater canoeing experience had taught him several valuable lessons. Always stay on your back and keep your feet in front of you after turning over in a major rapid so you can push off the rocks and obstacles with your feet instead of banging into them head first. This maneuver will usually help prevent a serious injury from occurring because scrapes and bruises are a lot easier to deal with than a major head injury or a broken bone would be.

It would be very difficult to get a seriously injured person to a hospital out of this area in a timely manner because of the isolation and lack of communication. The only option available would be to put the injured person in a canoe and paddle them non stop to the takeout point.

The most interesting story during that first trip on the lower canyons happened early on the fourth morning after they had set up camp on the Mexican side of the river. The sun was starting to make it's glorious appearance when he opened his eyes early that morning and the first thing he saw was a horse standing over the top of him. The horse's head was barely above his face. The horse was snorting and staring at him while liquid was constantly dripping out of his nose into Wild Bill's face.

The unexpected sight of a horse's head directly above his face made him jump in fear. Wild Bill quickly rolled out of the sleeping bag as fast as he could and stumbled forward while trying to straighten up. He finally was able to regain his balance and was surprised to see two Mexican Cowboys on horseback who had rode very quietly into the river camp.

It was a very awkward situation when he excitedly tried to communicate with the Mexican Cowboys using his limited Spanish vocabulary. They were basically just asking for food and water. The other three sleeping campers finally got up and everyone enthusiastically offered to share with them what they could out of their limited food supply. A few warm beers were offered and the Cowboys happily accepted. They eventually became very friendly and everyone enjoyed the limited conversation. The Mexican Cowboy's ended up being the only two people they saw that entire week.

Another interesting encounter with a group of young men from Mexico happened three years later during the sometimes annual lower canyons trip. Wild Bill was part of a large group of paddlers that was just a few miles from the take out spot below Dryden when they suddenly noticed a group of young men waving at them from the Mexican side of the river. The canoe group was very hesitant to pull over and see what they wanted but the group of young men on the Mexican side of the river were yelling and waving at them to come over and talk with them.

It was a group of nineteen male teenagers and an older man who appeared to be the team leader. They seemed harmless and the older man was trying very hard to explain what the problem was. The limited Spanish vocabulary was once again a stumbling block but Carlos was part of the group on that trip and he could speak fluent Spanish. The older Mexican man started talking to Carlos.

The older man kept pointing at a small aluminum flat bottom boat that was on the river bank next to them and Carlos finally understood what he was asking for. The leader of the group was trying to tell Carlos that they were scared of the river and he was frantically asking for help. The river in that area was very swift and a steep rock wall about fifteen feet tall was on the Texas side.

Wild Bill looked at all of those young men and his first instinct was to say no and head on down river. The canoe group quietly had a serious discussion among themselves and decided to take a vote. The secret vote was taken and they decided to help the young teenagers get across the river. The young men excitedly loaded into the canoes one at a time and they paddled them across to the Texas side of the river. It took several round trips because they could only take one passenger across at a time. The current was very swift and you had to angle the canoe across the turbulent waves.

The young men were very happy when they jumped out of the boat on the Texas side of the river. They pulled t-shirts out of their back packs that had American sports team logo's on them and they quickly changed. These young men still had twenty miles of very rough terrain that was covered in thick brush and cactus to walk across before reaching the nearest highway.

The older man told Carlos that there would be a van waiting for them at the highway to take them to the Midland and Odessa area. They had jobs waiting for them there.

The last one was safely paddled across and the young men all smiled and waved before they quickly gathered into a group and headed out for the long walk to the highway. The strange sight of a 100 peso bill laying on the bottom of the boat surprised Wild Bill. Everyone in the canoe group was glad to see these young men get across the river safely and they did not expect anything in return.

Wild Bill still has that 100 peso bill stored away and it is a funny reminder of his once in a lifetime experience as a "coyote". Everyone in the group agreed that they would never do that again but it seemed to be the right thing to do at the time. The river crossing at that spot would have probably turned into a bad situation with a tragic outcome if the young men had tried to cross by themselves.

This section of the Rio Grande river was normally very isolated and desolate and it was a very rare occurrence to see anyone during the week long canoe trip. Things were a lot different during that time and the travel back and forth across the border was not as intense and out of control as it is now.

Wild Bill and his crazy cousin Jerry teamed up together for a lower canyon canoe trip on the Rio Grande river and that trip produced many memorable stories. A large group of canoeing friends had put in two days ahead of them and they we were in a hurry to try and catch up with them.

After a long day of paddling they were closing in on the hot springs rapid. Jerry had consumed several too many of Milwaukee's best that day and he was struggling to stay in the boat and stay focused. The class three rapid was just ahead of them. Wild Bill did not participate in the drinking contest and he was able to stay focused on the rock lined rapid just ahead.

They were able to successfully navigate through the rapid upright after barely clearing the numerous rocks at the start of the rapid and then violently banging into the large boulder at the bottom of the drop. Jerry was trying to pull his limp body up off the bottom of the boat after the hard collision. Wild Bill slowly paddled the partially submerged canoe over to the Mexican side of the river to find a campsite next to the springs.

Jerry laid down on the sand covered bank to take a quick nap after Wild Bill managed to help him get out of the canoe. Wild Bill ventured over to the springs to spend some quality time lounging in the warm springs. Jerry was snoring loudly when he returned and Wild Bill covered him with a sleeping bag and then laid out in his own sleeping bag a few yards away.

It was a beautiful night for star gazing and Wild Bill was focused on the amazing sight of glowing stars and planets that were lighting up the dark night. Wild Bill got up early the next morning to get the camp coffee going while Jerry was still snoring loudly a few yards away. He ventured over to wake him up when the coffee was ready and the unusual sight of large paw prints in the sand next to Jerry's sleeping bag quickly got his attention.

The sight of fresh cat prints all around Jerry's sleeping bag was breath taking. The large Mountain Lion had circled around his sleeping bag several times during the night before heading over to the springs for water. The fresh paw tracks were not there when they had set up camp the night before.

There was no blood on Jerry's sleeping bag when Wild Bill tried to wake him up. Jerry was slow to respond but eventually started to crawl out from under his sleeping bag with no noticeable injuries. The fresh tracks were all around him and it was just amazing that he did not end up as a cat meal. The only thing that probably saved him from being cat nip was either the bad body odor or the loud snoring. The foul smell and the loud noise is what had apparently scared the Mountain Lion away.

Another interesting story from that same time period occurred during a November canoe trip through Santa Elena canyon near Lajitas. The small group Wild Bill was paddling with was a few hours below Lajitas when they noticed a group of people gathered on the Mexican side of the river. They seemed to be having a big party because the sound of Tejano music and loud voices could be heard echoing way up river.

The loud par-tiers started signaling at the canoe group to paddle over towards them. Wild Bill and the canoe group cautiously paddled closer to see what they wanted. They appeared to be very friendly and were trying to tell them in Spanish to get out of the canoes and come join the party.

They paddled the canoes over to the bank and joined the group. One of the par-tiers wanted Wild Bill to come over to the fire pit and check out what they were cooking. There were two large holes in the ground that were surrounded by simmering wood chips and they were covered by pieces of tin.

Wild Bill's new friend uncovered one of the pits to reveal a large cows head that they were baking in the hole. The "head cook" then handed him a fork while he began to dig into the cows brain area with his fork. Wild Bill was a part time cattle rancher but he never had the opportunity to eat the meat directly from a cows head before and this was a new experience for him.

The meat was seasoned well and tasted pretty good. Everyone in the small canoe group cautiously joined in on the free meal. Sometimes it can be very difficult to eat something that is looking straight at you while you peel away the meat from the brain area. Fresh home made tortilla's were also passed around to make tacos with. The cow head tacos were an unexpected treat that was appreciated.

Everyone was laughing and having a good time. The conversation was very friendly in spite of the limited Spanish vocabulary. It was starting to get late so the paddlers had to say goodbye to their new partying friends and start heading down river to find a campsite. The take away from this experience was that the local people from both sides of the river in the Big Bend area always seem to be very friendly and helpful even towards a bunch of strange looking characters paddling down river.

Trying to navigate through the rock slide rapid in Santa Elena canyon can be very difficult in moderate to high water levels. The rapid is full of large boulders that you have to carefully maneuver around and you can not see from one end of the rapid to the other because of the large rocks that block the view. Wild Bill learned the hard way after a couple of bad wipe outs that the best way to successfully run this rapid is to climb one of the large boulders at the start and make a mental note of what route to take. It is very important to locate the boulders that need to be avoided at all cost.

The stargazing at night on the lower canyons section of the Rio Grande river is just amazing. Wild donkeys braying loudly along with an occasional mountain lion scream echoing down river make the nights very interesting. The opportunity to eat fried or grilled catfish every night is a possibility because of the great fishing. There are several primitive hiking trails along the lower canyons that offer beautiful views of the surrounding mountains and desert terrain but you have to be focused on your surroundings and try to avoid any close contact with the rattlesnakes.

Wild Bill survived those early trips paddling down the lower canyons. The amazing stories would probably make an interesting book. The unique experiences he had in this area helped to create a life long interest and fascination with the Rio Grande river and Big Bend National Park.

A whitewater raft and canoe race was held in the Lajitas area for several years. The race started in Colorado canyon about 25 miles above Lajitas along the most beautiful drive in Texas. The flow rate on the Rio Grande river below Presidio was consistently on the high side. Guided raft trips were a big business in the area at the time and the local outfitters would organize an annual raft and canoe race.

The raft race was the primary event and it started first and then the canoe race followed. There were several Texas Water Safari teams that would show up and participate in the canoe race because a substantial amount of prize money was involved. The turnout for the race was usually very good.

Wild Bill had the opportunity to compete in the canoe race a couple of times during this interesting time. Shane and Wild Bill entered the Colorado Canyon canoe race in 1987. They were able to successfully keep their tandem unlimited canoe upright through the intense rapids and canyon wall sweepers all the way down the 25 mile race course. They crossed the finish line in fourth place overall and finished right behind a well known Texas Water Safari racer named Fred Mynar.

They won a hundred dollars and then the prize money was quickly spent at the big party and celebration that followed the race in downtown Lajitas. Clay Henry, the mayor of Lajitas was there to watch over the festivities. Clay Henry was the famous beer drinking goat that could down a Lone Star long-neck in a matter of seconds. Visitors and tourists would purchase long-neck's at the historic Lajitas Mercantile and then watch in amazement while Clay Henry guzzled them down one after the other non stop. Clay Henry would stand next to the coral fence waiting patiently for the next long-neck to be stuck into his mouth with his female goat entourage standing close by watching the show.

A well known Tejano band from Mexico was floated across the river in rafts and flat bottom aluminum boats in order to play music at the big concert and dance that night in Lajitas. The old western town was crowded with people from both sides of the river and they were gathered there to celebrate and party after the races were over. Tejano music was loudly played and could be heard echoing down the Rio Grande river. The party lasted late into the night and continued on into the early morning hours. Clay Henry would hang in there as long as the long necks kept coming.

Wild Bill and Jack crashing through large waves on the Rio Grande
river

Clay Henry, the mayor of Lajitas, downing a long neck in front of the crowd

Wild Bill and Jack paddling through hot springs rapid

Wild Bill trying to keep the boat upright in the upper maddison rapid

CHAPTER 4

1982: The first Texas Water Safari and the dreaded "DNF"

1982: Wild Bill's first Texas Water Safari and the dreaded "DNF"

The long range plan to enter the "World's Toughest Boat Race" for the first time suddenly came together in June of 1982. Shane and Wild Bill started discussing the possibility of teaming up and doing the Texas Water Safari. Shane had a well used and abused sawyer fiberglass canoe and they decided to use it for the race. There was very little planning or training that went into this first race. The bad thinking was that since they paddled a lot on the weekends and had done several week long trips on the Rio Grande river they should be able to handle a 265 mile canoe race.

Shane and Wild Bill were familiar with the upper San Marcos river and the lower sections of the Guadalupe river but they were not very well prepared for that first race. The team came together very late in the game and there was no plan. They rigged the boat out for the race in Wild Bill's front yard one day before the Friday check in.

They were going to use double blade paddles that they had made themselves from plastic single blade paddles. Tom had given them a few suggestions and some advice for the race but they were basically on their own to figure things out because everything was a secret back in those days. There were very few water safari racers that would give you advice or show you how to rig racing boats out.

The first weekend in June rolled around and they showed up for the check in at Aquarena Spring Lake. Shane and Wild Bill paid their 25 dollar entry fee and a sheet of paper with the rules and required equipment was handed to them.

The final canoe rigging and the required inspection was just about over when a water safari veteran that they did not know came up to the boat and looked over what they were doing. The uninvited guest shook his head and was staring at Wild Bill with a serious look on his face when he said, "you're not going to make it, come back next year and try again".

Shane and Wild Bill were stunned by the rude comments but they did not immediately respond. The uninvited guest started staring at the six pack of beer that they checked in and had stored away under the seat. "I have always wanted to do that but I couldn't justify the extra weight".

The rude comments were starting to make Wild Bill very angry. They reluctantly shook the uninvited guest's hand before he turned and walked away. They did not know who this guy was and he did not introduce himself.

Shane and Wild Bill did not know that many of the water safari veterans would walk around and check out the way the novices were rigging out their boats before the race. They would then get together and have a contest between themselves. They would start making bets and predictions on how far down the race course the novices they were checking out would make it.

Pat Oxsheer had made a blunt assessment of their race preparations and said that they didn't have a chance to finish this race. The comment that really hurt was, "come back next year and try again". Wild Bill couldn't figure out if it was the home made paddles or the primitive food inventory of sardines, crackers and Vienna sausage that made him say that. Pat was right on the money with his blunt assessment of their race preparations but he did not want to hear it.

Pat and Wild Bill would become friend's several years later after Pat moved to Terlingua and became a river guide on the Rio Grande river. They laughed about the rude comments several years later after Wild Bill reminded Pat of the conversation and jokingly thanked him for the motivating words of encouragement. Wild Bill never forgot those comments and has used them for motivation.

Shane and Wild Bill drove to cotton seed rapid and hiked down to the river after the water safari check in was finished. They needed to check out the rock infested rapid to try and figure out the best route through. Wild Bill made a very bad decision and jumped off the cement wall that was located just above the rapid. He landed awkwardly and stumbled forward before falling face first into the muddy river bank.

The right knee buckled under him and was severely injured because of the awkward landing. The knee started to swell up as big as a small watermelon. It was stiff and very painful when he tried to bend it. The only option available was to wrap it up tightly with gauze the best way he could.

The thought of not starting the race never entered his mind because he was determined to be in the boat and start his first Texas Water Safari on Saturday morning. They spent the night at Tom's camp ground and tried to sleep in the bed of the truck and on the ground with sleeping bags because the tight budget they had for this race did not include any extra money for a motel room.

The race started in Aquarena Spring Lake on Saturday morning with 51 teams entered. The never ending portages and obstacles on the upper San Marcos river forced Wild Bill to hobble and stumble on the damaged knee while he tried to help carry the boat around all of the hazard's. Wild Bill was able to help carry the boat when necessary and the painful knee injury did not affect his stroke rate. An occasional aspirin would be the answer to help alleviate some of the pain problems.

Jack Lenz was their team captain and his job was to throw military canteens full of water in front of the boat when they paddled by the checkpoints. Jack didn't want to wade out into the river so he would just toss the canteens into the water in front of them. Shane and Wild Bill would then try to quickly pluck them out of the river when they paddled by.

They had no racing experience and very little training but they were able to maintain a good stroke rate and boat speed with their home-made double blade paddles. The most important thing was that they did not make any major mistakes at the rapids or portages.

The field was spread out and they were in the top 15 and were doing pretty well for novices with no experience. They were trying very hard to maintain a steady stroke rate with their homemade double blade paddles but eventually started slowing down some and dropped back a few positions.

Wild Bill picked up one of the floating canteens out of the river when they passed by the Luling checkpoint and to his surprise it was full of beer. This should have disqualified them right then and there but they were excited and very happy to be drinking cold beer out of a canteen.

They were laughing while they threw the beer canteen back and forth between themselves. The beer foam was dripping off of Wild Bill's face. They quickly picked up the stroke rate but the alcohol induced spurt of energy would soon ware off and they would be physically struggling again. The six pack of beer that they had started the race with ended up floating down river somewhere after a sudden wipe out and swim on the upper river.

The beer handoff was illegal but Jack could see that they were just about done with this race and he was trying to give them a quick boost. Marathon canoe racing and drinking alcohol do not go very well together. This was just another self inflicted hurdle to overcome. The bigger problem was the lack of training and not knowing how to pace themselves in a marathon canoe race. They were basically a couple of novices that didn't know what they were doing.

There were two major log jams on the lower San Marcos river that were located just above Gonzales 90. The first log jam portage was very difficult. It required the beer drinking canoe racers to drag their boat over several large logs and then climb up a very steep bank.

Wild Bill could barely bend his swollen knee. The only way he could get up the steep embankment was by grabbing large tree roots and limbs and pulling himself up as hard as he could. Shane was dragging the boat up the steep bank with little help from him.

They finally reached the top of the ridge and Wild Bill was able to help carry the boat through the dense trees and brush. The re-entry into the river was very comical. The river bank where they were standing suddenly collapsed because of the weight and they slid down the steep embankment and plunged back into the river.

Wild Bill was trying very hard to keep his feet in front of him while pushing off the large tree trunks and thorn bushes with his arms and legs to avoid a head on collision. The boat suddenly came sliding down the bank behind them and was violently banging into the trees before it crashed into the river right on top of them. This was just another nail in the coffin. They cautiously climbed back into the boat and started heading down river.

The stroke rate was starting to dramatically slow down when they limped in to the Gonzales area dejected and defeated. The lack of training and racing experience caught up with them after 80 miles of nonstop paddling and forced them to make a regrettable decision. They both agreed to pull out of the race at Gonzales after the terrible reality started sinking in that they were not physically up to the challenge of a 265 mile non stop canoe race.

The dreaded "DNF" acronym was then written in by their names. That was a terrible decision that still bothers Wild Bill today. The only positive experience from that first race was that he learned what not to do and that marathon canoe racing is hard work.

The terrible sight of a "DNF" acronym placed next to his name on the official finishers list that year caused him to eventually question his motives. The Texas Water Safari is a lot like life in general because it is full of ups and downs and you are constantly trying to overcome obstacles.

There were two ways to proceed at this point. Forget about the bad experiences in this race and move on to something else or step up and do better next time. Thank the Lord that Wild Bill chose to step up and try harder the next time.

Wild Bill had to go through a major knee surgery two weeks later to repair the ACL and meniscus damage to his right knee. There was a lot of long term damage to the knee that he would have to learn to live with but he was able to eventually get back to work and family responsibilities after the surgery and rehab was over. The first Texas Water Safari finish would have to wait until later.

That entire experience was mostly negative but it was the catalyst that drove him to "come back and try again next year". Wild Bill learned the hard way that when you compete in an endurance event like the TWS you need to be ready both physically and mentally.

The "DNF" acronym motivated him to train harder and try to enter the race again in 1983 but Darla was due to deliver their first child on the same weekend the water safari was scheduled. That could be chalked up to bad timing. There was no way Wild Bill could fully commit to the race because Darla and their first child took priority.

That meant that he would have to stay home and watch the race from the Floodplain Ranch river bank on that first weekend in June. Wild Bill watched Tom and Red pass Pat Petrisky and his four man team to take over first place overall. Pat Oxsheer and his three man team were close behind in third place. Howard Gore, Bucky Chatham and Mark Gore came rowing by a little while later in fourth. The next few hours were spent sitting on the bank entertaining himself by throwing sticks into the river for his river dogs to retrieve.

Shane and Jack paddled by Floodplain ranch in fifth place overall. Wild Bill wanted to make them laugh and repay Jack for the illegal hand off from the year before. Ice cold drinks were offered to them out of his ice chest but they respectfully declined. Wild Bill had to round up all of his river dogs and walk back to the house to check on Darla because their first child was due anytime and he could not take the chance to venture away from home very far.

Wade was born into this world two weeks after water safari weekend and he is a blessing from the Lord. Wild Bill was focused on his beautiful family and his life was dramatically changing. The Texas Water Safari was still in the future plans but it would have to be placed on the back burner for now.

CHAPTER 5

1984: Record low water levels and My first finish

1984 came around very quickly and Wild Bill needed to make a decision. Sit out another year or make the commitment to try and finish "The Worlds Toughest Boat Race" for the first time. The motivation was there to enter the race but he didn't have a boat or a game plan. Wild Bill contacted Tom to see if he had any recommendations on a solo racing canoe. Tom was the person to contact for racing equipment and advice. They had a long friendly conversation about the water safari and Tom told him to come on over and check out his inventory.

Wild Bill decided to start making serious plans for the race but none of his canoeing friends seemed to be interested in teaming up with him for a tandem run. Darla was not very happy with the solo idea when he finally told her of his tentative plans and asked for her permission. Darla reluctantly gave her approval but the bigger problem was that money was tight and there would be very little available for the purchase of a racing canoe.

The plan to enter the race in the solo division started to slowly come together. Wild Bill made the trip to Tom's place in Martindale to look over the solo boats he had for sale. There wasn't enough money available in their limited funds to purchase one of the new solo racing canoe's that Tom was trying to sell him. Tom finally showed him a well used and abused solo racing canoe that was stored away out of sight. Tom affectionately called the pieced together fiberglass racing canoe, Old Blue.

Old Blue was a fiberglass sawyer design and it was very long and narrow. Tom started into a detailed explanation of the racing history behind Old Blue. Tom said that pieces of Old Blue had won seven water safari's over the years. The boat had originally been a tandem racing canoe that had been expanded into a three man and then finally had been cut down to a solo model.

The boat had patches and seams all over it because of the many additions and subtractions. Tom then paused for a moment and told Wild Bill that he hated to see it go but he would consider taking 200 dollars for it. The deal was quickly made with a handshake and with a personal check.

Old Blue was loaded up on the truck and was heading for its new home in Thomaston. One more important transaction needed to be made before leaving. A new racing canoe would also require a new racing paddle. Wild Bill had no choice but to purchase a brand new double blade racing paddle with wooden blades. That ended up costing almost as much as Old Blue did. The long drive back home would give him the needed time to come up with a believable explanation for Darla.

The first serious attempt for him to compete in the Texas Water Safari was finally coming together. The excitement he was feeling when leaving Tom's place that day was putting a big smile on his face. Wild Bill had a solo racing boat that came with a history of success and a brand new paddle. The more pressing issue would soon be answered. Would Darla feel the same way?

Old Blue and Wild Bill got off to a shaky start while he tried to adjust to the boat balance. Sitting in a very long and narrow solo racing canoe can be a difficult adjustment. Training runs down to Nursery from Floodplain ranch became the training routine leading up to the pre-lim race in May.

Wild Bill finished second solo and in the top ten overall in the 40 mile pre-lim race. The confidence level was very good after that race and his boat balance seemed to be improving after every training run. Tom mentioned his name as being a dark horse threat in the solo division during a Victoria Advocate interview that was published just before the water safari started.

There was no way he was going to beat Steve Landick. Steve was a well known canoe racer from Michigan that was entered in the race that year and he was a big threat to be the first solo paddler to ever win the water safari. Steve had just finished a 28 thousand mile paddling adventure across the United States. The well documented adventure paddle had taken him down several different rivers and had taken him several years to complete.

Texas was in a prolonged drought in 1984 and the river levels were very low when race weekend came around in early June. Wild Bill had put a lot of training time in on the lower Guadalupe river but not very much on the San Marcos river because of the lack of a training partner that could help shuttle vehicles. The anticipation and excitement was growing and Wild Bill was getting ready to embark on his first serious attempt at finishing the "World's Toughest Boat Race".

This was a race that he had been thinking about since 1972 when he found what was left of a wood strip rowing canoe during a fishing trip on the Guadalupe river. This was his chance to get rid of that feeling of failure that still haunted him after the 1982 race. The dreaded "DNF" acronym was placed next to his name after dropping out of the race at Gonzales because he was dejected and defeated. The "come back next year and try again" opportunity was just about to begin.

The race was about to start and Wild Bill was lined up on the second row. Tom led everyone in a beautiful prayer and then handed the microphone over to the race starter. Tom would routinely do all of the pre-race announcements and lead the prayer before running to his boat to start the race. This would usually force him to start the race somewhere close to last. Tom had won the race a couple of times with Pat Oxsheer and would win a few more with Red Motley. Tom's racing partner in 1984 was his wife Paula and they would be a very competitive team in this race.

Forty three teams were lined up in rows of six to start the race and the number of teams entered was down because of the intense drought and the very low river levels. It has been debated over the years whether or not the 1984 TWS had the lowest river levels on record for the race. Wild Bill believes that the 1984 race had the lowest river levels in the history of the TWS and it only got worse. The best evidence to back that up with is that he was there and experienced it firsthand. Wild Bill's passion for paddling on the Guadalupe and San Marcos rivers started way back in the mid 1970's and he had never personally seen the river levels this low before or since that time.

The twenty second Texas Water Safari started in Aquarena Spring Lake with Ralph the swimming pig watching over the start and loudly grunting in excitement. The starting gun went off and the racers cautiously paddled by his floating platform. Ralph was a well known celebrity and would sometimes jump in the lake after the starting gun fired off and then he would become another obstacle that the racers had to carefully avoid.

This was Wild Bill's first serious attempt at being competitive and finishing the "World's Toughest Boat Race" and he was determined to not make any boat damaging mistakes or push himself to hard early in the race. It became obvious to all the participants that this was going to be a race of pure endurance and attrition because of the low water levels and extremely hot temperatures.

Wild Bill was trying very hard to find the deeper channels while he navigated down the upper San Marcos river. The boats were spreading out after the start and everyone was trying to hold their position and maintain a steady stroke rate. Wild Bill was moving along pretty well and was in the top fifteen. There were some close calls at old mill and cottonseed rapid but he successfully maneuvered around the large rocks that were showing because of the low water levels.

Shane was Wild Bill's team captain and he could only give him water with no ice and no additives. The race rules required that everyone had to start the race with all of your food and supplies checked in and secured in the boat. The mandatory safety equipment had to be shown to a race official at the check in and secured in the boat. The designated team captain was the only person that could legally touch the boat and they could only give you water and encouragement.

It was a long and grueling first day of canoe racing. Everyone was trying to navigate down a river that had turned into nothing more than a creek with very little flow. Old Blue would come to an abrupt stop when Wild Bill tried to paddle over the shallow gravel bars while trying to find the deeper channels. This never ending problem was slowing the race down considerably.

Paddling through the shallow water was forcing Wild Bill to constantly jump in and out of the canoe and then start running down river while dragging the boat through the shallow spot behind him. The constant jumping in and out of the boat activity was just adding more stress to the overall physical strain on his body. The amount of effort that was required to get through that first day on the upper San Marcos creek was taking a heavy toll on everyone.

The glorious sunset on the western horizon was lighting up the sky with magnificent colors when he approached Ottine dam. Wild Bill successfully portaged around the old dam on the left side without any major problems. Old Blue had a lot of scrapes and gouges on the hull after all of the abuse that was inflicted on the first day but there were thankfully no leaks. Wild Bill managed to make it down to the Palmetto park low water bridge checkpoint just after dark.

There were a couple of major log jam portages to contend with between the Sladen cemetery bridge and the Gonzales 90 checkpoint. Wild Bill was able to reach the San Marcos and Guadalupe river confluence just before dawn on Sunday. It was time to smile and down a warm can of coke in celebration because he had finally got off that creek and was now on a real river. Wild Bill paddled in to the checkpoint at the Gonzales gravel bar around eight o'clock on Sunday morning.

Wild Bill caught up with another solo paddler who was struggling and was getting ready to drop out. The first twenty three hours of the race were spent mostly paddling by himself and Wild Bill desperately needed someone to talk to. Robert was struggling and was depressed but Wild Bill convinced him to stay in the race and paddle with him on down to Hochheim.

Robert's team captain joined in the discussion and helped to talk him into staying in the race. Wild Bill's sleep deprived thinking was that they would be headed down a real river instead of a creek. The Guadalupe river should have more water flow but he was wrong. The flow rate was no better than what he had just endured through on the San Marcos river.

It was probably worse because of the wider sections and long open stretches. Robert and Wild Bill followed each other and they tried to find the deeper channels and avoid the shallows and the gravel bars. It was an exercise in futility because they had to jump in and out of their boats many times in order to drag it through the shallow water. It took almost nine hours to get to the Hochheim check point from Gonzales because of the time spent dragging their boats through the shallow spots.

Robert and Wild Bill became canoe racing friends and his company through this long section of the race course was greatly appreciated. Wild Bill was very disappointed when Robert decided to stop at Hochheim to rest for a while. There was no time to rest and it was still daylight so Wild Bill continued on because he was determined to keep paddling without taking any prolonged breaks. Tom had given him some great advice during one of their water safari discussions. Tom told Wild Bill that you should never give in to the temptation of taking rest stops and wasting valuable time. " Take a no doze pill and keep paddling because you can sleep at the finish line".

Wild Bill kept paddling towards Cheapside with his brand new double blade racing paddle. The sun was beginning to disappear on the western horizon on Sunday afternoon. Wild Bill had just made it through the Cheapside checkpoint when one of the most bizarre events that he has ever experienced happened. Thirty six hours of continuous paddling down a dried up race course with very little water flow was starting to catch up with him.

The hallucination stories he had been told about from water safari veterans because of the lack of sleep and mental fatigue were some of the craziest stories he have ever heard. This happens to just about everyone at some point during the race and you just have to ignore it and paddle through it.

The sun was making it's glorious disappearance on the western horizon and Wild Bill was moving along at a steady stroke rate just before dark when he looked over to the left bank and the strangest thing he had ever seen was taking place. Six men in dark suits with nice top hats were carrying something along the river bank and they were all waving at him. It looked like a casket and it was glowing in the late afternoon sunlight.

Wild Bill closed his eyes and then opened them again to verify what he had just seen. The funeral procession was getting much closer. The six bearded men were smiling and waving their big top hats at him. They were carrying a glowing casket along the river bank.

Wild Bill picked up the stroke rate even more and was desperately trying to put some distance between himself and the pall bearers. Wild Bill reluctantly glanced over a third time and they were right next to him waving and smiling.

The stroke rate increased dramatically and Wild Bill was paddling as hard as he could. Every time he glanced over towards the funeral procession they were right next to him. They were smiling and waving their big hats at him. The sight of six bearded men with big top hats carrying a bright colored casket was overwhelming him emotionally.

Wild Bill was terrified when it finally dawned on him that they were waiting for him to drop dead so they could put him in the casket and finish the funeral procession. The empty casket was meant for him and these well dressed bearded men were just trying to fill it with his dead body and finish the job. Wild Bill's heart was pounding and he was gasping for air.

The funeral procession would not go away and it continued following him down river for over thirty minutes before total darkness set in. Wild Bill was stressed out so much that he didn't even take the time to turn on his headlight because he just wanted the pall bearers and their casket to go away.

Shane and Darla were patiently waiting for him at the highway 72 bridge near Cuero. Wild Bill was still in shock and was having a hard time trying to explain to them what had just happened. Darla was shaking her head in disbelief when he told her about the funeral procession. In hindsight, that would have been a great funeral to be a part of but he was not ready to be placed into a coffin yet. That was the most bizarre and scariest thing that he have ever seen.

Wild Bill survived the funeral procession incident and was closing in on the Victoria riverside park checkpoint. This was 50 hours into the race and he had not wasted any time resting or taking breaks at the check points. There is really no good way to prepare yourself for staying up this long with no rest and things started changing in a hurry.

Wild Bill was moving along at a good stroke rate when all of a sudden his mind went into neutral. The sudden mental meltdown caused him to lose focus and forget what he was supposed to be doing. The focus on paddling down river as fast as he could disappeared and Old Blue slowly drifted over to a gravel bar. Wild Bill stepped out of the canoe and that is the last thing he remembers.

Gib and Averyt paddled into the checkpoint and told Wild Bill's team captain that they saw a solo paddler laid out on a gravel bar in the direct sunlight. They asked him if he was OK when they paddled by. The sleeping solo paddler waved at them and didn't say anything.

Wild Bill paddled into the checkpoint about 15 minutes behind them. Shane was very glad to see him after the conversation he had with the tandem team that just left. The short rest stop is apparently what Wild Bill needed because he felt much better and he was ready to tackle the most difficult section of the race course. The massive log jams below Bloomington were next in line.

Wild Bill's headlight had not been working very well and the new plan going forward was to catch up with Gib and his partner and follow them through the log jams. It was getting close to dark on Monday when he finally caught up with them about halfway between Victoria and the swinging bridge checkpoint near Bloomington.

This was about 60 hours into the race. The 60 hour milestone is significant because after this many hours of nonstop canoe racing your focus and mental state will usually start fading away. Wild Bill's mental awareness and decision making was going downhill in a hurry even though he had taken the short break above Victoria. The unscheduled pit stop was not helping very much now.

Wild Bill was trying to draft their boat and his bow would occasionally bang into their stern. Gib was getting irritated with him. Wild Bill was trying very hard to stay right behind them because his headlight was not working anymore.

Wild Bill suddenly rolled out of Old Blue because his boat balance and mental state had deteriorated to a breaking point. Gib and Averyt slowed down after they heard the loud splash and turned to see him swimming in to the shoreline. The quick swim temporarily brought him out of his delirious state and he was quickly back in the boat and right behind them again.

The same scenario happened again just a little while later. That is when Gib talked Wild Bill into putting his life jacket on so he wouldn't end up being alligator bait.

Wild Bill convinced Averyt that they were all lost and they should just turn around and head back to the last checkpoint. Gib kept correcting him and angrily told Wild Bill to please stop distracting his partner. The comical conversation continued and it seemed to be helping everyone stay alert.

Wild Bill following Gib and Averyt to the swinging bridge checkpoint. Shane was patiently waiting there for the quick water hand off. The mile long log jam was going to be a long portage because of the low water conditions and he was very fortunate to be drafting a team that had a good headlight. There were several large alligators with red glowing eyes closely watching them while they dragged their racing canoe's along the very uneven and tree lined river bank. Gib and Averyt seemed to be amused at the rambling comments that Wild Bill was making and they enjoyed the conversation and company as much as he did.

The sun made its glorious appearance on Tuesday morning and Wild Bill was by himself again. Gib and Averyt left him behind. The 72 hour mark of the race was approaching and Wild Bill was struggling again. The sun will make its appearance and the exhaustion and physical pain from the race will still be there but the mental awareness and focus that disappeared the night before will sometimes make a sudden comeback.

Wild Bill realized that he was getting close to the last checkpoint at the Tivoli hwy 35 bridge and it motivated him to push harder and not think about the pain. Shane and the bank crew were waiting for him at the checkpoint and they relayed the bad news that it was a very rough bay and that he would definitely need to snap on the spray skirt.

The sight of his lovely wife, his dad and his team captain standing there put a smile on his face. There were only fifteen hard miles left and his first Texas Water Safari finish would be a reality. Wild Bill's energy level was not very good at this point because he had run out of food the night before and the last peanut butter and honey sandwich was long gone.

There was a rough bay crossing left and his goal of finishing "The World's Toughest Boat Race" would finally be accomplished. Darla encouraged him to hang in there and she would be waiting at the finish line to celebrate his first finish. That conversation gave him more determination and the stroke rate started increasing when he paddled through Seadrift cut and entered San Antonio bay.

The southeast wind was blowing 20 to 25 miles per hour and it was going to be a rough bay crossing but he had trained this section and he knew what needed to be done. The three to four foot waves were giving him a lot of trouble. Paddling a long and narrow racing canoe through turbulent waves can be very difficult and challenging.

Wild Bill made a good decision to go straight across the bay and then work his way along the shoreline towards the mouth of the barge canal. It was very important to stay out of the barge canal and avoid a disqualification. Following the shoreline enabled him to avoid a large section of rough open water but he still had to pull over to the bank a couple of times to dump water out of the boat. It took a lot of effort and determination to finally make it to the barge canal point upright.

The barge canal point would prove to be the roughest part of the bay crossing. There was a large tug boat pushing a long line of barges off in the distance. The barges were headed for the barge canal entrance and Wild Bill figured that he had plenty of time to get across before the barges closed in.

The large waves were breaking over the bow when he started crossing the mouth of the channel. It didn't take long for Wild Bill to realize that he was in trouble when he started feeling the water level rise over his shoes in the bottom of the boat.

The spray skirt was helping a lot but water was still seeping in when it pooled up on top of the nylon skirt. The foot pump that was mounted in the boat was not able to keep up even though Wild Bill was pushing on it as hard as he could. The bad situation was steadily getting worse.

Old Blue was suddenly upside down and Wild Bill had to crawl out of the tight fitting spray skirt. Wild Bill was completely submerged underwater and was desperately holding his breath. Wild Bill was swallowing a lot of bay water and was starting to panic when he was finally able to free himself and swim to the surface. Large amounts of bay water were violently being regurgitated out of his mouth while he was gasping for air. The large waves were trying to pull the boat out of his reach.

Wild Bill started kicking his feet while trying to hang on to the boat. There was very little progress being made while he tried to swim and pull a semi-submerged racing canoe to the nearest shoreline. The situation was getting much worse because the line of barges that he had not paid much attention to earlier were now bearing down on him. Panic was setting in while he continued to swim as fast as he could with one hand and Old Blue was tightly gripped by the other.

Wild Bill was not making much headway because the large waves were continuously crashing into him. A hard decision had to be made at this point. Let Old Blue go and swim to safety or hang in there and try to pull it out of harm's way. The water safari race rules state that you have to finish with at least a piece of your boat intact and with the race number still attached. The sleep deprived and warped thinking at the time was that if he let the boat go it would probably be run over by the barge's and would end up at the bottom of the canal in pieces and would never be seen again.

Wild Bill made the quick decision to start waving his arms at the tug boat that was pushing the barges and try to get their attention. He was waving his hands and arms as fast and as furious as he could but the first barge was almost on top of him. The decision was made to give up and abandon Old Blue. The tug boat engines suddenly started slowing down and the captain blew his air horn.

The barges were almost on top of him when the tug boat engines were shut down. The first barge almost came to a complete stop because of the weight they were pushing. This sudden turn in events gave Wild Bill just enough time to keep swimming and pulling the semi-submerged racing canoe to the nearest shoreline and safety.

Wild Bill was finally able to stand up in chest deep water and he waved back at the tug boat captain in gratitude. The tug boat captain blew his horn and they powered the engines back up and headed into the canal. The near collision with a convoy of barges was just another near miss that was barely avoided. Wild Bill was in a marathon canoe race that never seemed to end and he still had a couple of miles to go to the finish line.

The Seadrift seawall was within sight. Wild Bill was slowly paddling through the large waves along the seawall when Old Blue went completely under again. The finish line was just ahead and his bank crew was there patiently waiting. Will Bill decided to walk Old Blue in to the finish line from that point because his boat balance was gone and his energy level had bottomed out. He had not eaten anything for over eight hours and was barely able to paddle anymore.

The only people waiting for him at the finish line were his lovely wife, his Dad, his team captain and one race official. Wild Bill managed to awkwardly climb the stairs at the finish line with some help from Darla. There was a big smile on his face when it started to sink in what had just happened.

The official finishing time was 82 hours and 15 minutes. The more important take away was that he had just completed the hardest thing he had ever done in his life. Wild Bill had just finished "The World's Toughest Boat Race" for the first time.

This was a marathon canoe race that required a lot of physical endurance and mental toughness and he made it. There was no crowd gathered at the finish line. The volunteer race official walked up to him after the hugs and handshakes with his small bank crew started to slow down. The race official looked at him with a smile on his face and said, "good job", "we will be looking forward to seeing you again next year". The race official handed him the ninth place finishers plaque and shook his hand.

It was a beautiful wood plague that is shaped like the state of Texas and it had these words engraved on the front. 9th place, 1984 Texas Water Safari, The World's Toughest Boat Race.

That 1984 finisher's plaque is still his most prized trophy. It was time to load up and head back home for some much needed rest and any celebrating would have to wait.

There were only seven teams at the awards banquet that was held at a local restaurant in Seadrift. Fifteen teams finished the race that year. Roy and Jerry won the race in a USCA C-2 after passing Steve Landick at Cheapside. Steve had been leading up to that point but he had to pull over and take a break due to the extreme heat and low water level conditions. Roy and Jerry were the first and last USCA C-2 team to win the Texas Water Safari.

Wild Bill finished in third place in the solo division behind Steve Landick and Mike Riley. Mike came in seventh place overall and was the last finisher to make it to the banquet in time.

That was the hardest canoe race that Wild Bill ever competed in. Finishing the "Worlds Toughest Boat Race " for the first time was a major accomplishment and it gave him a better understanding of how to overcome all of the ups and downs that life can sometimes throw at you. It was time to put the double blade paddle down and focus on his beautiful family.

The Lord was working on him through the positive influence of Darla's family and several other Christian friends. Wild Bill was moving in the right direction but because of his stubbornness it was an ongoing process that was slowly moving forward. Thank you for your patience Lord Jesus.

A new family tradition started after the water safari was over. Wild Bill, Darla and their one year old son Wade loaded up in the truck and headed to southern Colorado for a two week camping trip. It was the first of many camping trips that the family embarked on after the race was over. The sometimes annual family camping trip would usually include a whitewater adventure on several famous rivers across the country.

Wild Bill paddling old blue down the lower Guadalupe river in 1984

CHAPTER 6

1985: Where did the nickname Polecat come from?

1985 came around very quickly. It was time to start making plans for the water safari again. Wild Bill's job was located in the oil fields around Refugio, Texas and one of his co-workers seemed to be very interested in water safari stories. They would occasionally get together in the parking lot after work and drink beer. Gene would laugh at the crazy stories that Wild Bill enthusiastically talked about from his experiences in the 1984 race. These after work wind down sessions would usually take place about two times a week. The parking lot beer drinkers would eventually become friends with one of the most interesting characters they had ever known.

Pat Kelly was a well known person around Refugio and he was a member of the volunteer fire department. It was a very common sight to see Pat wandering up and down main street or cleaning the building and equipment at the fire department. Pat was mentally challenged and he fit in very well with Gene and Wild Bill.

Everyone in town liked him because of his very funny laugh and different personality. The locals would treat him with respect because of his dedication to the volunteer fire department. Pat started hanging out with the parking lot beer drinkers at the after work wind down sessions. Gene would do whet ever he could think of to get Pat laughing. The loud and funny laughing between them would cause everyone else to start laughing in response. Pats unique personality and loud laughing was contagious and everyone looked forward to him stopping by for a visit.

The local Dairy Queen was right next door and someone in the group would go get an ice cream cone for Pat in order to keep the party going for a little while longer. The conversations shifted all over the place and would usually always ended up with everyone laughing so hard that tears would be streaming down their faces.

Pat was very interested in Morse code at the time and he would always try to give everyone there a detailed training lesson in Morse code. Pat said that the number 807 means beer in Morse code. The parking lot beer drinkers were always drinking beer when Pat joined them so he started calling them team 807 instead of calling them by name. Wild Bill needed to come up with a unique boat number for the water safari and the number 807 made a lot of sense. That was the number he ended up using for every race he entered after that until the imitation Cowboys took it over.

Pat ended up having a lot of influence on water safari nicknames and boat numbers. Gene was proud of his belching ability and would put it on full display for everyone to hear during the parking lot parties. Wild Bill wanted to be competitive so he would chime in with load noises from the expulsion of gas from the backside of the body. The releasing of air and gas from all of the exit points of the body would soon turn into a contest. Pat would join in with his crazy laughing while downing his ice cream cone. The competition between the three of them was intense and the loud laughing, belching and gas releasing could be heard echoing across the large parking lot.

The parking lot contest motivated Pat to give Wild Bill the new name, Polecat. The embarrassing talent he had was developed over the years from the contests that he participated in at the annual family reunion. Wild Bill had several uncle's that were very good at this and they would initiate a family contest. The extended family would quietly gather outside around the campfire after supper.

Wild Bill and his cousin's would try to be competitive in the gas releasing contest but they did not have the experience and talent that his uncle's had. That is probably something that should not be bragged about but it is part of his TWS story and it needed to be told. Texas Water Safari racing friends have asked him many times over the years where did the nickname Polecat come from. Polecat's answer is that his good friend Pat described it best, "you can smell him before you see him".

Pat gave Gene a new name during one of the parking lot beer parties. Three Dots was the Morse code name that Pat liked to call him. They would start laughing and then point at each other with three fingers when the new name was mentioned. Polecat agreed that this was a very good nickname. Gene eventually had to accept it and that was his new name going forward whether he liked it or not.

Three Dots and Polecat transferred out of the Refugio area to other company locations a few years later and they both had to sadly say goodbye to their good friend. Pat was a unique character and he ended up having a lot of influence on the TWS in a round about way. Three Dots and Polecat love to tell funny stories about their old friend from Refugio with the loud and different laugh. Three Dots agreed to sign on and be Polecat's team captain for the 1985 Texas Water Safari.

Darla gave birth to Brandon in January 1985 and he is a blessing from the Lord. Polecat had a two year old son and a baby in the house and it was going to be very difficult to get enough training miles in to compete in the water safari. Darla reluctantly gave her permission for him to enter the race.

Polecat was eventually able to get the necessary practice time in and Old Blue was going to get one more shot at winning the solo division. The water levels for the 1985 race were much better than the year before and were in the moderate range. The positive thinking was that Polecat had a chance to be competitive in the solo division after a year of experience. That experience should give him a better understanding of the race course and how to prepare himself for 265 miles of nonstop paddling.

Ralph the swimming pig was proudly watching over the start of the 23rd Texas Water Safari from his floating platform in Aquarena spring lake. Polecat had a year of experience behind him and his confidence level was very good. Tom led everyone in prayer and then he shot the starting gun off. The game plan was to start fast and not make any major mistakes that could ultimately cost valuable time.

Rio Vista dam was the first major obstacle to get around and he was determined to paddle over the dam and through the rapid without portaging. Polecat was able to paddle over the dam upright but he took on a significant amount of water and Old Blue was completely submerged. The crowd was cheering when he quickly jumped out of the submerged canoe and swam through the rapid.

The good news was that there was no noticeable major damage inflicted to the boat. Polecat swam through the rock infested Rio Vista rapid with his boat and was eventually able to get over to the nearest bank and dump water. The whitewater mentality that dominated his thinking during the race would usually get him into trouble. Polecat's previous canoeing experience was mostly from paddling through intense whitewater rapids on different rivers and this gave him the false confidence that he could paddle through anything.

That is not a good game plan when you are in a fragile racing canoe. Polecat has learned the hard way that it makes more sense to be cautious and not take unnecessary risks while navigating a long and fragile racing canoe down the upper San Marcos river.

The excitement and the adrenalin rush that you feel after the start of the race along with the large crowds that are watching will sometimes lure you into making some bad decisions and taking unnecessary chances. Paddling down river as fast as you can is very important but keeping your racing canoe free of damage and not wasting valuable time making repairs is equally just as important.

The first day did not have all of the wild and crazy events that he experienced the year before. Three Dots was doing a good job as the team captain and was very busy entertaining the other bank crews and team captains with his Pat Kelly laughing impersonation. Polecat's dad and the party bunch were having a good time following the race. There was a lot of self inflicted pressure on Polecat to keep the party going.

The first day ended with the field spread out. Polecat was trying to keep up a fast stroke rate with his double blade paddle and stay close to the solo leaders. John and Peter were in a big battle for first place in the solo division and Polecat was having a hard time trying to stay close to them.

The sun made it's glorious appearance on Sunday morning. This turned out to be a very long hard day of racing because of the hot temperatures and isolated stretches of river below Hochheim. Polecat was paddling by himself with no one to talk too. The sight of Darla and Wade and all of the river dogs at Floodplain Ranch helped put a big smile on his face. The sun was beginning to disappear on the western horizon when he paddled up to the primitive boat dock.

Three Dots was quickly changing out the water jug while Darla and Wade tried to encourage him. The river dogs were barking in excitement when Polecat shoved off and started paddling down river. The light from his bedroom window was shining across the river. Polecat waved and thanked everyone for being there. Wade was yelling out words in toddler language but Polecat knew exactly what he was trying to say. "Go Polecat go". Two river dogs suddenly jumped in and tried to follow him but Polecat was too fast for them and they eventually had to stop and head back home.

There was a long night of canoe racing straight ahead and Polecat needed to pick up the stroke rate and put some pressure on the division leaders. The wild hallucinations started making their ugly appearance late that night and it was hard to stay focused. Wild, scary looking creatures were staring at him from the river bank and large cartoon characters were dancing and laughing on top of the cypress trees. Thank the Lord that there was no funeral procession waiting for him to drop dead.

The sun made its glorious appearance on Monday morning and Polecat caught up with a tandem racing canoe that only had one person in it. Mike was paddling by himself after his partner had pulled out of the race near Victoria. Mike was completely out of food and he was struggling to paddle the long tandem racing canoe down river by himself. The lack of food was slowly draining his energy level and he was just about to the point of dropping out of the race.

Polecat knew Mike because of his family owned campground and canoe rental business on the upper San Marcos river. That was a good place to go for boat repairs and racing supplies after Mike's parents had purchased the property from Tom Goynes. Mrs. Spencer operated the business and she is the friendliest person you will ever have the opportunity to meet. She has a passion to follow the water safari and take pictures of the race teams while they navigate through all of the hazards and obstacles along the race course. Mrs. Spencer was the Texas Water Safari official photographer for many years and she would follow the race all the way down to Seadrift.

Polecat was excited to finally have someone to talk to. They were paddling through the isolated sections of the race course below the swinging bridge check point. Polecat slowed down the stroke rate and paddled along side Mike to try and start a conversation. Mike was by himself but he was not technically in the solo division because he had started the race with a partner in the tandem division.

It was early Monday afternoon when they paddled into the log jam cut area. There was just enough flow rate going through the cuts to avoid having to make the long and difficult portage around the mile long log jam. Polecat had trained in this area a lot and he knew which way to go. Mike followed him through the narrow, brush lined channel into Alligator lake.

This unique area has always been Polecat's favorite section of the race course. The great memories of back when he was eleven years old started to dominate his thinking while they cautiously made their way through the logjam area. Polecat's dad operated several oil wells and tank batteries in the area during the mid 1960's. The young Polecat would occasionally go with him and his job was to open and close the seven gates that had to be driven through in order to reach the oil wells and tank batteries. They would launch a flat bottom boat and put lines in the river after the work was done.

This section of the Guadalupe river was fished very hard by commercial fishermen in 1967. The young Polecat and his dad would talk to them occasionally when they were running their lines. The commercial fishermen would proudly show them the 60 to 80 pound flat head catfish that they were catching in Alligator lake. That made a big lasting impression on an eleven year old boy. The commercial fisherman told them that it was very difficult to get a fishing boat through the narrow cuts and into Alligator lake but it was worth the effort because of the great fishing. Those comments convinced the young Polecat's dad to never attempt a fishing trip into Alligator lake. The memories from those days always put a big smile on Polecat's face when he is paddling through the area.

Large alligators and water moccasins will be patiently waiting on the river bank for their next potential victim when you paddle by. This section of the race course is where the best water safari stories come from. This unique section of the race course is well known to water safari veterans as the race equalizer because teams will usually end up slowing down through this area because of the logjams and the mind numbing hallucinations. Strange things will happen sometimes when you push yourself to your physical and mental limits with no rest.

Mike was having a very difficult time and was starting to fall further behind. Polecat suddenly heard him yell out in excitement. Mike had just found a couple of sandwiches in zip lock bags floating by his boat. Mike was downing them as fast as he could and Polecat could hear the excitement in his voice. It was a cold case mystery how those sandwiches managed to fall out of Old Blue and end up in the river. Polecat was very happy that Mike had found them.

The dominate smell of salt water was in the air and was very strong. Polecat paddled in to the Tivoli bridge checkpoint and Three Dots informed him that San Antonio bay was choppy but was not extremely rough. That was good news and would be the direct opposite of the rough bay crossing that he had to endure through last year in his first finish.

Polecat finished in tenth place overall and third solo in 60 hrs. and 41 minutes. That was a big time improvement from the previous year but he was disappointed in the final results and his overall performance. Finishing in the top ten was worth celebrating but the goal of winning the solo division would have to wait until next year. Tom and Red won the race in a tandem unlimited canoe. John Bugge won the solo division with Peter Derrick coming in second. These guys were very fast and Polecat was going to have to shift into a higher gear to be competitive in this division. Polecat needed more training time and a lighter racing canoe in order to get his name on the solo division trophy.

The finisher's banquet was held at a local restaurant in Seadrift with fourteen teams finishing in time to be there. The banquet attendance was very small and barely filled up the small restaurant. There were a few interesting stories told when teams were called up to receive their finishers plaque. Polecat did not tell any stories when Tom called him up to the front to receive the tenth place award. Mike was called up to receive the eleventh place finishers plaque and he gave Polecat a lot of undeserved credit for taking the time to slow down and encourage him when he was struggling. Mrs. Spencer walked up to Polecat after the very short banquet was over and thanked him for encouraging her son to stay in the race and to keep moving forward towards the finish line. There was nothing mentioned ever again about the peanut butter and honey sandwiches that mysteriously appeared floating down river. Some secret stories should always stay tucked away under the Cowboy hat.

CHAPTER 7

1986: A new racing canoe, boat crashing and "Struggling" to get to the finish line.

1986 came around very quickly. Polecat decided to go check out Tom's inventory of solo racing canoe's once again. Old Blue needed to go into retirement and it was going to be replaced with a lighter and faster solo model. Tom was more than happy to show Polecat a brand new Landick solo boat that had just arrived. The Landick model was made out of a very light material called Kevlar and was named after the 28,000 mile man from Michigan, Steve Landick.

Polecat was very impressed with how light it was compared to Old Blue. The price was agreed to after some negotiating and Polecat was now one of the first water safari paddlers to own a Landick solo racing canoe. It was already rigged out with a rudder and foot peddles but it needed a spray skirt. Polecat asked Paula if she had the time to make the spray skirt. Paula was the go to person for water safari spray skirts and you usually had to get on a long waiting list. The bigger problem was going to be how to explain the purchase of a brand new racing canoe to Darla.

Polecat tried to explain it to her as a long term investment. The new solo racing canoe would probably be the last one he would ever own. Darla shook her head in disbelief and reluctantly gave her approval. Thank the Lord that they are still together after 43 years of marriage.

Old Blue was put up on the canoe racks at home for the last time and went into a forced retirement. It is still proudly hanging there today. Old Blue is a reminder to Polecat of how different the racing canoe's were back then and how hard those first two water safari finishes were.

The training started early that year in order to get used to this very unstable solo boat. The boat was designed for a smaller and more compact person and it became pretty obvious that a big guy like Polecat was going to have to drastically improve his boat balance in order to keep it upright.

Polecat was able to get in the river at home and train at least once a week over the next few months. The forty mile pre-lim race was held in early May and Polecat finished in the top ten overall. The confidence level was very good and the positive thinking going forward was that he was going to finally be a force to be reckoned with in the water safari solo division.

The 1986 Texas Water Safari started in Aquarena Spring lake with 51 teams entered. Polecat was lined up on the second row. Tom gave the final instructions and led everyone in the opening prayer before shooting the starting gun. It was a fast start and Polecat was paddling as hard as he could with his double blade paddle in order to stay in front of the bigger boats that were directly behind him.

A tandem canoe suddenly slammed into the stern of his new racing boat from behind. The hard hit and the quick turn in direction caused the boat to become very unstable. The boat was turning sideways and was being forced into the bank. This is the nightmare situation that everyone tries to avoid at the start of the race. A long racing canoe getting stern hooked from behind will usually not have a good ending. The unstable boat will probably capsize and then you will be ran over from behind by the other teams that are trying to paddle by. Valuable time will be wasted while you try to swim the boat in to the nearest shoreline.

Polecat was being forcibly rerouted straight into the lake shoreline. This all happened so fast that he never had the time to check and see who was doing this evil deed to him from behind. Polecat was quickly being driven straight into a floating platform where Ralph the swimming pig was standing. Ralph was proudly watching over the start of race from his observation deck with his handlers.

Polecat slammed into the floating platform and knocked Ralph into the water. The boat rolled over and Polecat was ejected out of his seat into the deep lake water. Ralph started swimming towards him but suddenly changed directions and headed towards the other canoe's that were paddling by. This was a very embarrassing situation because Polecat had to start swimming in to the shoreline with his half submerged racing canoe in tow behind him.

Ralph did not seem to be upset because he was grunting in excitement and started swimming towards the other racing boats as fast as he could. Ralph's handlers were frantically trying to call him back with no success. Several racing canoe's were trying very hard to avoid him any way they could. The large crowd that was watching the show from the shoreline was laughing and cheering. They were being cheaply entertained with the unscheduled comedy show. The passing teams were shouting at each other to make some room so they could avoid hitting Ralph and the swimming Polecat. Ralph turned around and started heading back towards the swimming Polecat. The scary thoughts of having to wrestle with a swimming pig in the deep lake water motivated Polecat to pick up the swimming pace even more.

The swimming Polecat finally reached the nearest shoreline and was able to stand up and dump the water out of the submerged canoe. Polecat quickly looked around and noticed that he was now starting the race dead last. Ralph was still swimming towards him because all of the other boats had paddled by. Polecat needed to get back into the boat and get out of his way. The comedy show finally came to an end and the swimming Polecat was now in last place.

The reality was that he needed to pick up the stroke rate and catch back up to the pack in order to get back into the solo race. Polecat was trying very hard to make up for the lost time while he paddled through the portages, obstacles, hazards and rapids that dominate the upper San Marcos river. Polecat was eventually able to make his way back into the top ten and was slowly closing in on the solo leader. Oxsheer rapid was the next potential hazard just ahead.

The confidence level was slowly coming back and the boat speed was getting better when another major setback happened. Polecat successfully avoided hitting the visible rocks that lined the start of the rapid but then paddled over a large rock that was partially submerged and grounded to a sudden stop. The large jagged rock was gouging and grinding into the Kevlar hull directly under the seat area.

The sound of cracking Kevlar was very loud. The new racing canoe was filling up with water and then both of the wood gunnels in the middle of the boat snapped. There was nothing Polecat could do at this point except to quickly jump out of the boat to prevent more damage. It was too late.

Polecat pulled his damaged solo boat over to the shoreline and turned it upside down to survey the damage. The rock did not penetrate all the way through the Kevlar but it had caused extensive hull damage. The gunnels on both sides of the boat next to the seat were broke in half. They would have to be repaired and reinforced in order to continue the race.

Panic was starting to set in. Polecat scouted around the immediate area to find something to reinforce the gunnels with. A couple of strong tree limbs were laying on the ground close by. They could be modified and used to reinforce the damaged gunnels. A sharp pocket knife and a few zip ties were vital to this operation and Polecat was fortunate to have both in the emergency repair kit.

A roll of duct tape, zip ties and a sharp pocket knife are essential items that were always included in the repair kit and checked in before the race. The teams he had just worked so hard to pass were starting to paddle by one by one. Polecat broke the tree branches to the desired length and then zip tied them into place to reinforce the damaged gunnels. The repaired canoe was finally launched back into the river but Polecat was once again in last place.

The boat was not leaking but it definitely had noticeable movement in the damaged hull area directly below the seat. The boat damage was severe but Polecat was determined to get the stroke rate and boat speed back up to where it should be and he tried to not dwell on the negative stuff. The sun made its glorious disappearance on day one and Polecat was still in the race.

The previous two water safari finishes had been mostly a test of physical and mental endurance. This race was shaping up as a test of overcoming equipment damage and failure. Polecat was basically paddling a racing canoe that looked like a banana boat coming down river. The bow and stern were both elevated higher than normal because of the fractured hull and the loss of support to the middle of the boat directly under the seat area. The repaired gunnels were helping to support the damaged area but the tree limbs and zip ties would loosen up and move back and forth in turbulent water.   The bad situation was depressing and it seemed to be getting worse.

The terrible and evil thoughts of quitting the race started to infiltrate Polecat's thinking but then he remembered how depressed he was after dropping out of the 1982 race. The bad thoughts finally started to fade away because he did not want a repeat of the terrible feelings of failure and disappointment. Three dots was encouraging Polecat to hang in there and keep paddling.

The constant movement in the damaged area would end up requiring several more unscheduled repair stops. Polecat would try to reinforce the gunnels and the damaged hull with whatever makeshift items he could find along the river bank. Large rocks were eventually placed in the bow and the stern in an attempt to help eliminate the severe angle and straighten out the banana boat.

The sun made it's glorious appearance on Sunday morning. Polecat was paddling the banana boat down river as fast as he could. The steady pace would occasionally be interrupted with a quick stop in order to make more boat repairs. This was causing a lot of valuable racing time to be wasted.

Polecat humbled himself and thanked the Lord in prayer for helping him get through the night. Then he prayed for the strength and toughness that would be required to finish what he had started.

The personal relationship he had with the Lord Jesus was in its early stages and it was becoming very important for him to strengthen that relationship through faith and obedience. A life changing event was going to happen one month later when he accepted Jesus as his Lord and Savior and was baptized at his Church. "Thank you Lord Jesus for saving a sinner like me".

The second day was very hot and humid. Polecat was double blading his not so new solo racing canoe through the Cuero area and was headed for Floodplain Ranch. The very high expectations for this race were now in the trash can. Polecat was focused on just getting from one checkpoint to the next without breaking his damaged solo racing canoe completely in half.

Floodplain Ranch was just around the next bend on that late Sunday afternoon. Darla was standing there with Wade and Brandon. They were all patiently waiting for the depressed Polecat to show up. Three Dots quickly changed out the water jug while the depressed Polecat tried to understand what his young sons were saying. "Go Polecat go", were the only clear and distinct words he could make out. Darla was laughing and was encouraging them to yell louder. Polecat's river dogs were howling in excitement while he tried to talk to them. The enthusiastic reception he was getting was helping to bring Polecat out of his self induced depression.

The interesting idea of putting Brandy in the bow and Candy in the stern to level the boat out started to creep into his warped thinking. They would be good company and could possibly trim the boat out some more and help eliminate the banana shape. The explanation he could use at the finish line was that he found these mutts somewhere along the race course and they needed a ride.

This made a lot of sense to Polecat at the time and he briefly considered calling them into the boat. They could bark and howl at the coyotes while he paddled them down the lower Guadalupe river and into San Antonio bay. The reality was that the hitch hikers would be grounds for disqualification because they were not on the check in list and the finish line was 90 miles down river. They probably couldn't sit in a boat for that long. Polecat had no choice but to leave them behind.

The loud sounds of "go Polecat go" and Three Dots doing his Pat Kelly laughing impersonation could be heard echoing down river while Polecat paddled out of sight. The sight of his beautiful family put a big smile on his face. The Floodplain ranch water hand off had given him a much needed shot of adrenaline and a big boost in confidence.

The next seventeen hours of the race were extremely hard and mentally challenging. Polecat tried to stay focused on paddling his severely damaged racing canoe down the lower Guadalupe river without inflicting any more damage. The dream of winning the solo division was long gone and that was replaced with a personal challenge to finish the "World's Toughest Boat Race" in a banana boat.

The south wind was blowing hard when Polecat paddled into the last checkpoint at the Tivoli bridge on Monday afternoon. Three Dots gave him the bad news that it was going to be a rough bay crossing. Polecat snapped on his brand new spray skirt and was not very confident that he was going to make it to the finish line. The damage to the hull was so bad that sitting in the not so new solo racing canoe was kind of like sitting in an inflatable kayak that had a bad leak in it. The only positive thing that could possibly happen at this point was when the boat finally broke completely in half maybe he could swim in to the finish line with a small piece of the bow that still had the boat number attached to it. That should be good enough for his third straight finish.

The bay was very rough and turbulent. Polecat was surprised when he started paddling over the top of the large waves with very little trouble. The damaged hull would severely bend in the middle and reshape itself into a V shape when it bottomed out in the hole in between the three to four foot waves. The banana boat was floating over the top of the large waves and whitecaps instead of plowing straight through them. The bay crossing was a slow process. Twenty five mile per hour winds and large waves were pounding into the banana boat and there was still five miles left to bay front park.

This unique experience reminded Polecat of when he was in a white water raft in the middle of an intense rapid. The raft would reshape itself in between the large standing waves before expanding back out when it cleared the top of the white caps. Paddling across a rough San Antonio bay is just like being in a very long and turbulent whitewater rapid. Polecat was expecting the damaged canoe to break in half at any moment but it was still upright and in one piece.

The finish line was within sight. Polecat had successfully made it across the longest open section of the bay without capsizing or swamping out. The waves seemed to be getting larger when he paddled across the barge canal point and made the gradual turn towards the finish line at Seadrift. Three Dots and the party bunch were patiently waiting at the flagpole to congratulate him. Darla was yelling out encouragement from the seawall when Polecat paddled the banana boat across the finish line. Polecat awkwardly climbed out of his not so new racing canoe and stumbled up the steps. Darla had a big smile on her face when she cautiously embraced the foul smelling Polecat and kissed him. This was a great ending to a not so great race.

Polecat crossed the finish line in twentieth place overall with a finishing time of 57 hrs. and 5 minutes. The valuable time that was wasted because of the boat damage and all of the repairs had cost him any chance at being competitive in the solo division. Polecat still managed to finish third in the division for the third straight year. John Bugge and Mike Shively won the race in a tandem unlimited canoe. Peter Derrick won the solo division and Butch Bailey came in second.

Polecat was very fortunate to have been able to finish this race at all. The awards banquet was held at a small local restaurant in Seadrift. Thirty two teams finished in time to be there. Several racers and team captains checked out the not so new solo racing canoe after the awards banquet was over and were very impressed that Polecat had made it in to the finish line with so much damage.

There was an unofficial contest that quietly took place among the water safari racers to determine which team had made it to the finish line with the most damage and with the best repair job. It looked like it was going to be a close contest between Polecat and the first place mixed team. John Mark and Carol had overcome a lot of extensive damage to their canoe and they were in the running for the bragging rights. The results of the secret vote were revealed and Polecat was the clear winner. Polecat did not know that he would be very competitive in this contest for the next several years.

Polecat and Darla at the finish line in 1986

Polecat dumps water after a wipeout on the upper San Marcos river
in 1986

CHAPTER 8

1987: The original "Cowboys" (Three Dots and Polecat)

1987 came around very quickly. Polecat made the very easy decision to part with his not so new solo boat. It was a fast model but it ended up not being a good fit for a large man. Tom and his shop team were able to repair the damage and then Polecat put it up for sale. Tom was able to sell it for him pretty quickly. Polecat immediately used that money to purchase a used we no nah ICF tandem unlimited racing canoe that Tom had for sale at his place.

There wasn't any money passing through Polecat's hands during this transaction because it was basically an even trade. That was a good thing because he didn't have to worry so much about explaining this expense to Darla.

The used ICF tandem unlimited boat had been through one water safari but it was in good overall condition. The even trade meant that Polecat would be making the jump into the tandem unlimited division after three unsuccessful attempts to win the solo division.

It was time to try something different and hopefully that would bring better results. Three Dots was chomping at the bit to get into the race after being a team captain for the last two years. Three Ddots and Polecat were now teammates and they had big plans to do well in the 1987 water safari.

Three Dots had transferred with the company to Levelland, Texas and it was going to be a challenge to get together for training runs. Three Dots would have to drive the 500 miles from west Texas and meet Polecat somewhere along the race course when their days off lined up.

They were able to work through the logistics problem and get together several times for training in the weeks leading up to the race. The new division they were moving into was going to require some single blade paddle training along with the usual double blades. Polecat's three previous water safari finishes were all primarily done with a double blade racing paddle.

Double blading for 265 miles is very hard on the wrists, hands and shoulders. The stiffness and soreness that occurred in the arms and shoulders would take a while to recover from. It was very common to not even be able to start the vehicle with the right hand after the race. The right hand would be almost useless and you would have to reach over and use the left hand to turn the ignition key. This was a common problem that had to be dealt with for several weeks after the race was over until the hand strength finally returned.

The common strategy that the unlimited teams used during the water safari was to use single blade paddles around fifty percent of the time and then pull out the double blades in the long and open sections of the race course.

The 40 mile pre-lim race came around in early May. Three Dots and Polecat were confident that they could be competitive in the tandem unlimited division. They ran a fast race and ended up finishing in the top five. Three Dots and Polecat did pretty well in their first race together and the water safari was just a month away. That is when everything changed.

A large tropical disturbance from the Gulf of Mexico came through the area in late May, just a few days before the Texas Water Safari was scheduled to start. The large amounts of rain associated with this storm caused the river levels to start rising dramatically. Polecat had to shift his attention to the potential flood that was coming his way in a hurry.

Polecat lives on a small ranch next to the Guadalupe river near Thomaston. The family had to be evacuated and furniture was moved to higher ground. The first weekend in June was when Three Dots and Polecat were supposed to be racing down river but the race had to be postponed due to very high river levels up and down the entire race coarse. Tom made the announcement that the race would be re scheduled for July fourth weekend.

Three feet of muddy river water made its way into the house on the first weekend of June. Darla and the two young boys had to move into Victoria and stay with her parents for several weeks. Polecat spent the entire month of June ripping out damaged flooring, insulation and sheet rock. There was no water safari training going on during that time.

The thought of pulling out of the race briefly entered his mind but he had committed to something and his racing partner was depending on him to show up. July fourth weekend is usually one of the hottest weekends of the year in south Texas and it was no different that year. The river levels along the race course were slowly coming down even though the constant rainfall didn't seem to be easing up very much. The 49 teams entered were hoping and praying that the water levels would come down just enough to start the race.

TWS race week finally showed up. The constant rain finally stopped and the river levels were dropping. The race was given the green light by the safari board. The entered teams showed up for the check in and safety briefing. Tom did most of the talking at the check in and he warned everyone to not even think about suing the Texas Water Safari if something bad happened to them during the race. Tom emphasized to everyone that he had several lawyer friends that would volunteer their time and would fight you all the way through the court process. The water safari did not have insurance coverage and that was probably the only reason they were able to start the race on that July 4th weekend. Several sections of the lower Guadalupe river were still in moderate flood stage.

Three Dots and Polecat were lined up on the first row because of the strong finish they had in the pre-lim race. The starting gun went off and they shot out of the first row very quickly with their double blade paddles. They were very motivated to start the race as fast as they could. Polecat briefly looked over at his friend Ralph the swimming pig and smiled. Ralph was grunting in excitement while he proudly watched over the start of the race and his handlers were holding him back.

Polecat looked around at the competition and noticed that they were leading the race. This was an exciting sequence of events because he had never been in the lead before. Polecat yelled out to Three Dots to put the pedal to the metal. It was very close but Three Dots and Polecat were the first boat to reach the island portage at the end of spring lake.

The excitement of being in the lead didn't last long. Several other very fast tandem teams caught up with them and quickly paddled by. It really wasn't something worth bragging about but the start put a big smile on Polecat's face. Three Dots and Polecat were moving along at a very good stroke rate and were in the top five overall when things changed in a hurry.

There was a large crowd watching from the bank when they approached cottonseed rapid. The rapid was going to be very difficult to paddle through without taking on large amounts of water because of the high river level. Three Dots and Polecat could hear the crowd loudly shouting that the "Cowboys" were coming. That was the first time that they had ever heard that name being used to describe their team.

They wore expensive cowboy hats during the race. All of the other canoe racers wore caps or safari type hats that made them look like they were going on an African safari. This was Polecat's fourth straight year wearing a well used cowboy hat with a chin strap attached. This just seemed natural for him because the wide brim kept the sun out of his face and off his neck.

The only downside of wearing a large wide brimmed cowboy hat was that it could easily be knocked off your head when you paddled under low hanging tree limbs and thick brush. The harsh reality of losing your hat or sunglasses in this race was that it would eventually become a big problem. The scorching hot south Texas summertime temperatures will eventually take a toll on you. It is very important to secure your hat and sunglasses firmly to your head and to take very good care of them.

Three Dots and Polecat were focused on cotton seed rapid. They cleared the upper section before running up on one of the partially submerged rocks that was located at the bottom of the rapid. They were able to keep the boat upright and slide over the rock but it ended up punching a pretty good sized hole through the bottom of the boat.

The boat was full of water and they had no choice but to quickly pull over to the nearest bank and dump the water out. The large hole was right below where Three Dots' foot rest was located. Large amounts of water were gushing through it and was filling the boat up with river water.

Three Dots yelled out to Polecat that they needed to try and fix the damaged area before continuing. Polecat did not want to do that and waste valuable time. The yelling back and forth continued. Polecat finally asked Three Dots if he could just place his foot over the damaged area and push the frayed Kevlar back into the punctured hole to stop the leak.

Three Dots was able to push the damaged Kevlar back into the hole with his foot. That was good news but he was going to have to keep constant pressure on it with his foot in order to stop it from leaking. This sounded like a good idea to Polecat. Three Dots was going to have to stay in an awkward position with his foot pushing down on the damaged area. It did not leak very much as long as he kept applying constant pressure.

The Cowboys with the big hats were still moving along at a good stroke rate down the lower sections of the San Marcos river. Three Dots was constantly complaining about the numbness and pain he was feeling in his foot because of the awkward position it was in. The difficult decision had to eventually be made to pull over and repair the damaged area. The bottom of the boat had to dry in the sunlight for a few minutes before the hole could be repaired with multiple layers of duck tape. Two tandem teams paddled by during the boat patching procedure.

The hard lesson that Polecat learned from the year before was that you should always take the necessary time and fix it right the first time so you don't have to keep pulling over and repeating the process. The damaged area was not leaking anymore and the duct tape patch was holding. The Cowboys with the big hats paddled into the Guadalupe river confluence near Gonzales not long after dark. Three Dots and Polecat reached the gravel bar checkpoint and caught up with a team from North Carolina . They were doing very well in their first water safari.

Janet and Sandy were two young ladies that were racing in the USCA C-2 division. The women's division was just starting to take off. The women who started this trend helped change the race for ever. There had been several women over the years that had done very well in the mixed division but an all women's team was a new trend and it was here to stay. The first all women's team to finish the water safari consisted of Carol Keirnan and Nova Hall in 1976 and they finished in 9th place overall. Teddy, Celeste, and Donna were a very competitive multi women's team in the 1986 water safari. Marie McKay finished first in the women's solo division that year.

Janet and Sandy were whitewater river guides on the Nantahala river in North Carolina. They were moving along at a very fast stroke rate. Three Dots and Polecat were pushing hard to stay in front of them but they were able to stay right behind the Cowboys with the big hats. Janet and Sandy were determined to stay ahead of Donna and Teddy, another strong women's tandem team that was not very far behind.

The conversation was friendly and was keeping everyone alert. Three Dots and Polecat enjoyed listening to the stories about their river guide experiences and what motivated them to enter "The Worlds Toughest Boat Race". The first night on the Hochheim stretch can be a big mental challenge after a long day of canoe racing on the San Marcos river. The excitement after the start and the intense physical effort you have to put into the race on the upper sections of the river can be very difficult. Trying to navigate a long and fragile racing canoe through all of the obstacles, portages and hazards will usually drain you both physically and mentally. "Take a no doze pill and keep paddling" is the good advice from Tom that Polecat has always tried to follow.

Three Dots started bellowing out his version of Willie Nelson's greatest hits while everyone else chimed in as background singers. Three Dots takes pride in his belching ability but he can sing pretty good also. The singing brought back the great memories of when they were part of a sellout crowd at a Willie Nelson concert in Corpus Christi on a very cold night in the winter of 1985.

They gathered next to Willie's touring bus and stood there in the cold drizzling rain after the concert was over. The small group of fans standing there were very surprised when Willie came out of the bus and started a long conversation with them. Willie agreed to sign Darla's cowboy boot and Carlos' shirt collar. Three Dots and his girlfriend were the only ones that Willie invited on to the bus after the boot signing because of the limited room on board. Willie was impressed with Three Dots constant laughing and sense of humor. Darla still has that boot stored away as a souvenir.

Three Dots was loudly singing some of Willie's greatest hits while they paddled towards Hochheim. The singing and laughing kept everyone focused and moving down river. Janet and Sandy stayed right behind the singing Cowboys for several hours. Three Dots and Polecat were finally able to pull away from them and then watched the beautiful sunrise on Sunday morning.

Polecat led the short prayer and thanked the Lord for helping everyone make it through the first 24 hours of this marathon canoe race. The jalapeno dried sausage and canned peaches were passed back and forth in celebration. Polecat is a coffee addict and it is always a major disappointment to not be able to sip on a hot cup of coffee early on Sunday morning. The reality was that he would just have to be satisfied with a warm can of coke that was stashed away in the food bag under the seat.

The Texas Water Safari is a very competitive race but everyone involved understands how difficult it is and that common experience creates a unique bond with the other racers and bank crews. Team captains have been traveling all night from one checkpoint to the next with little or no rest. They are very important members of the team and the racers depend on them for water and encouragement. Polecat has a lot of respect for team captains and has always admired the commitment they have to their team and this great race.

The stroke rate was picking up and the Cowboys were trying to take advantage of the higher water levels and finally being in familiar territory. Polecat stared at his flood damaged home when the Cowboys paddled by his river house near Thomaston. The repairs were on hold during water safari weekend but would soon be ramped back up. It was very difficult to paddle by there without stopping for a quick break but there would be plenty of time to rest at the finish line.

The Cowboys with the big hats were able to pass a couple of tandem teams on that very hot July afternoon. Three Dots and Polecat found themselves in a good back and forth battle with Horsefly and his partner Martin. There were five teams that were very close to each other when the sun started to disappear on the second night below Victoria.

Bucky and his partner Terry were in that group. Bucky was a well known water safari veteran from Seadrift and he did several races on a very fast rowing team that finished in the top three in previous years. Bucky always had great stories to tell and he liked to tell Polecat about his commercial fishing business in Seadrift and then he would share detailed, secret water safari advice. The top secret advice would always end with, "Don't tell anyone about this". Bucky volunteered to supply the shrimp and organize the cooking team at the awards banquet after it moved to bay front park.

The very high water levels on the lower sections of the race course were helping everyone maintain a fast stroke rate and boat speed. The logjam cuts and Alligator lake were next in line. The massive logjam in this area was always growing and moving and had been growing even bigger recently because of the flooding that occurred in early June. Bucky and Terry were right behind the Cowboys with the big hats when they approached the logjam area. They turned off their bow light and quickly disappeared into the "secret" cut that no one else knew about.

The Cowboys did not see Bucky and Terry again after they took the secret cut. The Cowboys were able to beat them to the finish line.

Three Dots and Polecat had not trained in the area because of the house remodeling that had to be done after the June flood. The bow light was not working very well and the Cowboys were forced to rely on headlights that were strapped to their cowboy hats.

This was the first water safari that Polecat had participated in with a partner and he was used to being by himself and having no one to talk to for hours on end. Three Dots was starting to freak out because of the wild hallucinations and crazy things he was seeing. Hallucination alley is the common term that veteran water safari racers use when describing the river coarse below Victoria.

Polecat had to assure Three Dots that these crazy things he was seeing were not real. Polecat's advice to him was to just keep paddling and enjoy the party. It is hard to ignore the demon like faces that are staring at you from the top of the trees and the imaginary obstacles in the river that are not there. The wildest images that your imagination can come up with will suddenly appear all over the place when you start losing focus and slide into a bad case of mental fog because of the lack of sleep.

Polecat has experienced hallucination alley at different times during the three solo races that he had previously finished and learned the hard way to just smile at the crazy images and keep paddling. The image of the funeral procession that was following him in the 1984 race was the worst one. The pall bearers were waiting for Polecat to drop dead so they could put him in the casket and finish the funeral. That was one of those terrifying hallucinations that Polecat had to overcome and learn from. Three Dots was trying to explain to Polecat in detail what he was seeing. Polecat enjoyed listening to the crazy stories and just kept encouraged him to paddle through it.

The Cowboys reached the Tivoli bridge checkpoint just before daylight on Monday. The smell of saltwater drifts through the air when you get closer to San Antonio bay and the finish line. The Cowboys were trying very hard to catch Horsefly and his partner when they snapped on the spray skirt in Seadrift cut. There were a couple of tandem boats not very far behind and that was helping them to stay focused on keeping the fast stroke rate going. The wind had been blowing pretty hard all night and the Cowboys were in a hurry to get to the finish line before it picked up even more.

San Antonio bay was very choppy and the wind was starting to pick up even more when the Cowboys paddled up to the mouth of the barge canal and pulled up on the shoreline to dump water. The foot pumps that were mounted in the boat could not keep up with all of the water that was leaking in. The Cowboys noticed another team that was pulled up on the bank not very far from them. Three Dots yelled out to them, "which way to Seadrift" while the Cowboys quickly dumped the water out of the boat. Polecat yelled back at him to be quiet because he knew where Seadrift was.

The canoe on the bank next to them was a tandem mixed team. Polecat recognized John Mark and Carol from last years race. There was a loud team discussion going on between them and that was something that the Cowboys did not need to get involved in.

There are many famous water safari stories over the years of how people in this race got the dreaded "DNF" acronym placed next to their name because of losing their boat or losing their minds in the last few miles of the race.

Mike was in the USCA C-1 solo division and was in the top ten when he lost focus and his mental state deteriorated after leaving the Tivoli checkpoint. There was no GPS tracking devices or cell phones being used then. Mike pulled up on the bank somewhere between Tivoli and San Antonio bay and started wandering aimlessly around the shoreline. There was no way to communicate with him and he was several hours overdue at the finish line when a search team was finally organized to go and try to find him. They found his boat and started searching the desolate, brushy area. They finally located him walking around in the thick brush not knowing where he was or what he was doing. Thank the Lord that an alligator did not find him first.

Bill had a bad experience in San Antonio bay when he swam and walked in to the finish line after losing his solo boat in the rough turbulent waves. Bill swamped out and capsized and then tried to swim into shallow water with his boat in tow. A tough decision had to be made, save himself or keep battling the large waves and try to save the boat. Bill made the right decision and he let the boat go. The phrase, "It ain't over till it's over" applies to this race in many different ways.

The Cowboys with the big hats did not want to add their names to this list. The finish line was only a few miles away and the wind and waves were getting worse. Polecat told Three Dots that the finish line is that way and he pointed off in the distance. It was time to get back in the boat and finish this thing. The Cowboys started paddling over the large waves and suddenly found themselves involved in a back and forth battle with John Mark and Carol. The finish line was within sight.

The Cowboys with the big hats finished in tenth place overall with an official time of 48 hrs. 55 minutes. John Bugge and Mike Shively won the race in a tandem unlimited. Janet and Sandy, the Cowboys new friends from North Carolina finished in 12th place overall and were just a few minutes ahead of Donna and Teddy. Polecat was very happy with the fourth straight finish but was a little disappointed with being the third tandem unlimited team to cross the finish line. Three Dots had his ups and downs but ended up doing pretty well in his first race.

The Cowboys were in the running for the unofficial award of the most damaged boat and the best repair job that makes it in to the finish line. The competition was intense for the bragging rights and the secret vote that was taken did not reveal a clear winner.

The 28 teams that finished in time seemed to really enjoy the fried shrimp lunch at the bay front park finish line in Seadrift. Owen West temporarily shut down the festivities when he paddled in to the finish line after the banquet started. Everyone that was there lined up along the seawall and enthusiastically cheered him in.

Telling funny and interesting stories of your water safari experience when you were called up on stage to receive your award and patch was starting to take off. This seemed to be well received by everyone at the banquet. The funny story telling was slowly becoming another unofficial contest.

The race was finally over and Polecat had to get back to the flood repairs that were waiting on him back home. The family was able to move back in after the repairs were finished several weeks later. This was the second time in six years that record setting floodwaters from the Guadalupe river had severely damaged Polecat's home and it would not be the last time.

Three Dots and Polecat at the Gonzales checkpoint in 1987

Polecat and Three Dots get fresh water jugs from Jack at the
Hochheim checkpoint in 1987

CHAPTER 9

1988: Why am I doing this race? A gut wrenching reality check.

1988 came around very quickly. Three Dots wanted to team up with Polecat again after the top ten finish in 1987. The five hundred mile gap between them made getting together for regular training runs very difficult. Polecat transferred into the offshore production division of the company and was now working in the Gulf of Mexico out of Surfside, Texas. Three Dots would have to travel down to south Texas and they would meet up when they could for training runs.

Polecat's top priority was to help Darla raise their two young son's during his off week from offshore. Thank the Lord that Polecat has a wife that understands the time commitment that is required to be competitive in the Texas Water Safari. Darla has reluctantly allowed Polecat to be AWOL from his family responsibilities during the training season. The TWS has always been a team effort within the family and Darla is a very important member of the team.

Three Dots and Polecat were able to overcome the different work schedules and the long distance between them to get the necessary training miles in together leading up to the 1988 race. A very interesting training run happened in May while checking out the section between the swinging bridge checkpoint and Tivoli. The Cowboys were just about to reach the logjam cut area when a severe thunderstorm rolled in right over the top of them. It is not a good thing to be on the river when lightning is striking all around you. This scenario has happened a couple of times over the years during the race and Polecat would just grit his teeth and keep on paddling. That can be very hard to do when lightning is striking the trees right next to you. The competitive TWS racing mentality would kick in and force Polecat to keep paddling forward down river and try to ignore the chaos.

The difference was that this was a training run. Large golf ball sized hail started raining down on top of the Cowboys along with severe gusts of wind. There was no discussion or debate between Three Dots and Polecat and they quickly headed for the river bank to seek shelter. The Cowboys were in the middle of nowhere and there was no shelter to be found close by. It would not be a good idea to hide under a tree with lightning strikes and high winds all around you.

The Cowboys decided to turn the racing canoe upside down and crawl underneath it to escape the hail storm. The large hail that was pounding on the Kevlar boat bottom was deafening. Three Dots and Polecat tried to shield themselves from the hail storm with the canoe while holding it down on top of them with a tight grip because of the gusting high winds.

Polecat was worried about potential boat damage from the large hail. It seemed like the hail storm would never end when all of a sudden it stopped. They crawled out from under the boat to inspect the damage and were surprised to find just some minor dings in the hull. Large tree limbs were splintered and knocked down all around the area. Polecat lowered his head in prayer thanking the Lord Jesus for helping them get through that terrible hail storm with no injuries or major damage. The hail storm ended up causing over an hour delay in the training run and the Cowboys were going to be very late getting to the takeout spot at Tivoli. Polecat's dad had been waiting for several hours at the bridge to pick them up and was starting to get worried.

Polecat's dad has volunteered many times over the years to be a shuttle driver for the Cowboy training runs. Dad was willing to do whatever he could to help because he loved to follow the Texas Water Safari and he was Polecat's biggest fan. Dad followed the race from start to finish and would be at every checkpoint give verbal support and encouragement. The TWS was always a big annual event for him and he would usually turn the race into a four day camping trip and party with his friends.

Polecat's dad was a Korean war veteran who suffered a severe head injury during an intense battle in South Korea in 1950. The near fatal injury from an explosion would cause him numerous medical problems for the rest of his life. Thank the Lord that he survived the battle and a brain tumor operation several years later. That operation caused him to completely lose the hearing and feeling on the left side of his face. Dad survived all of this and lived a long life. Dad worked in the Texas and Louisiana oil fields while raising a family. Polecat and his sister were blessed to have a father that was such a good example of how to overcome the bad things that life can sometimes throw at you.

Dad would team up with Jack and Connie and several other partying friends and they would follow the Cowboys all the way to Seadrift. Connie's loud voice could be heard echoing up river when she would shout out, "Where are the Cowboys"? The party bunch was the funny name that Three Dots and Polecat called them. Three Dots and Polecat would always put a lot of pressure on themselves to keep paddling through all of the ups and downs in the race in order to make sure the party bunch had a good time all the way down to the finish line.

The 1988 Texas Water Safari started with 51 teams lined up in rows of six. The very low river levels were going to create a much different race course than what the Cowboys had experienced the year before. Tom led everyone in a beautiful prayer and then shot off the start gun. There were several very fast tandem unlimited teams entered in the race along with a strong multi man team consisting of Joe, Fred and Brian Mynar.

It was going to be a challenge for the Cowboys to be competitive in the unlimited division. There were no significant screw ups or near misses early in the race on the upper river. That dramatically changed later that day when the Cowboys approached the Palmetto state park checkpoint. The food supply that the Cowboys checked in was much different than what they had used in the past. The egg and potato tacos, peanut butter and honey sandwiches, Vienna sausage, sardines in Louisiana hot sauce, jalapeno dried sausage and canned peaches had been replaced by MRE's. The Military meals that were ready to eat were stored away in the boat and weighed much less than the usual stuff.

The Cowboys recruited their good friend Carlos to help them find the MRE's. Carlos was an officer in the army reserve and was able to get the Cowboys several cases of MREs at a cheap price. The Cowboys used them during training runs and the high calorie meals tasted pretty good. They even had a small single serving bag of ground coffee in some of them. Polecat's favorite was the Cajun jambalaya and rice meal that also came with several interesting side packets.

Three Dots and Polecat were moving along at a good stroke rate with their double blade paddles and were in the top ten after a long day of canoe racing on the San Marcos river. That is when everything started going downhill in a hurry. Three Dots was not feeling well and was having bad stomach problems. The Cowboys cleared the Palmetto state park checkpoint and were headed down river towards Gonzales.

Three Dots gut problems were getting much worse and he suddenly started to violently throw up with no warning. It was not a very pleasant experience to watch Three Dots throw up in the bow of the boat with the terrible smell of regurgitated MRE's polluting the air around them. Three Dots was finally able to get back to paddling when the puking eased up a little. The bigger problem would be if he could eventually recover from the gut problems he was experiencing and not let it force him out of the race. Three Dots seemed to be getting better and was able to drink some water when the Cowboys neared the Gonzales 90 bridge. The plan was to pull over very quickly and change out water containers before heading on down to the confluence of the San Marcos and Guadalupe rivers.

Three Dots decided that he needed to step out of the boat and sit in the water for a minute. Polecat reluctantly agreed to the unscheduled waste of time. Carlos was standing on the bank and was encouraging Three Dots to hang in there and keep paddling through this difficult time he was experiencing. Three Dots abruptly emptied his gut again in front of the small crowd that was there.

Polecat was trying to eat his MRE just a few feet away. The violent gut emptying incident forced Polecat to quickly turn his head so he wouldn't have to watch the show. There were several other team captains and race fans there and they had to scatter to avoid the wild spectacle. That was the last gut cleaning episode and the Cowboys were finally able to start paddling down river again.

Three Dots was doing much better when the Cowboys reached the Gonzales gravel bar checkpoint. They had once again caught up with their friends from North Carolina, Janet and Sandy for the second year in a row at the same spot. Janet and Sandy had a year of Texas Water Safari experience behind them and it was going to be a good battle trying to pass them.

Three Dots was feeling much better and he started bellowing out his favorite Willie Nelson songs. The Cowboys were trying to distract the girls from North Carolina while they paddled by. Polecat was very happy that Three Dots had overcome his stomach problems and now they had a good battle going with another fast team to keep them motivated through the first night. The singing and funny conversation's with Janet and Sandy seemed to go on for a while before everything changed.

The Cowboys rounded a gradual turn in the river and suddenly noticed a large Cypress tree laying completely across the river just above the water line. The downed tree was blocking most of the river and the current was very strong around it. The Cowboys did not train on this section of the race course because it normally doesn't change very much. If anyone knew about this hazard before the race started they were probably keeping it a secret. It was very common for water safari racers to keep critical race information like this a secret.

The Cowboys were just a few minutes ahead of their North Carolina friends and the downed tree came up on them in a hurry. The current was very swift and the tree was partially submerged in the turbulent water. Three Dots did not see the potential hazard until it was too late and the Cowboys ran their boat right up on top of the downed tree and suddenly came to a grinding stop.

A large broken limb that was attached to the trunk of the tree punched a large hole completely through the Kevlar bottom near the middle of the boat. The Cowboys stopped dead in their tracks. Three Dots was violently ejected out of his seat and into the river by the sudden stop. The loss of his weight in the bow caused the stern of the boat to start sinking.

Polecat had to make a quick decision to jump out of the boat because it was getting ready to wrap around the trunk of the tree. Three Dots was swept down river with his paddle still in his hand. Polecat was able to hang on to the tree trunk with one hand and to his paddle with the other.

Polecat was trying very hard to keep his head above the turbulent water. Janet and Sandy were approaching the hazard and Polecat yelled out to them to head river right to avoid the downed tree. They were able to successfully paddle over to the far right along the bank and avoid the same fate.

Polecat was able to slowly start pushing the boat forward over the tree trunk before the partially submerged stern went completely under. The boat was very close to the point of being sucked under the tree trunk. Polecat was finally able to push the boat forward and over the tree trunk before any more damage was inflicted.

The swift current pulled him under the tree and he frantically tried to stay afloat. Polecat's head popped up above the water line on the downstream side of the tree while he hung on to the submerged racing canoe for dear life. Polecat was gasping for air when he finally reached calmer water. Three Dots was then able to swim over and help him drag the boat over to the nearest bank.

Janet and Sandy pulled over to make sure the Cowboys were OK. Three Dots and Polecat dragged the severely damaged racing canoe up on the steep bank and turned it over to find a long rip and gaping hole completely through the Kevlar bottom.

Janet and Sandy asked if anyone was injured. There were no noticeable physical wounds. This disaster was going to test the Cowboys mental toughness more than anything else. Three Dots and Polecat thanked their North Carolina friends for stopping to check on them. The Cowboys encouraged them to head on down river before another team passed by. Three Dots yelled out that the Cowboys would soon catch back up and pass them after the repair job was finished. They both laughed and paddled off into the darkness.

Three Dots and Polecat dragged the boat up the steep bank until they could find some level ground. It was going to be difficult to get the Kevlar bottom dry enough to be able to apply a duct tape patch and get it to stick. The tree crashing incident happened around three am in the morning.

Three Dots came up with the good idea to start a camp fire close to the boat. That should help with the drying process. The Cowboys had matches in several of the MRE meal packets. They needed to find some fire wood to start the process. They managed to get a pretty good fire going and then positioned the racing canoe to where it was close enough to help dry the damaged area.

Three Dots and Polecat sat down next to the fire and painfully watched several water safari teams pass by. This was a very difficult and depressing time for them because their high expectations for this race seemed to be going up in smoke. The Cowboys were physically and mentally drained and they did not have a plan going forward.

The camp fire Cowboys eventually fell asleep. A lot of wasted time passed by when Polecat suddenly heard Three Dots yell out, "get away from me". Polecat sat up to see an armadillo climbing over his leg. The sight of a strange looking critter crawling over his leg made him quickly jump up. The scared armadillo was frantically trying to escape the area. The uninvited guest had bumped into Three Dots back before changing directions and crawling over Polecat's leg. That was the wake up call the camp fire Cowboys needed in order to regain some mental focus.

The Kevlar bottom was finally dry enough to proceed with the patch job. Polecat started the process of applying layered strips of duct tape to the damaged area. That was the only roll of tape they had, so if it did not hold the race would be over. Three Dots and Polecat downed another MRE and put out the campfire before dragging the boat back into the water.

There was a lot of valuable time wasted there but it was still dark and the Cowboys were anxious to get back into the race. The patch job seemed to be holding as the sun made it's glorious appearance on that beautiful Sunday morning. Polecat led the team prayer and then they sang Amazing Grace.

The Cowboys eventually caught up with a young mixed team that had passed them the night before. That was just what the Cowboys needed in order to regain some much needed momentum and confidence after the tree crashing incident. Three Dots and Polecat picked up the stroke rate and were catching up with them when they noticed that the young women in the bow was sun bathing and taking pictures of the sunrise. The young man in the stern was paddling at a strong stroke rate while his partner was soaking in the sun and taking pictures.

Three Dots started up a pleasant conversation with them. The young couple said that they had passed a team during the night that had a nice campfire going on the bank. Three Dots could not help himself and had to ask them a question. "What place are y'all in"? The nice young man answered that they were in 25th place. Polecat immediately went into shock and a deep depression.

The tree crashing incident had set them back 16 places and they were now paddling with the teams that were just trying to finish within the 100 hour time limit. This was the first time Polecat had ever been this far back in the pack and it was a very humbling experience.

Three Dots and Polecat looked at each other in disbelief. They quickly paddled by the friendly mixed team and headed for Hochheim. This was supposed to be the breakout race that Polecat had been hoping for since 1984. It quickly deteriorated into a race where the Cowboys found themselves paddling with the teams that were just trying to finish.

There was very little conversation going on between Three Dots and Polecat while they tried to come to terms with the harsh reality. They paddled in to the Hochheim checkpoint around mid morning on Sunday. Jack and the bank crew had been patiently waiting for several hours.

Everyone was very happy to see the Cowboys because they were way overdue. Three Dots quickly gave them a brief explanation of what had happened the night before during the tree crashing incident. The small crowd just kept staring at the layers of duct tape that extended from one gunnel to the other over the middle of the canoe. The Cowboys did not want to hear it but Jack gave them the bad news. They were currently in 24th place with several tandem teams just a few minutes ahead.

Jack quickly changed out the water containers and the Cowboys headed down river. The next section of the race course down to Cheapside was a very awkward time because of the disappointment and depression. Polecat felt pretty good physically after the campfire nap but Three Dots was a basket case mentally. Three Dots had overcome dehydration and stomach issues on Saturday but the tree crashing incident was dragging him down mentally. The conversation became very negative at this point while the blame game and finger pointing started to take over.

Three Dots was ready to pull out of the race at Cheapside and Polecat was starting to agree with him. The depressed Cowboys were both in agreement that the best thing they could do at this point was to quit at Cheapside. The demoralized Cowboys did not know that Darla had assembled a large group of friends and family at the Cheapside checkpoint to support and encourage them.

Three Dots and Polecat pulled in to the checkpoint and started slowly climbing out of the canoe. Darla was standing close by and sternly asked, "what are you doing"? Three Dots responded to her that the Cowboys were pulling out and that this was the end of the race for them. Darla stared at Three Dots in disbelief and then said something that pierced through Polecat like a sharp sword. "Your nothing but a couple of Wimps"! Darla was very upset and the crowd standing there watching the drama unfold did not say anything. Polecat's depression was getting much worse and he kept his head down. Darla continued, "We have been waiting here for several hours to support you and now your going to quit"? Darla was on a roll and the chewing out continued, "All you care about is a Texas Water Safari plaque that will hang up on the wall and no one will ever look at it again".

Three Dots was very irritated with Darla and her harsh words and he began to argue with her. This was not a very pleasant conversation and it was getting worse. Polecat was blown away by her comments and he just sat there quietly in the boat while Three Dots and Darla argued with each other. Polecat looked up at the crowd and noticed several close friends and family standing there with very sad expressions on their faces. This motivated Polecat to finally intervene in the intense argument and try to calm things down.

Polecat yelled at Three Dots that this was not the time or place to pull out of the race. "Stop arguing with her and get back into the boat". "Let's head down river so we can talk about this some more". Three Dots and Darla were still exchanging heated comments when he finally got back into the boat and the angry depressed Cowboys started paddling down river.

Polecat's lovely wife had just called him a "Wimp" in front of a large crowd. Polecat was having a very hard time trying to figure out why she would do that. The Lord stepped in and helped Polecat understand. Darla made those comments out of love. Darla knew how much this race meant to him and she remembered how bad he felt after pulling out of the 1982 race. The harsh comments she yelled at him were true and accurate. The boat was not leaking and the Cowboys were physically OK after 30 hours of canoe racing. The only reasons why they were thinking about quitting was because of all the time that was wasted after the tree crashing incident and the places that were lost.

Polecat quietly asked himself, "why are you doing this race"? The Texas Water Safari is much more than just about trophies and recognition. Polecat has learned over the years that competing in this difficult canoe race can help you deal with all of the crazy things that life can sometimes throw at you. The TWS can help give you the valuable experience needed to overcome obstacles, setbacks, equipment damage, injuries, physical problems and mental fatigue. The list goes on and on and on.

Polecat's canoe racing friends say that the TWS is the hardest thing that they will do all year. The consensus is that once you finish this race everything else you have to deal with doesn't seem so bad. Polecat's personal testimony is that the Texas Water Safari has pushed him way beyond what he thought he was ever capable of doing. This marathon canoe race has given him a different perspective on the limits that he has placed on himself.

The good and bad experiences during the race have significantly strengthened his personal relationship with the Lord Jesus. Reaching out to the Lord through prayer during the good and the difficult times of life will always get an answer from him in his own time and in un-expected ways. The Lord does not care about what place you are in and you don't have a relationship with God on your terms. Christians have a relationship with God on His terms, which is faith and obedience.

Polecat started to come out of his depression after focusing on all of these positive things. Three Dots was starting to calm down some. The Cowboys picked up the stroke rate and paddled towards Cuero. Three Dots was still dwelling on all of the negative stuff that had taken place. Polecat was trying to be positive after remembering the reasons why he was doing this race. The "woe is me" attitude was slowly fading away. The Cowboys were overlooking the good things that had happened.

Three Dots had overcome a bad case of dehydration and stomach issues that would have forced most people out of the race. There were no serious injuries and they were able to successfully patch a badly damaged racing canoe after nearly wrapping it around a downed tree. There were a lot of positive things to talk about instead of dwelling on the negative stuff.

The Cowboys caught up with another tandem team and their stroke rate and boat speed picked up some more. The stroke rate slowly kept increasing when they were able to pass another tandem team a little while later. The Cuero dam portage was next in line and the Cowboys carefully portaged the repaired racing canoe over the dam. They tried very hard not to scrape off any of the multiple layers of duct tape that was stretched across the damaged hull area.

There was another team at the dam and the Cowboys were able to pass them during the portage. The party bunch was patiently waiting at the Highway 72 bridge. They were yelling out encouragement when the Cowboys arrived. Three Dots and Polecat affectionately call this place the Peacock bridge because the landowner just downstream of the bridge has a large flock of Peacocks. Three Dots started calling out to the Peacocks with his very loud squawking imitation and our feathered friends started to respond. Connie yelled out, "call the Peacock's Glenn". There was nobody there named Glenn but everyone knew who she was talking about.

The Cowboys were still in the race and the party bunch was having a good time. Life was good and everything was slowly getting back to normal again. The pressure of keeping the party going and giving them something to cheer about was helping to push the Cowboys on down the race course.

The stroke rate and boat speed started picking up even more when the Cowboys left the Cuero 236 checkpoint and paddled towards Victoria. They were able to pass two more tandem teams in the process and the attitude in the boat was dramatically changing for the better.

The Cowboys paddled up to Floodplain Ranch and Polecat could see his bedroom window from the river. The overwhelming thoughts of crawling into a soft bed will sometimes cause Polecat to lose focus but the competitive racing mentality had returned and the Cowboys were focused on the race again.

The river dogs were gathered on the bank when they paddled up to the primitive boat ramp. Polecat tried to talk to Spook, Candy, Brandy and Shadow. They were barking with excitement and enthusiasm and then they all jumped into the river and tried to follow the Cowboys after the water hand off. They could not swim fast enough to keep up. Polecat looked back and told them to go home. The bad thoughts of dumping Three Dots and replacing him with the river dogs started to creep into the back of Polecat's sleep deprived mind.

The rejuvenated Cowboys reached the Victoria riverside park checkpoint and noticed that two teams they had been chasing all day were pulled over and resting. Three Dots and Polecat had already wasted enough valuable time during the tree crashing incident. Jack very quietly changed out the water jugs and everyone tried very hard to not disturb and wake up the resting canoe racers.

The rejuvenated Cowboys were now back in the top twenty. They needed to keep the good stroke rate going through hallucination alley and pass a few more teams. The mental focus was good at this point. The crazy hallucinations that usually make their ugly appearance through this section of the race course did not show up as dramatically as they normally do. The unscheduled campfire nap from the first night was helping to keep everyone alert.

The Cowboys were able to pass another tandem team when the sun made its glorious appearance on Monday morning. The early morning cooler temperatures and bright sunshine were giving the rejuvenated Cowboys a big boost and they were able to catch up with their racing friend Kent and his partner Johnny.

Kent is a good friend from Luling and Polecat always enjoyed talking to him after the race was over. Kent and Polecat had a lot in common because they both worked in the offshore oil industry. They also enjoyed competing against each other in the "Worlds Toughest Boat Race".

Polecat and Kent's sons would soon be competing against each other on the football field during the Cuero, Luling football rivalry several years later. Kent always did pretty well in the water safari. Kent would run the race in the standard division with a different partner every year. Polecat once asked him out of curiosity where was he finding all of these different teammates. Kent answered that he would usually recruit his water safari teammates at the local bars in Luling and then give them a tryout on a training run. Kent smiled and told Polecat that some of them worked out and some didn't. Kent's name is on the standard division trophy several times.

Three dots and Polecat were getting close to the salt water barrier dam and noticed two teams just in front of them. There was a very large log jam piled up just in front of the dam and it had the entire river blocked off. The two teams in front of the Cowboys were confused about where they were and how to proceed. They had convinced themselves that they needed to turn left and paddle into the man made canal that heads off towards hog bayou and eventually into the surrounding swamps.

Three Dots and Polecat were very motivated and confident at this point. They told the lost teams to follow them. The Cowboys portaged the massive log jam and the submerged dam on river right. There was another tandem team that had made the bad decision to turn into the man made canal and they were still missing. The saltwater barrier dam was very isolated and on one was there because it was not a checkpoint and there was no public access.

The party bunch had been partying all day long and they were very excited to see the Cowboys when they paddled up to the Tivoli Bridge checkpoint. Jack relayed the information that the bay was choppy and that there was a multi man team just a few minutes ahead of them.

The spray skirt was pulled out and snapped on during a quick pit stop at the mouth of Seadrift cut. The sun was disappearing over the western horizon when the Cowboys caught up with the multi man mixed team. John Mark, Carol and Corky were pulled up on the shoreline at the mouth of the barge canal. This was the second year in a row that the Cowboys had caught up with John Mark and Carol at the same spot. There seemed to be a serious team meeting going on between them and there was no reason for the Cowboys to stop and get involved in their heated conversation.

They quickly got back into their boat when they noticed the Cowboys paddling by. Three Dots and Polecat had to shift into a higher gear and they tried to out sprint them to the finish line across the very choppy bay. The flashing yellow light at the flag pole was in view. The Cowboys finished in an official time of 61 hours and 49 minutes. That was good enough for fourteenth place overall and fourth place in the tandem unlimited division. Fred and Brian Mynar won the race. Janet and Sandy came in eleventh place and were the first women's team.

Polecat slowly climbed out from under the tight fitting spray skirt and then fell face first into the turbulent waist deep water. It was very difficult to stand up after sitting in a racing canoe for two and a half days. Polecat was finally able to stand up and slowly stagger up the steps at the finish line. Darla ran up to him and they hugged each other tightly with tears streaming down their faces. Darla wiped away the tears of joy from Polecat's face. They just kept hugging each other for several minutes and no words were needed. The stored up emotions were flowing out. Polecat regained his composure and he thanked her for the harsh words that she had laid on him at Cheapside.

The only reason the Cowboys were standing at the finish line was because of the soul searching reality check that she forced them to think about. Three Dots thanked her and apologized for becoming so angry. It didn't really matter what place the Cowboys ended up in because they had overcome sickness, severe boat damage and self inflicted depression to make it to Seadrift.

The 1988 TWS ended up being two different races combined into one event. The race started with big goals and high expectations. The Cowboys had to overcome a lot of hurdles before finishing strong. It was time to get cleaned up and get some much needed rest.

Polecat told the story of the tree crashing incident and the boat repair campout at the finishers banquet. The crowd seemed to really like the part of the story when the armadillo came out of the brush and woke them up after running into Three Dot and crawling over Polecat.

The Cowboys easily won the unofficial award of the most damaged boat and the best repair job. Polecat turned the boat upside down and pulled all of the duct tape off so everyone could see the intensive damage after the banquet was over. The we no nah brand name on the side of the racing canoe was partially scraped off due to all of the damage.

Polecat wrote, "we no nah ta" in large letters in its place. That was a very good description of the Cowboy team. There was another valuable lesson learned during the 1988 Texas Water Safari. Polecat never used MRE's again.

The water safari was over and the family vacation was the next thing on the calendar. Darla and Polecat loaded up their two young son's and headed out on a two week camping trip. It was way past time for him to return his undivided attention and focus towards his beautiful family.

Three Dots and Polecat had a long phone conversation a few months later. They were both in agreement that they needed to look into the possibility of moving into the USCA C-2 division. The unlimited racing canoe they had used for the last two races was severely damaged in the tree crashing incident and it would have to be put into retirement.

Jerry Nunnery was the go to person when you wanted to talk about the USCA C-2 division. Jerry and Roy were the only team to ever win the Texas Water Safari in a USCA C-2 in the 1984 race. The TWS racing community was very small and everyone knew each other during that time.

Polecat called Jerry a few months later to ask him if he knew where a used USCA C-2 could be found for sale at a decent price. Jerry was surprised to hear from Polecat and said that he had a used racing canoe that he was willing to sell at the right price. Jerry lived in the Freeport area and worked at one of the local plants.

Polecat made the long drive over to Freeport a few days later to look at the boat and to try and make a deal. Polecat had to stop at a convenience store in the area and ask for directions after getting lost but finally was able to drive up into his driveway while Jerry was working out in his garage. Jerry waved at him to come on in while he continued his workout routine.

The workout he was doing was very intense and impressive. Jerry was sitting in a chair in the middle of his garage with a single blade racing paddle in his hands. The paddle had a wire cable attached to it just above the blade and the cable stretched out for fifteen feet before it threaded through a rotating pulley that was attached to the roof next to the garage doors. The wire cable then went straight down and was attached to a five gallon bucket that was on the cement floor. Large weights could be added or subtracted to the bucket in order to increase or decrease cable tension.

Jerry proudly showed Polecat his home made workout invention and invited him to try it out. Jerry added a lot of weight to the bucket and challenged Polecat to imitate his water safari stroke rate and technique when using a single blade paddle. Polecat did a quick warm up and then started paddling as hard as he could. The weight in the bucket was putting a lot of pressure on his shoulders and mid section. Polecat switched from one side to the other after ten strokes on each side.

The workout seemed to go on for a while and Jerry was acting like a coach. Jerry would yell out instructions to increase the stroke rate and switch sides. Polecat was pretty tired after about fifteen minutes of this intense exercise and started slowing down before coming to a complete stop.

Jerry was smiling after coaching the work out and he told Polecat that you have to be able to consistently do 60 strokes a minute during the water safari in order to be the first boat to Seadrift. Jerry and Roy won the race in 1984 and had to paddle through some extremely low river levels. Polecat was closely listening to his advice because Jerry evidently knows what he is talking about. Polecat's take a way from Jerry's advice was that he was going to have to pick up the stroke rate in order to get his name on the USCA C-2 trophy.

The training exercise and coaching tips were greatly appreciated but it was getting late. Polecat had to eventually change the subject and ask to see the racing canoe he had for sale. The boat was a we no nah mixed USCA C-2 and it was in very good condition. The boat had been used in some short races and during training but it had never been used in the water safari.

Jerry proudly showed Polecat the boat that they used to win the 1984 race. It was on a canoe rack in the back of the garage and Jerry said that there was no way he would ever part with that boat. Polecat made an offer on the USCA C-2 he had for sale and then there was some friendly negotiating before a final price was agreed upon. Jerry was telling some very interesting water safari stories from past races when the deal was finalized and the boat was loaded on the truck for the ride home.

Jerry has a good sense of humor but he gets very serious when discussing water safari strategy and preparation. Polecat thanked him for the training advice and for letting him try out his homemade paddling machine. The long drive back home would give Polecat some time to try and figure out how he would explain the purchase of another racing canoe to Darla.

CHAPTER 10

1989: Low water levels, High expectations, and a terrible finish

Paddling a USCA C-2 racing canoe down a winding river with single blade paddles and with no rudder attached was going to be a little different than what Polecat was familiar with and would take a lot of practice time. Polecat's double blade paddle with the wooden blades would have to be put up on the rack at home and retired. The badly damaged we no nah ICF tandem canoe would be repaired later but would never be used in the water safari again. The retired ICF tandem canoe has survived through several floods and hurricanes over the years and is still on the canoe rack next to old blue in the barn. It is just taking up space but it does bring back the great memories of those early races.

Three Dots and Polecat started making training plans for the 1989 Texas Water Safari. Three Dots would still be commuting from Levelland and that meant that the Cowboys would have to put in a lot of training miles when they were able to coordinate the days off.

The 1989 TWS training season was in full swing and one of the training runs turned out to be a very interesting adventure. The Cowboys decided to do a night training run on the Gonzales to Hochheim stretch of river. This was the same area where the boat pinning disaster happened in last years race. The plan was to start just before dark at Gonzales and do the majority of the training run at night. Polecat rigged up a make shift bow light that should be good enough for a training run but would definitely not be used in the water safari.

The training run was moving along smoothly while the sun was starting to disappear on the western horizon. The Cowboys were trying to maintain a very fast stroke rate and keep the USCA C-2 headed down river in a straight line. This type of racing canoe will sometimes track from one side to the other when the river depth and current changes. There is no rudder to help steer the boat and that makes it more of a challenge to keep the boat moving forward in a straight line. The bow and stern paddlers have to work together in sync to successfully navigate through the many rapids, shallow spots and turns in the river. This was going to be a big change in paddling technique and would require a lot of practice.

Three Dots turned on the temporary bow light and it was working good enough to see the obstacles down river. The bow light suddenly quit working about an hour after dark. It was a very dark night with no moon and the Cowboys were forced to pull over to try and get the bow light working again. Three Dots reached in to the dry bag to pull out the backup head light but soon realized that it had been left behind in the truck at Gonzales.

Frustration started setting in while they tried to figure out what to do next. They eventually gave up on trying to fix the light and decided to head on down river at a slower pace and cautiously limp on in to Hochheim. This was only about half way into the long training run and there was nothing but open pasture land and cows on both sides of the river. The bad situation was getting worse and the Cowboys had to accept the fact that trying to paddle down river on a very dark night with no lights was not a good idea.

There were a couple of near misses and close calls before the Cowboys pulled the boat over to the bank and had a team meeting. The only two options available were to camp out on the bank and wait for daylight or walk to the highway and try to hitch hike back to the vehicle in Hochheim. The bad decision was made to carry the boat to the highway and then try to hitch a ride to Hochheim. This terrible idea was based on the assumption that it was only a mile or so to the highway. The Cowboys had no idea at the time that it was over four miles from the river to the highway from there. The overland portage would go through some very dense brush and overgrown pasture land. Hopefully there would be a road not to far away that could be followed up to the highway.

The Cowboys were taking their time and were trying not to damage the new racing canoe while carrying it through the dense vegetation. The sounds of wild animals running through the dense brush caused Three Dots and Polecat to suddenly stop because they could not see exactly what was happening in front of them. The lost Cowboys started worrying about a pack of wild hogs attacking them or maybe even accidently stepping on a copperhead snake. The water safari mentality of pushing through any obstacle with reckless abandonment and laser like focus took over.

It took a long time to get through this brushy area next to the river. The lost Cowboys finally made it through the brush with no damage to the boat and with only a few scratches and cuts to the arms and legs. The area finally opened up into a large pasture and the walking pace increased but the uneven terrain caused the lost Cowboys to occasionally trip and stumble to the ground because of the tall grass and critter holes. The boat had to be lifted up over several barbed wire fences that lined the pastures. A few more deep cuts were added during this process because of not being able to see very well with no light. There was no road access anywhere close by so the lost Cowboys had to carry the boat several more miles through rough pasture land and over many barbed wire fences. The cow herds were cautiously watching the lost Cowboys from a distance and the Brahman bulls were ready to charge if their territory was challenged by the rough looking characters wearing Cowboy hats.

Three Dots and Polecat were both getting very tired of carrying the boat for this long so they would stop and switch sides in order to be able to use the other arm for a while. This over land portage would end up taking over three hours to complete. Polecat had never carried a canoe that far and for that long. It kind of turned out to be a challenge of its own. The lost Cowboys were determined to get their new USCA C-2 cruiser to the highway with no damage. They finally made it to the highway and hid the boat in the thick brush and marked the spot in their weary minds.

The next step would be to try and hitch a ride with someone to the Hochheim bridge. It was three o'clock in the morning and there was not much traffic on the highway. Three Dots and Polecat started walking down the shoulder of the highway towards Hochheim. The river bridge takeout was over seven miles down the road from here.

Three Dots would awkwardly stick out his thumb as an approaching vehicle zipped by but no one would even slow down. It kind of sounded like they would even accelerate more when they passed by. Nobody was going to stop and pick up a couple of rough looking characters wearing cowboy hats. They had dried mud and blood stains all over their clothing and bodies. It was a long seven mile walk but the tired Cowboys finally made it to the bridge where the truck was parked.

The sun started making it's glorious appearance on Sunday morning. The night training run had basically turned into an unscheduled triathlon. Twenty miles of paddling was followed by a four mile over land boat portage through some very rough terrain. That was followed with a seven mile walk along the edge of the highway. This was all done with no lights on a very dark night.

The triathlon was finally over and it was time to round up vehicles and find the hidden race boat. Three Dots and Polecat headed for Floodplain ranch to get some much needed rest. It was very hard to stay awake and make the drive back home after the long night. The Cowboys did not know that another crazy event was about to happen.

They drove up to the Floodplain Ranch entrance and noticed several sheriff deputy cars parked alongside the county road at the neighbors place. Polecat's heart rate jumped and panic was setting in because he was worried about Darla and the boy's because they were at home by themselves.

Three Dots and Polecat stopped and watched the deputies put on their bullet proof vests and load their weapons. Polecat cautiously stepped out of the truck and identified himself to the deputies before approaching them. The deputy would only tell him that there was an armed suspect that had barricaded himself in a cabin on the river and he would not surrender to the authorities.

Polecat asked the deputy if he could turn into the next gate and check on his family because they were at home by themselves. The deputy gave him permission to proceed with caution and to isolate everyone indoors until further notice. Polecat immediately started praying to the Lord Jesus for his families protection. Darla and the boys were fine and they didn't even know there was anything going on at the neighbor's place. Darla told Polecat that there had been a big party with a lot of noise going on over there the night before.

A sheriff's deputy finally came over a few hours later and said that the suspect had surrendered and the standoff was over. The neighbor's did not live there full time but they had a river cabin that was used occasionally on the weekends for family gatherings.

The story came out later that the suspect had chased down his wife and her sister with his tractor while they were trying to leave. The intoxicated tractor man managed to catch up with them at the property gate and turned over their car with the front end loader on his tractor. The women were able to crawl out from under the upside down vehicle and run for their lives. They escaped across the pasture while the intoxicated tractor man continued to search for them. They had to run for their lives up the county road on foot to another neighbor's place over a mile away. They hid out in a water well house until daylight and then asked the neighbor for help. The sheriff's office was then called in for assistance. This was a bizarre ending to a crazy weekend.

The 1989 Texas Water Safari started on the first weekend of June with fifty teams entered. Three Dots and Polecat were entered in the

USCA C-2 division. The Cowboys were able to get in the necessary training for this race and they felt good about their chances to do well in this division.

Tom was going over the final race instructions on the loud speaker while the Cowboys were doing a quick warm up paddle in Aquarena Spring lake. Three Dots and Polecat decided to pull over to the floating observation platform where Ralph the swimming pig was standing and briefly talk to their good friend. Ralph was grunting in excitement while Polecat tried to thank him for his support of the Texas Water Safari. Ralph's handlers and the people standing close by were laughing loudy while Three Dots and Polecat had a long conversation with their friend. The grunting got significantly louder when Polecat tried to recruit him for next years race. Three Dots would have been kicked of the team and Ralph would have replaced him. The crowd was laughing but Polecat was serious.

The river levels for the 1989 race were very low because of another prolonged drought. The levels were not near as low as they were in 1984 but this was definitely going to be a negative factor and would ultimately cause a lot of DNF's. Three Dots and Polecat both figured that these very low water conditions would end up working in their favor.

Tom fired off the starting gun and the field spread out pretty quickly. The Cowboys were moving along at a good stroke rate and were in the top ten through the never ending obstacles and portages on the upper San Marcos river. Darla and Polecat's two young sons, Wade and Brandon were following the Cowboys down the race course and were having a good time playing in the shallow water at the checkpoints. Polecat would always have a big smile on his face when he heard Wade and Brandon shout, "go Polecat go". This race has always been a big family event and the memories of seeing them having a good time along the race coarse and hearing them cheering the Cowboys on are a constant reminder of how much of a blessing they are.

The first day moved along without any major problems. There were a couple of close calls and some minor boat damage inflicted while the Cowboys navigated down the narrow and slow river. Three Dots and

Polecat were in a back and forth battle with several tandem teams and with a solo paddler named John Dunn. John was a young and talented canoe racer who had recently finished his military commitment in the Army and finished well in the 1988 TWS. Tom had become John's mentor and coach and was a positive influence on him. John was doing well in the solo division and the Cowboys had several friendly conversations with him while he drafted behind their boat on the lower end of the San Marcos river.

A severe thunder storm could be seen off in the distance when the Cowboys approached the Gonzales checkpoint late Saturday night. It was time to shout hallelujah when the Cowboys merged into the Guadalupe river and waved goodbye to the San Marcos creek. Jack quickly changed out the water jugs at the gravel bar checkpoint and the Cowboys paddled straight into a very intense and severe lightning storm.

Lightning was striking all around them. Three Dots and Polecat jumped and yelled every time a bolt of lightning struck the trees close to them. Strong wind gusts were trying to push the Cowboys into the river bank and a hard rain was blowing into them. The sting from the blowing rain was painful and Polecat lowered his head to try and deflect it from his face with the brim of his hat.

The Cowboys were paddling hard trying to keep the boat headed down river while the strong wind gusts and driving rain was pounding into them. The ringing in Polecat's ears from the loud thunder seemed to be getting worse and he could not hear anything that Three Dots was trying to tell him. The water safari competitive mentality of getting through obstacles any way possible and as fast as you can kicked in and took over Polecat's thinking. There was no way the Cowboy's were going to pull over and waste valuable time while waiting out this powerful storm.

Three Dots and Polecat passed two teams that were huddled up under their boats on the bank. The Cowboys continued to paddle hard down river and were barely able to keep the boat straight and off the bank because of the high winds. The storm raged on for a while before finally easing up some. The temperature went down dramatically during the storm. It kind of felt like being in a winter storm in early June. Polecat's body was violently shaking because of being soaking wet and the sudden drop in temperature.

There were no dry clothes to change into and the only other option was to put life jackets on for extra warmth. The Cowboys quickly put their life jackets on and continued down river. The storm finally ended and the weather calmed down but they had to leave the life jacket's on for several hours in order to help get the body temperature back up to normal. That was by far the worst lightning storm Polecat had ever personally experienced. Thank the Lord that the Cowboys were able to paddle through it without getting toasted.

Three Dots and Polecat pulled into the Hochheim checkpoint to change out water jugs and Jack told them that Mark and Grady had a big lead on them. The Cowboys needed to pick up the stroke rate in order to close the gap. The jalapeno dried sausage was pulled out of the food bag under Polecat's seat while they paddled down river and celebrated a beautiful Sunday morning. Three Dots started singing country and western gospel songs. Polecat thanked the Lord Jesus in prayer for helping everyone get through that terrible lightning storm the night before. "Amen".

The storm had very little impact on the low river levels and the Cowboys were going to have to keep a fast stroke rate going in order to have any chance of catching up with Mark and Grady. The peanut butter and honey sandwich, sliced peaches and a can of warm coke tasted pretty good on that beautiful morning. Polecat really wanted a cup of hot coffee but the warm coke would have to do.

It was a very hot and humid day when the Cowboys paddled through Cheapside and headed for Cuero. John Dunn was not far behind and the Cowboys were determined to stay in front of him. Connie was yelling out to Three Dots, "call the Peacock's Glenn" when the Cowboys approached the Cuero 72 bridge. Three Dots answered her request and eventually was able to get the Peacocks to answer his crude squawking noises.

The party bunch was having a great time sitting on the bank laughing and cheering. There is always a lot of self inflicted pressure on the Cowboys to keep the party going. Dad, Jack and Connie were having a good time following the race and it was up to the Cowboys to keep the party going.

Polecat was very excited when they pulled over at Floodplain Ranch for a quick water hand off late Sunday afternoon. Darla and the boys were cheering loudly and the river dogs were jumping in excitement. Spook, Candy, Brandy and Shadow were barking and howling while Polecat tried to talk to them during the quick hand off. They desperately wanted to jump in the boat and Polecat briefly thought about adding them to the team. They would be good company but they probably couldn't paddle fast enough to adequately replace Three Dots. They couldn't sing as well as Three Dots could but they would be very entertaining when they howled in harmony with the coyotes.

The second night turned into a mental challenge and the wild hallucinations made their ugly appearance. The motivation to catch up with Mark and Grady was helping the Cowboys stay focused. This was Polecat's sixth straight race and Three Dots' third. The Cowboys had some experience with wild hallucinations and how to deal with them. Three Dots would go into great detail describing to Polecat what the imaginary creatures he was seeing in the tree tops looked like. Polecat was impressed but it would eventually turn into a contest between them on who was seeing the wildest looking creatures. There was no clear winner of the hallucination contest.

The sun made it's glorious appearance on Monday morning and the Cowboys were in seventh place overall and the second USCA C-2. The field was spread out because of the low water conditions but the Cowboys were not very far behind the sixth place tandem boat. It was going to be difficult to catch Mark and Grady because they had a pretty large lead on the Cowboys at this point. The primary focus shifted to the tandem team that was just a few minutes ahead of them. The Cowboys were headed into the logjam area below the swinging bridge checkpoint on Sunday afternoon. The logjam cut ended up being a long and difficult portage because there was not enough flow going through the area. Alligator lake was not runnable because of the very low river levels.

Polecat started to notice a dramatic change in the way Three Dots was acting. Three Dots started saying crazy things that didn't make any sense. Then he would stop paddling with no warning and dig around in his food bag. The sudden body movements were making the boat unstable and it forced Polecat to concentrate on keeping the boat upright.

This odd behavior started all of a sudden. Polecat tried to talk to him and get him re-focused on the race again. Three Dots has always had mental challenges but this odd behavior was something that Polecat had not seen before. It was time to panic because the Cowboys had slowed down considerably and Three Dots was aimlessly foraging around in his food bag and not paddling. This caused Polecat to get very angry with him and start yelling out orders.

Three Dots was now in la-la land and he would start babbling nonsense and stop paddling. The conversation was very difficult but Polecat was finally able to convince him to take a no doze tablet to see if that would help cure his mental breakdown. The Cowboys paddled up to the Tivoli bridge checkpoint and Three Dots seemed to be improving a little. Jack told us the bad news that San Antonio bay was very rough and would be very difficult to cross. Jack said that several teams in front of them were talking about going the long way through Trailer cut and bypassing Seadrift cut because of the rough bay conditions.

Polecat had no experience going that way but fondly remembered the story that Tom had told about his crazy experience when he and his partner lost focus and portaged into the Union Carbide plant cooling pond back in one of his first races in the 1970's. The story goes that they were not making good decisions and were confused about where they were when they portaged into a cooling pond that had a man made levee around it. Tom said, "I shouldn't have even considered going that way because I had never trained that long route through the bay and my teammate was struggling".

John Dunn caught up with the Cowboys at the checkpoint and seemed to be very motivated. There was no time to waste for a friendly conversation at this point and everyone quickly headed out for the finish line. This was right at the 60 hour mark in the race. Three Dots needed to clear his head and get back into the game so the Cowboys could have a chance to pass a couple of teams during the rough bay crossing. The 60 hour mark is a significant milestone. Polecat's previous race experiences were proof that your mental awareness can start to rapidly diminish at the 60 hour mark and cause you to lose the ability to make good decisions. There are many great stories of water safari racers over the years suffering through severe mental fatigue and not being able to finish the race. The 60 hour syndrome is what Polecat likes to call it. This is just one of the many reasons why the Texas Water Safari earned the name, "The World's Toughest Boat Race".

Three Dots and Polecat made the terrible last minute decision to head for Trailer cut. The Cowboys had to portage over two small log jams in the river just downstream from the Tivoli bridge. The mosquitoes were so bad that they completely covered the Cowboy's severely abused bodies during the portage. It was a waste of time trying to swat them away because there was too many to contend with. All you could do was try and keep them out of your eyes and nose. Three Dots was having a hard time with this and convinced Polecat that they needed to take the time to jump into the river and try to get the mosquito swarm off their bodies. Polecat would not normally agree to waste valuable time doing this but the 60 hour syndrome was starting to creep into his decision making.

The Cowboys quickly jumped into the river to get some relief from the mosquitoes. Polecat poked his head up above the water line and gasped for air just in time to see Three Dots long nose barely sticking above the water line. Three Dots long nose was completely covered with mosquitoes. It was the only part of his body above the water and it was covered with a swarm of mosquitoes. This very odd sight made Polecat laugh while Three Dots just floated there motionless for several minutes.

The 60 hour syndrome was starting to creep in and take over. There was no insect repellent in the boat so the Cowboys were just going to have to grin and bear with it and get back to paddling. The sun was disappearing on the western horizon when the Cowboys paddled by the Seadrift cut entrance and headed into Trailer cut. This was going to be a new experience for Polecat and would prove out to be a very bad decision.

The mental fog was rapidly setting in and the decision making was getting much worse when the Cowboys paddled into an area that they were not familiar with. Polecat was very confused and nothing looked familiar to him because the terrain opened up and there were several old fishing shacks in view on the right bank.

Polecat had a terrible feeling come over him that they were lost and they needed to stop at one of the fishing shacks for directions to Seadrift. Polecat was not thinking clearly and neither was Three Dots. The Cowboys paddled over to the bank and walked up to one of the old fishing shacks to see if anyone was at home. The warped thinking was that maybe they could give them directions on how to get to Seadrift. No one was there. This was just a fishing camp and the house was a small cabin on piers that was not occupied on a regular basis.

Three Dots and Polecat started looking around the outside of the cabin and noticed a huge pile of junk metal not far away. The mentally fatigued Cowboys suddenly became fascinated with the large pile of junk metal and for no reason started dragging large individual pieces of metal out of the stack. Three Dots eventually tried to piece together some of the larger pieces and shape it into a metal jigsaw puzzle.

Polecat spotted a pile of fire wood and found some matches in the emergency container that was stored away in the canoe and got a nice camp fire started. The mentally confused Cowboys continued piecing together the metal jigsaw puzzle. The contest to see who could put together the most interesting pile of junk metal art got more intense and the Cowboys were enjoying the competition against each other. Three Dots ended up putting together something that resembled several rusted out crab traps piled on top of each other. The large stack of junk crab traps that he put together was crowned off with a pile of rusted outboard motor parts. Polecat tried to challenge him with an interesting pile of junk tractor and implement parts that he tried to piece back together..

The Cowboys did not know why they were there and did not care. Life was good and they were both having a great time pulling junk metal out of the pile and trying to put the pieces back together.

Several large critters cautiously crawled out of the brush to investigate what the noise was all about. Red eyes were glaring at the Cowboys from the nearby marsh. Time didn't matter anymore and there was no concern about how much time was being wasted. The only thing that seemed to matter was dragging large pieces of metal out of the pile and putting the beautiful puzzles together.

The competition continued on for several hours. Three Dots and Polecat would occasionally take a break from the intense battle and stand by the warm campfire to observe their beautiful art work. The Cowboys mental awareness had completely bottomed out and it was time to party and have a good time. There was no clear winner of the metal art puzzle contest named because no impartial judges were available at the time to declare a winner of the unique competition.

Polecat suddenly had a disturbing thought occur to him. The Cowboys were supposed to be in a canoe race and not on a camp out. Jack and the bank crew had been patiently waiting at the finish line in Seadrift for several hours while the mentally challenged Cowboys were having a party. The Cowboys were way behind schedule and no one knew where they were.. There were no GPS devices and no cell phones available. The only thing the bank crew could do was worry, wait and pray. The Cowboys were missing in action and there was no search team looking for them.

Polecat started coming back to reality and told Three Dots that they were supposed to be in a canoe race. They needed to get back in the canoe and get to the finish line as fast as possible. The mentally challenged Cowboys put the camp fire out and looked over their metal art one last time. They had wasted several hours at the camp site putting junk metal together and it was way past time to get back into the race. Three Dots and Polecat never slept a wink during the camp out.

The sun was starting to make it's glorious appearance on Tuesday morning and the mental fog they were in was starting to clear up some. The decision was made to head back to Seadrift cut and take the route they were familiar with. The bright sunlight started bringing back some of the limited mental capabilities that they had lost the night before. The Cowboys were back in the race and they headed into San Antonio bay. Polecat told Three Dots that they were probably in last place. The bigger problem would be to get to the finish line before Darla got very upset with the long wait.

The Cowboys caught up with a solo racer named Mike Riley. They ended up getting into a good back and forth battle with Mike to the finish line. The bay conditions had calmed down considerably compared to the day before and the Cowboys were making good time across the choppy bay. The finishers banquet had just started and there was a large crowd gathered at the finish line.

Three Dots and Polecat finished in the official time of 76 hours and 35 minutes. This was good enough for fourteenth place overall and second place in the USCA C-2 division. Darla and the boys were there to greet them. Darla was upset but was happy to see the Cowboys cross the finish line. They had been at the finish line all night. They slept in the truck while patiently waiting for the Cowboys to finish. Darla would not hug Polecat because he smelled a lot worse than his nickname.

The Cowboys were twelve hours behind schedule and had lost seven places in the process. It was good to be there and Polecat lowered his head and thanked the Lord Jesus for helping them and the bank crew get to the finish line safely. Polecat learned from this experience that if you want to see a big crowd cheering for you and your team at the sea wall, plan it out to where you can get there around banquet time. The crowd was applauding when the Cowboys were finally able to climb the seawall steps and make their way over to the stage just a few minutes after finishing the race.

Polecat was having a hard time standing up straight because his joints were starting to stiffen and tighten up after 76 hours of physical and mental abuse. Three Dots nodded his head at Polecat to step up to the microphone and say something to the crowd. Polecat thanked Jack and the bank crew for their help and support before starting in with the story about the camp out at Trailer cut. The Cowboys entertained themselves for hours by dragging junk metal out of a large pile and pieced it back together to create some interesting metal art. The crowd seemed to enjoy the story but really liked the mosquito story. Three Dots large nose was the the only part of his body sticking out of the water and it was completely covered with a swarm of mosquitoes.

Joe, Fred and Brian Mynar won the race and Mark and Grady won the USCA C-2 division. There were only nineteen teams that finished the race that year due to the very low water conditions and the Cowboys were the last team to make it to the finishers banquet before it started.

Three Dots and Polecat were no help loading up the boat and equipment after the banquet was over. Polecat was sitting in a lawn chair and was barely able to stay awake when Mike Shively walked over and started up a friendly conversation.

Mike won the solo division and was in fourth place overall. Mike and his partner John Bugge had previously won the water safari a couple of times. Mike was an instructor at the Texas A&M veterinarian school and Polecat had the opportunity to have some interesting conversations with him at the finishers banquet in previous races. Mike had a funny sense of humor but he was a very serious and intense Texas Water Safari racer. Mike congratulated Polecat on another finish and said that he really enjoyed the metal art and mosquito stories.

Mike then said, "the mosquitoes would not have been so bad if y'all would have been a little faster". Mike smiled and shook Polecat's hand before he turned and walked away. Polecat is not sure if that parting comment was meant as a joke or if he was serious. Polecat just nodded his head in agreement because Mike was right. The Cowboys were in a good position to finish seventh or better with less than fifteen miles left to the finish line and they mentally fell apart and imploded.

The sixteen hour split time across San Antonio bay set a new Texas Water Safari record for the longest bay crossing on record. That record stood for many years before it was finally broken. That is probably a record that should not be bragged about but it's the only record setting time Polecat ever helped set in the Texas Water Safari.

Darla helped load the foul smelling Polecat into the truck and they headed for home to get some much needed rest. Polecat does not remember the drive back home. They arrived at Floodplain ranch and Darla tried to wake Polecat up using every tactic she could think of. Polecat would not respond. She finally gave up and rolled the windows down. Darla left Polecat sitting slumped over in the front seat of the truck and told him good night.

Darla has told Polecat many times over the years that she supports his participation in the Texas Water Safari and is willing to help when ever she can. She has no sympathy for the self inflicted mental and physical abuse that he puts himself through.

Polecat woke up a few hours later and he was still sitting in the truck. Polecat was still wearing the same foul smelling water safari clothes that he had put on five days earlier. It took him a few minutes to collect his thoughts and realize that he was at home. Polecat desperately needed to go take a hot shower and get in bed. The faithful river dogs were standing guard next to the truck and were anxiously waiting for Polecat to wake up and give them some much needed attention. The muscles all over Polecat's body were stiff and tight and that caused him to stumble and fall down after slowly stepping out of the truck. Spending the night sitting in an upright position in the passenger seat of a truck did not help improve the muscle pain and stiffness that he was experiencing. It made it worse.

This was an appropriate ending to a memorable race and it was going to take a lot of time to recover from all the physical and mental abuse that he had put himself through.

Three Dots called a few weeks later and told Polecat that he needed to take a break from canoe racing. Polecat would have to find another racing partner. The traveling back and forth from west Texas for training was very hard and expensive and the last race had taken a heavy toll on him. Three Dots said that he would consider being the team captain again but Polecat would have to find another partner to team up with for next year's race. Three Dots and Polecat were still good friends. Three straight races as teammates ended with a lot of crazy events and unbelievable stories.

CHAPTER 11

1990: "The Running man" and my first Houston Marathon

Polecat started spending a lot more time in the weight room during his time off at work. The offshore production platform he worked on had a very nice workout facility on board and it was a good place to waste time. There was very little time off available while at home because of two young sons that Darla desperately needed help with. Polecat had been an occasional runner in the past but was feeling the motivation to start increasing the distance.

The most common trip would be a six mile run to the post office and back with river dogs following in hot pursuit. The county road in front of Floodplain ranch was not very busy. Polecat and his pack of dogs would occasionally head out early in the morning on foot and paws to pick up the mail at the post office. The postmaster knew everyone's name and would usually hand Polecat his mail when he entered the building before all of the river dogs had a chance to follow him inside.

Polecat's neighbors gave him a new nickname that seemed appropriate. The Running man was the name he was known by all around the Thomaston area. The six mile runs started stretching out into ten miles and then that eventually expanded into an occasional twelve mile round trip to the Thomaston river bridge.

The faithful pack of river dogs would drop out one by one along the longer course and would wait for the Running man to return before rejoining the group. Precious was the only one that could hang with the Running man for the entire twelve miles. The Thomaston river bridge several years ago was a one lane suspension bridge that had a wooden deck. It was listed as a historical site by the state of Texas. The historic bridge was a popular destination for locals and tourists. They would stop and take pictures of the unique and interesting design. The one lane suspension bridge was removed a few years later and was replaced by a cement two lane design.

Precious and the Running man were taking a quick break at the bridge before starting the long run back home when she saw her reflection in the door of a car that was slowly driving by. Precious suddenly charged the car and jumped towards her reflection and violently slammed head first into the passenger door. The car door was seriously damaged but the violent collision did not seem to hurt her. Precious ran back towards the Running man wanting his attention.

The Running man tried to ignore her and give the car owner the impression that he did not know this crazy dog. The young lady stopped and looked over the door damage before walking over to the Running man. "Is that your dog"? the young lady asked. The Running man reluctantly admitted that Precious was his dog and he apologized for her bad behavior and the damage. The conversation was friendly and contact information was exchanged. The Running man told her that he would pay for the door repair. The home owners insurance policy ended up paying for the damage because Precious was determined to be part of the Floodplain Ranch property. The insurance agent said that he had never heard of or personally been involved with a claim like that before.

The running addiction got more and more intense as 1989 came to an end. The Running man has been asked several times over the years why does he run so much. The answer comes from one of his favorite movies. Forest Gump was asked the same question in the famous movie and his answer was, "I just like running". That simple answer seemed to fit the Running man. The long runs with his river dogs were starting to get even longer and the pace was faster when the new year started.

Crazy cousin Jerry lived in the Houston area and he would come to Floodplain ranch sometimes for short canoe trips and horse shoe tournaments. Jerry won the Texas state doubles horse shoe tournament championship several times with his partner and he was also a former motorcycle racer in his younger years. Crazy cousin Jerry is what the rest of the Stafford family calls him because of his unique personality. Jerry would frequently head out on weekend motorcycle rides on his Harley along with a large group of motorcycle friends from the Houston area. The Running man always looked forward to the annual Stafford reunion and the all night long horse shoe tournament.

The family reunion is where Jerry tried to talk the Running man into entering the Houston Tenneco Marathon in January. Jerry offered his spare bedroom as a place to stay if Darla would allow him to enter the race in January 1990. The Running man had not put much serious thought into running a marathon and he had no idea how to train for a 26.2 mile race.

The training and planning for a long distance event like that should have started months earlier. The scheduled days off from work fell in line with the start of the marathon and that just added fuel to the fire. Darla shook her head in disbelief when the Running man told her that he was thinking about entering the 1990 Houston marathon. Darla likes to say that the Running man has a relentless and never ending desire to find extreme ways to punish his body and this was just another stupid example of that bad behavior.

Darla and the Running man drove up to the George Brown convention center in downtown Houston on a warm Saturday afternoon in January and he entered the Houston marathon just one hour before the entry deadline. In those days you could walk up to the entry desk at the convention center in person and enter the race on the day before the Sunday morning start. There were over four thousand runners entered in the 1990 Houston Tenneco marathon. Darla and the Running man spent the night at crazy cousin Jerry's house and he volunteered to drive them to the early morning start at the convention center. Jerry and Darla would then follow him down the race course.

The marathon contestants started lining up around six thirty in the morning on the road directly in front of the convention center on that clear and cool Sunday morning. Race volunteers were spread out for several hundred yards along the starting line and they were holding up signs that had estimated finishing times written on them.

The Running man noticed a do not cross yellow caution tape stretched out behind a large group of runners. This is where the world class runners from all over the world were grouped together and they were separated from the rest of the field.

The longest training run the Running man had ever done was only fifteen miles long and he had no idea what his estimated finishing time would be. The Texas Water Safari competitive mentality took over and convinced him to squeeze in right behind the caution tape and get as close to the starting line as he could.

The Star Spangled Banner was played and then the starting gun was fired off at seven am sharp. The world class runners took off and started sprinting like they were shot out of a canon. The Running man tried to keep up with them for a short distance but they quickly pulled away and were soon out of sight. It was kind of like trying to catch a scared deer that is running away from you.

The Running man realized that he had made a big mistake starting the race way up in the front of the pack. There are several highway over-passes that the marathon runners have to go over right after the start and the Running man was being passed by hundreds of faster runners on the narrow bridges. The space is very limited and the Running man was constantly being banged into from behind and was almost knocked down while the faster runners tried to quickly pass by. This was a lesson learned the hard way. Marathon runners should always line up with the group that is the closest to your expected finishing time.

Lining up right behind the best marathon runners in the world was not a good idea. The water safari mentality kicked in again and the Running man started violently slinging his arms and elbows and tried to open up some space between himself and the passing runners. The body bumping and tripping lasted for several minutes before the race course opened up again past the narrow bridges and the field started spreading out.

The Running man did not know how to pace himself for a marathon and he eventually fell in with a group of runners that seemed to be going the pace he wanted to maintain. The Running man asked a runner that was close to him what his expected finishing time was and he responded back that he was shooting for under three hours. Three hours was a little faster than what the Running man had figured on but the pace seemed comfortable at the time so he stayed with this group while they ran by the Rice University campus.

There were hundreds of people standing on the sidewalks cheering the runners on. Water stations were set up at the mile markers. There were several band's and solo singers along this section of the race course who were singing and playing very loud music. Race volunteers were yelling out encouragement and calling out your name and race number through loud speakers as you ran by.

The marathon was a big annual event in Houston and there was a lot of support from the local community. The Running man was starting to feel the burn and fatigue in his legs when the group he was running with neared the halfway mark. This was about as far as he had ever run before and it was only the half way mark of the race. The race course eventually started turning back towards Buffalo Bayou and the down town area.

The Running man started to slow down a little and the three hour group pulled away and left him behind. The next group of runners caught up with him and seemed to be moving along at a good pace, so he tried to hang with them for a while. The leg pain and fatigue was getting much worse when the group approached mile twenty. Mile twenty is a very significant milestone in a marathon. It is kind of like making it to mile two hundred in the Texas Water Safari.

The Running man was getting very tired at this point and was starting to struggle but was able to hang with the group he was running with. This is when your training usually kicks in and you focus on maintaining a steady pace. The Running man did not have the training to fall back on. The reality was that he was going to have to wing it and push himself through this difficult time in the race. Texas Water Safari experience started helping him get through this mental and physical challenge.

The Running man approached mile twenty and noticed several young women were in the middle of the road dancing and playing tambourines. The young ladies were professional belly dancers and they were in the middle of the road entertaining the surrounding crowd and the runners passing by.

The sight of young ladies with very little clothing on and playing tambourines was very unexpected and unusual. Several of the belly dancers stuck their hands out and offered to give the Running man a high five hand slap when he passed by. This was very surprising and the Running man enthusiastically stuck his hand out and tried to slap their hands.

The numbness and fatigue in his legs would not allow him to jump at the same time. Darla and Jerry were watching this comical scene take place from the side of the road. They yelled out encouragement and the Running man smiled and waved back to them. The last six miles in this race can be brutal when you try to keep a fast running pace all the way into the finish line.

The sight of runners laid out on the side of the race coarse trying to stretch out their aching muscles or battling leg cramps is a common thing to see on that last six mile stretch. Medical tents are set up along this section to help aid runners that can't go on any farther. The Running man was pressing on even though there was a lot of pain and muscle cramps shooting up and down his legs.

The outline of down town Houston was within sight. The race course was now following the edge of Buffalo Bayou. The Running man was able to pass several runners that were struggling and several more that were walking. The Texas Water Safari competitive mentality was definitely helping at this point. The Running man was focused on the finish line and not on the constant pain.

The Running man looked down at his feet and his brand new twenty dollar Nike running shoes were covered in blood and his toes were numb and had no feeling in them. Lessons were learned the hard way to never break in a brand new pair of running shoes on race day.

The down town multiple story office buildings and hotels lined both sides of the street. The Running man rounded the last corner and the finish line at the George Brown convention center was straight ahead. The finish line and the official time clock were getting closer. The Running man passed a few more struggling runners and then suddenly had to move over and sidestep a runner that was crawling on his hands and knees towards the finish line. The large crowd that was gathered along the last mile were cheering the crawling man on while he crawled ahead slowly on his bloody hands and knees. The Running man felt sorry for him and wanted to help the crawling man but that would have meant instant disqualification and the dreaded DNF acronym placed next to his name.

The Thomaston running man crossed the finish line in the official time of three hours, thirty seven minutes and forty one seconds. There was very little feeling left in his lower extremities and his feet were bleeding. The Running man started to awkwardly stumble while a race volunteer placed a thermal blanket over his back and shoulders.

Race officials and volunteers were lined up applauding and directing the runners who had finished into the large reception area. The Running man tried to sit down in a folding chair but was not able to bend his legs. The only option would be to lay down on the floor and rest his aching muscles. Darla and Jerry were patiently watching from behind a roped off barrier. They watched the Running man struggle to get up off the floor after resting for several minutes.

The race official that was standing at the rope barrier let them into the secured area to try and help the disabled Running man get back up. They had to kneel down and position themselves under each arm before they were able to slowly and carefully raise him up off the floor. The Running man was dead weight and could not help. Jerry and Darla had to drag him across the room towards the exit.

The Running man's leg muscles were knotted up and locked in place and would not function in a normal manner. The pain shooting up and down his lower extremities was overwhelming. There was a race official standing close by who offered to call for medical assistance if it was needed but the Running man respectfully declined.

The race official was able to clear a pathway through the large crowd and escort the rescue team to the nearest exit door and out of the convention center. The Running man had to grab on to a street light pole for stability while crazy cousin Jerry went to find his vehicle in the parking lot and then try to make his way back through the crowd to pick them up.

The Running man tried to sit upright in the back seat of Jerry's jeep but that was not going to work. The seat had to be laid down and the Running man was then able to slide in through the back tailgate and lay out in a horizontal position for the ride back to Jerry's house. Darla gave the Running man some Tylenol for the pain and then they loaded him into Darla's vehicle for the ride back home.

The quick exit from the convention center prevented the Running man from getting his finishers tee shirt and all of the other free stuff that was offered to the race finishers. That was not very important at the time because the Running man had just ran 26.2 miles as fast as he could and had finished his first Houston marathon.

The official 3:37:47 finishing time was good enough for 1,125th place out of 4,016 total finishers and that put the Running man into the top twenty seven percent. The more important milestone was that there was a large group of Texas Water Safari canoe racers entered in the Houston marathon that year and the Running man had beaten almost every one of them to the finish line.

The names are not important but the fact that the Running man was faster than they were in this race was a big confidence booster. The Running man turned the tables on the same people that had been consistently beating him in the Texas Water Safari. This was not a marathon canoe race but it was a race of speed and endurance and the Running man was able to out run them for 26.2 miles.

The Running man's finishing time in his age group was good enough to qualify him for the Boston marathon if he decided to enter that race. The Running man never pursued that because the Boston Marathon was held in April and that would interfere with Texas Water Safari training. The time and money involved to enter the Boston marathon and then at the same time train for the water safari would have been a very difficult thing to justify and explain to Darla. It took several days of rest and rehab for the leg muscles and feet to recover from the Running man's first Houston marathon.

The Thomaston Running man competing in the Houston marathon

CHAPTER 12

1990: A new safari partner and the breakout race

The Texas Water Safari training season was fast approaching and Polecat did not have a partner lined up for the race. If an experienced water safari team mate could not be recruited, Polecat just figured that he would have to suck it up and go solo one more time.

Polecat's sister Stephanie was a beautician at a hair solon in Victoria at the time and one of her regular customers was Mrs. Harras. At one of their many hair styling sessions, Mrs. Harras was telling Stephanie about her son that lived in the Houston area. The conversation rambled on for a while and then she casually mentioned that her son had participated in a very long marathon canoe race called the Texas Water Safari. That comment surprised Stephanie and she responded that her brother had also done the TWS several times. They both laughed and started exchanging stories about their funny experiences while following the race.

Stephanie mentioned that her brother was looking for a racing partner for this years race. Mrs. Harras replied that her son John Mark was also trying to find someone to team up with. Stephanie called Polecat that night and told him about the conversation she had earlier that day with Mrs. Harras. The ladies had agreed with each other that John

Mark and Polecat would be a good fit for the race. It is kind of funny and ironic that two ladies in a hair Solon were trying to put an odd couple together and make a Texas Water Safari team.

John Mark and Polecat knew each other because they had been involved in a couple of intense battles across San Antonio bay in 1987 and 1988. The unofficial bragging rights for the most severely damaged boat and best repair job had been a very close contest between their respective teams many times over the last few years.

The idea of teaming up with someone who had experienced a lot of the same problems that Polecat had to overcome in the race did not seem logical. John Mark and Polecat did not have much in common except for the fact that they both had a passion to compete in "The World's Toughest Boat Race". John Mark is a college educated engineer with an advanced degree and he lives in the big city of Houston. Polecat is a blue collar oil field worker that worked offshore in the Gulf of Mexico and lived with his family on a small ranch near Thomaston.

Polecat had a very nice we no nah USCA C-2 racing canoe that had made it through the 1989 race with minimal damage. Time was running out to find a team mate for the 1990 race. The start of the water safari was only three months away and Polecat really wanted to compete in the USCA C-2 division again. Polecat called John Mark from his offshore platform in early March and they had a very friendly conversation and an agreement was made to give it a shot and do a few training runs together to see if it would work out.

The Buffalo Bayou Regatta canoe race was scheduled for the next weekend in Houston and the decision was made to team up and use this race as the first training run. The Buffalo Bayou Regatta is a twenty mile long race in Houston that goes through some very interesting areas on the north side of town. This was a big annual event at the time and the race was very popular with the locals. Texas Water Safari teams would sometimes show up and enter the race.

The start of this race is very unusual because the teams are required to line up at the top of a steep embankment on the bank of the Bayou. The starting gun goes and off you have to drag your boat through some dense vegetation and a thick line of trees. Then you will have to slide down a very steep bank with your boat in tow behind you and try to avoid crashing into the trees before splashing into the deep Bayou.

The spectators and the local media love to watch the start of this race because it is very comical and entertaining. Watching canoe racers crashing into trees or each other while dragging their boats down the steep embankment is cheap entertainment.

John Mark and Polecat met up about an hour before the race started and made the last minute decision that Polecat would be in the bow because of the big weight difference. There was about a thirty pound difference in their weight so they had to quickly move the seats and foot rest in order to maintain a trimmed boat. It is very critical in canoe racing to not be bow or stern heavy because this will usually cause the boat to lose speed when you are navigating through the different water levels. Moving to the bow was a big move for Polecat because he had been the stern paddler in his last three Texas Water Safari races with Three Dots.

This move was going to take a lot of training time to adjust to. The bow paddler in a USCA C-2 has to use several different maneuvers and techniques and will constantly have to adjust the stroke rate in order to keep the bow headed in a straight line down river. The bow in a USCA C-2 has a tendency to tract one way or the other when going through turbulent water and fast currents.

The problem for this new team was that this was a race and they did not have any training time together to get all of this figured out. This was the first time together as a team and they were going to have to quickly get in sync and get down the bayou as fast as they could.

The starting horn blew and the new Cowboy team started dragging the boat through the thick tree line at the top of the hill before starting the slide down the steep embankment. Polecat was on his rear end and was sliding down the steep embankment with one hand firmly gripped on the boat behind him. John Mark was sliding down directly behind the boat and was trying to steer it away from the trees and thorn bushes that dominated the area. Polecat plunged feet first into the muddy bayou and went completely under.

Polecat's head quickly emerged out of the water and he checked to make sure that his expensive cowboy hat was still in place. The next step would be to grab tree roots to help support him and crawl back up onto the bank. John Mark was trying to push the boat into the water without submerging the bow or dipping the gunnels into the murky bayou. This was all happening very quickly. Polecat pulled himself back up on to the bank and then they both were able to jump into the boat without turning it over. The new Cowboy team looked around the immediate area and were amazed to see that they were one of the first boats in the water.

John Mark and Polecat quickly pulled out their single blade paddles and started heading down the bayou. The stroke rate was awkward at first because of the lack of training time together but they were soon able to get in sync and get a strong stroke rate going. There were a couple of boats directly in front of them after the wild start but the new Cowboy team was very fortunate they had avoided the chaotic stuff that was taking place behind them.

There were several boats upside down with people hanging on and trying to swim to the nearest bank. Loud voices were screaming and shouting at each other and were echoing down the bayou. This is what everyone had come to see. The Regatta was basically a sprint race down a very slow moving and open Buffalo Bayou.

John Mark and Polecat were in the top five and were doing pretty well in their first race together. They were concentrating on stroke rate and keeping the bow headed downstream in a straight line. There were a lot of spectators watching the race at public access areas along with an occasional homeless person that would be watching them from under the many bridges along the race course.

The new Cowboy team paddled into a narrow spot that was partially blocked by a large tree that had fallen over into the bayou.. Grady and his partner were right beside the Cowboys when both teams entered the very narrow opening. This was the only way open around the downed tree. The canoe's came to an abrupt stop side by side after grounding out in the shallow water.

John Mark and Polecat were frantically trying to paddle through the tight spot when Polecat's paddle blade accidentally came out of the water and slammed into Grady's head and shoulder. Grady and Polecat looked at each other with surprised looks and Polecat had no choice but to quickly apologize for the paddle slap to the face. Grady did not say anything directly to him at the time but it was obvious that he was not very happy with the accidental paddle slap to the head.

Grady and Mark had convincingly beaten Polecat and Three Dots in the 1989 Texas Water Safari USCA C-2 division. They were very good canoe racers and Polecat respected their ability. Grady and Polecat laugh about the accidental paddle slap to the head now and they have become good friends over the years. Grady's name is on the Texas Water Safari USCA C-2 trophy six times and Polecat is trying very hard to catch up with him but probably will never be able to match that milestone.

John Mark and Polecat finished in the top five of the Buffalo Bayou Regatta that year and they were very happy with the first training run together. The move to the bow position seemed to be a good move for Polecat and it worked out well in this race. The water safari training season was now in high gear and they needed to get in as many miles as they could.

John Mark was in between office jobs at the time and so that meant he had a lot of spare time to meet up with Polecat during the week to train. There was a long training run planned a few weeks later that would start above Luling and end somewhere close to Gonzales. The tentative plan was for Polecat to run into Gonzales on foot after they finished the training run to retrieve the shuttle truck that was left in the Whataburger parking lot.

The training run ended badly when the new Cowboy team crashed into a large rock that was partially submerged in a small rapid above Palmetto state park. The collision ended up ripping a pretty good sized hole into the bow of the boat just below the seat area. The Cowboys pulled over and tried to patch it up the best they could with the half role of duck tape that had been brought along for the emergency patch kit.

This was the situation that Polecat had hoped to avoid with his new partner. The two of them had a long history of severely damaging their racing canoe's during the water safari. This was just a training run but Polecat couldn't help but wonder if this was going to be a common occurrence with the new Cowboys. The temporary patch seemed to be holding up and they started heading for the Palmetto state park low water bridge.

The patch was starting to leak after the hard portage around Ottine dam. The new Cowboy team pulled over at the Palmetto state park bridge in order to check it out. There was no more patching material left. A team meeting was held and John Mark would have to stay with the boat and Polecat would head out for Gonzales on foot. The flawed thinking was that Polecat could start running the fifteen miles to Gonzales from there while at the same time trying to thumb a ride along the highway.

The Houston marathon finish was three months ago and Polecat was just now starting to feel the urge to run long distances again. The shoes Polecat had on were well used water shoes and not running shoes. Polecat eventually made it up to the highway and started running along the shoulder of the highway with his thumb stuck out. No one would even slow down. The odd sight of a rough looking character wearing a large cowboy hat and wearing shorts was apparently scaring them off.

The next ten miles took a while because Polecat would occasionally have to slow down and start fast walking in order to rest his aching feet. The sight of his truck in the Whataburger parking lot brought a big smile to his face. The training paddle and run finally came to an end after 35 miles of paddling and fifteen miles of running.. The jalapeno burger tasted pretty good and Polecat even brought one back for his new partner. Polecat had to wake John Mark up from his long nap under a shade tree next to the Palmetto state park bridge.

John Mark had been given the nickname Lone Wolf by his former team mate Carol because he likes to howl like a wolf at night during the water safari in order to stay alert. The nickname seemed to fit him and that would be his new racing name going forward whether he liked it or not.

The new Cowboys entered the 40 mile prelim race and finished in the top ten. The move to the bow was working out well and Polecat was getting more confident with every training run. The new Cowboys were definitely getting better as a team. They were finally able to avoid the boat damaging mistakes that seemed to be a common occurrence for both of them in past races.

The 1990 Texas Water Safari was scheduled to start on the first weekend in June with Polecat and Lone Wolf starting on the second row. The check in on Friday was awkward because the new Cowboy team had not planned out in advance exactly what they were going to check in. The rules stated that each team had to have a detailed list of the food and supplies they were taking and then be able to show each item to the race official at the check in. The amount of food that Lone Wolf had on his list seemed to be very excessive and would add a lot of unnecessary weight to the boat.

The Cowboys had to have a quick team meeting to discuss Polecat's concerns before proceeding with the check in. It was very common for teams to check in a lot of extra stuff on Friday and some of it would eventually be discarded before the race started on Saturday because of excessive boat weight. Lone Wolf had a medium sized Styrofoam ice chest that was crammed full of vacuum sealed food bags. The food bags looked like an assortment of freshly cooked meals that were straight out of the oven from his Mom's house. They sure looked good to Polecat and made jealous.

The bad thoughts of possibly borrowing or even stealing some of this from him during the race briefly entered his thinking. The reality was that the ice chest was stuffed full of freshly cooked meals and it was going to add way to much weight to the boat. Lone Wolf reluctantly agreed to discard some of it but it was still way to heavy.

Polecat checked in the usual stuff that consisted of peanut butter and honey sandwiches, egg and potato tacos, jalapeno dried sausage, canned peaches, granola bars, three cans of coke, dill pickles, GU energy gels, powdered Gatorade and a few candy bars. All of this stuff combined did not weigh near as much as Lone Wolf's ice chest.

The check in finally proceeded and went smoothly after the Cowboys came to a team agreement on the amount of stuff that could be stored away in the boat. The sometimes annual pre-race dinner at Herbert's was next on the list and then that was hopefully followed with a good nights rest at Tom's campground. Race day started early with a pot of strong coffee being brewed on the camp stove before loading up and heading over to the breakfast taco food truck to purchase several fresh potato and egg tacos.

It always seems chaotic on water safari race day at the starting line when teams make their last preparations and then launch their boats for a quick warm up in Aquarena Spring lake. The Cowboys did a quick warm up paddle and Polecat was able to convince Lone Wolf that they needed to head over and say hello to Ralph the swimming pig. Lone Wolf did not have the close connection to Ralph the swimming pig like Polecat did. Polecat had to explain to Lone Wolf just how important it was for him to talk to Ralph before the race started.

The Cowboys paddled over to the observation deck where Ralph was proudly standing with his handlers. Polecat took off his hat and thanked Ralph for his continued support of the Texas Water Safari. Three Dots was standing on the shoreline close by and tried to join in on the conversation. The large group of race fans standing along the bank were laughing at the funny conversation they were having with Ralph and his enthusiastic grunting in response.

Lone Wolf did not seem to be impressed with this waste of time and was ready to get lined up for the start. Polecat did not know it then but this would be the last time that he would have the opportunity to talk to his good friend, Ralph the swimming pig. Texas State University was the new owner of the Aquarena spring lake property and was implementing some major construction and remodeling plans. Ralph would be forced into early retirement and Polecat would never have the opportunity to talk to him again. The funny memory of accidentally knocking Ralph off his observation platform at the start of the water safari in 1986 and the many conversations with him over the years will always bring a big smile to Polecat's face.

Polecat and Lone Wolf were lined up on the second row as Tom started with the race announcements and then led everyone in prayer. The pre-race prayer is a great opportunity to lower your head in worship and personally thank the Lord Jesus for his many undeserved blessings. Tom is very good at leading the prayer. Tom will humbly ask the Lord to please watch over the racers, bank crews and race volunteers and help everyone get to the finish line safely.

The starting gun is fired off and the chaos begins. Racing canoe's start crashing into each other while trying to jockey for position. Several boats will end up upside down in Spring lake after the start due to collisions and turning over in the turbulent water that is created from so many long racing boats trying to paddle across a small lake as fast as they can. This is what the crowd at the start came to see and they are usually not disappointed. Forty five teams started the race. Lone Wolf and Polecat made it through Spring lake without any collisions and made a fast portage over the island.

Rio Vista dam was next in line after clearing the island portage at the end of spring lake. Rio Vista dam is runnable in a racing canoe for the teams that have the nerve to try. Lone Wolf and Polecat had already made the decision to run it as they approached the dam with a large crowd watching and cheering. A picture of the Cowboys was on the front page of the Victoria Advocate newspaper on Sunday morning. The picture showed the Cowboys paddling over the dam and managing to stay upright even though they had taken on a lot of water in the process. The headline above the picture said, "two Victoria area residents that are competing in the Texas Water Safari keep their hats on straight as they navigate the treacherous waters".

Lone Wolf and Polecat had a common water safari reputation. They both had a history of severely damaging their racing canoes and then being able to patch them up good enough to make it in to the finish line. The second training run together as a team had ended with a large hole being punched through the bottom of the boat after running up on a partially submerged rock. The competition in the USCA C-2 division probably figured that this common history would continue and would ultimately be their demise.

Lone Wolf and Polecat were very focused on the next obstacle in front of them and were not thinking about past mistakes. The move to the bow was working out pretty well and they seemed to be navigating the sweeping hard turns on the upper San Marcos river without having to slow down very much. The stroke rate was increasing and they were averaging somewhere in the fifty five stroke per minute range as they approached cotton seed rapid.

The famous Cotton Seed rapid at Martindale is always a good place for water safari spectators to watch boats capsize after crashing into the partially submerged cement dam or the large rocks that were once part of the cotton mill dam. The dam had been washed out and abandoned years ago.

Lone Wolf and Polecat both had a bad track record at this rapid in past races because of the bad decisions and the damage that was inflicted to their racing canoe's. The large crowd was yelling and cheering in anticipation and was expecting a big show from the new Cowboy team when they turned the corner and headed into the turbulent rapid. The Cowboys were in the top ten overall at this point and were a close second in the USCA C-2 division behind Ted and Larry.

The Cowboys carefully navigated through the cement and rock infested rapid with no serious problems and took on very little water. They both yelled out with excitement and relief after clearing this major obstacle with no damage. There was no valuable time wasted on boat repairs by the Cowboys today and the crowd seemed to be disappointed.

This was a big confidence builder for the new Cowboy team and they picked up the stroke rate and headed down river. The race course was at a moderate flow rate and this was helping the Cowboys get through these upper river portages and rapids with only a few minor problems.

Ted and Larry were maintaining the small lead they had on the Cowboys at the Luling highway 90 bridge checkpoint. The party bunch was having a good time and were waiting there to support the Cowboys. Three Dots quickly changed out the water jugs. Lone Wolf's dad was the newest member of the bank crew and Mr. Harras had been enthusiastically accepted into the group. Mr. Harras was not a partier but he loved following the race and taking pictures. Polecat's Dad and Mr. Harras became very good friends and they would hang out together while enthusiastically following the Cowboys down river.

Mr. Harras was the unofficial team photographer and he would sometimes climb large trees or go through thick brush and down steep river banks just to get a picture of the Cowboys going through difficult areas of the race course. Mr. Harras would be sitting on a tree limb or wading out into the swift water in some very isolated areas just to get a quick picture of the Cowboys paddling by. Three Dots, Mr. Harras, Dad, Jack and Connie were the core members of the party group and they were sometimes joined by other friends and family who would come and go throughout the long race.

Darla was six months pregnant with our third child and she was very limited on how much time she could spend following the Cowboys down the race course. Lone Wolf and Polecat were still moving along at a good stroke rate when the first day came to an end. There were no major mistakes made and no time was wasted on the upper river and that was keeping everyone motivated.

The Cowboys stopped for a quick water hand off at the Sladen cemetery bridge as the sun was disappearing on the western horizon. Three Dots gave them the good news that they were now in eighth place overall and were gaining ground on Ted and Larry.

This was when another major test of their race preparations unfolded when they strapped on the new and improved bow light for the long night of racing that was ahead of them. The bow light was powered by a small twelve volt battery that was connected with wiring and a cutoff switch to a light that was secured to the bow of the boat. The battery was heavy and was secured under Polecat's seat.

The system seemed to be working pretty well when they approached the Gonzales checkpoint. The bad track record the Cowboys had with bow lights had eventually forced them to ask questions and copy what other teams were doing. That is one of the benefits when you make the rounds and check out the rigging on other boats at the finishers banquet. If you make complimentary remarks about the way a boat is rigged out they will usually explain to you how they did it in detail. This is not possible at the check in because everything is a secret and hidden from public view.

The move to the bow position was working out well for Polecat but he was starting to experience a lot of physical fatigue from all of the bracing and the maneuvering that is required to successfully navigate a long racing canoe down the winding San Marcos river. This was the first time that Lone Wolf had raced in the water safari without a rudder to help him navigate through all of the obstacles and hard turns. Lone Wolf was doing a good job in the drivers seat without a rudder helping him and Polecat was setting a strong stroke rate up in the bow.

The word hut is yelled out several times every minute of the race so both paddlers can stay in sync when switching their single blade paddles to opposite sides of the boat. The sound of the word hut was endlessly echoing down river while the Cowboys tried to maintain a fifty five stroke per minute pace. This was the first water safari they had done together as a team and Polecat did not know that Lone Wolf had a history of mental fatigue and losing focus during the first night of the race.

There were hundreds of bugs zeroing in on Polecat's face and upper body because of the bright light that was secured on the bow directly in front of him. This is a normal occurrence at night during this race and the bow paddler just has to suck it up and deal with it the best way they can. A lot of water safari racers have a hard time with this but Polecat just looks at it as a challenge. The constant bombardment will usually help him stay focused and alert.

Mayflies are the most common and they will sometimes be so thick that they will partially fill up the bottom of the boat and plug up the bilge pumps. It is inevitable that a few of them will eventually find their way into your mouth and you will find out what these bugs taste like. The best way to look at this situation is that they are just adding some extra protein to your water safari diet.

Lone Wolf was howling like a wolf and was trying to keep himself focused on the river ahead. Polecat was bellowing out Willie Nelson songs and was trying to keep Lone Wolf entertained and alert. It does not matter how talented of a singer you are. All that matters is the louder the better.

Lone Wolf started rambling on about things that did not make any sense. Polecat tried to add some funny comments and keep the conversation going. The only thing that really mattered was that the stroke rate was good and we were headed straight down river.

It would have been nice to have Janet and Sandy close by to talk to but the field was spread out and the Cowboys were by themselves. The river is wide open in this section of the race course with only a few rapids and obstacles to deal with. Take a no doze pill and keep paddling is the great advice Tom likes to give young water safari racers. Lone Wolf was saying crazy things that made no sense and Polecat was singing like a drunk sailor but they were still moving down river at racing speed.

The sun made its glorious appearance on the eastern horizon and the Cowboys were closing in on the Hochheim checkpoint. Daylight will usually help bring you out of your delirious state of mind after a long night of paddling and singing and bug eating. The party bunch was patiently waiting at the checkpoint to cheer the Cowboys on. Three Dots yelled out the good news that they had closed the gap and were just a few minutes behind Ted and Larry. That unexpected news was a big confidence booster. Three Dots quickly changed out the water jugs and the Cowboys headed down river. The stroke rate picked up even more because the Cowboys were motivated and determined to catch the main competition and take over first place in the USCA C-2 division.

Jalapeno dried sausage was pulled out of the food bag in celebration of the beautiful Lord's day. Polecat started singing old gospel songs to praise and honor of the Lord Jesus. Lone Wolf joined Polecat in prayer and they thanked the Lord for his undeserved blessings and they prayed for God's protection for everyone that was still in the race trying to make it to the finish line in Seadrift. "Amen". There was no hot coffee available so Polecat had to settle for a warm can of coke and some jalapeno dried sausage for his Sunday morning breakfast.

Thirty minutes down river past Hochheim the Cowboys suddenly noticed a racing canoe that was pulled over along the edge of the left bank. Ted and Larry were apparently taking a quick break and were sitting in the river when the Cowboys paddled up to them. They looked very surprised and confused when the Cowboys paddled by them as fast as they could. "It sure is a beautiful Lord's day", Polecat yelled out as they sprinted by.

Ted and Larry jumped up out of the water and quickly got back into their boat to try and catch back up. Polecat was motivated to increase the stroke rate and not give them any hope. They thought that they had a big lead over the Cowboys and this pass was totally unexpected. This was the first time that the Cowboys had ever been leading a water safari division this far into the race and it was time to shift into a higher gear. Lone Wolf had previously won the mixed division with Carol but this was the first time he was this far up into the top ten and he was just as motivated as Polecat was. The Cowboys were putting everything they had into keeping the boat speed up and increasing the lead.

Three Dots and the party group were yelling in excitement when the Cowboys paddled into the Cheapside checkpoint in seventh place overall. More importantly they were the first USCA C-2. That was probably one of the fastest water hand offs that Three Dots had ever done before.

The second day of the race will usually end up being a day of survival because of the very humid and hot south Texas temperatures. Lone Wolf and Polecat were very motivated because of the possibility of winning our division and being the first tandem boat to the finish line.

Horsefly and Ron were in the tandem unlimited division and they were the only tandem boat left in front of the Cowboys. Three Dots told the Cowboys that they were closing in on them.

There were five multi man teams in front of them also but the Guadalupe river below Bloomington can be the equalizer and anything can happen down there. The very hot and humid Sunday afternoon temperature was making it a lot harder on everyone but the Cowboys were not slowing down. Horsefly and Ron were starting to struggle and the Cowboys caught up with them in the Cuero area.

Horsefly is a funny guy with a good sense of humor. Horsefly, Polecat and Lone Wolf would become teammates several years later but there was no time for conversation and the exchanging of water safari stories. The Cowboys quickly paddled by them.

The loud sounds of squawking peacocks were echoing down river when the Cowboys approached the Cuero highway 72 bridge. Connie was loudly yelling at Three Dots to "Call the Peacocks Glenn". The unique sound of Peacocks squawking in response to Three Dots comical attempts to call them could be heard from a good distance away. This was a great way to greet the Cowboys and it put a big smile on their faces. Polecat tried to enter the Peacock calling contest but he was no match for Three Dots. The sound of Three Dots and the Peacocks squawking back and forth to each other was getting more intense and everyone there was enjoying the entertainment.

The next scheduled pit stop was going to be at the highway 236 checkpoint and then on to Floodplain Ranch where Polecat's pregnant wife and two young sons would be waiting.

It was late on Sunday afternoon when the Cowboys finally arrived at the Floodplain ranch boat ramp. Several friends and family were yelling out encouragement and the river dogs were barking and howling in excitement. Precious was wanting to jump in the boat and go with the Cowboys but Polecat told her to stay home and watch over the family. Darla and the boys were standing there with Polecat's mother and they were encouraging the Cowboys to keep it going and finish strong. Polecat was staring at his bedroom window a few yards away and the bad thoughts of taking a short nap in his own bed was dominating his thinking. Wade and Brandon started yelling, "Go Polecat Go" and that brought Polecat out of his daydream and back to reality.

The sun was making it's glorious disappearance on the western horizon when the Cowboys approached mile 200 at the Victoria riverside boat ramp. The bow light was turned on and it was still shining brightly after several hours of abuse the previous night.

Three Dots told the Cowboys that they had widened the lead over the tandem boats behind them but they needed to pick it up another notch in order to catch the multi man team in front of them. This was good news and bad news and the Cowboys just tried to focus on the positive things.

The second night below Victoria can be a big mental and physical challenge after 36 hours of canoe racing. Lone Wolf and Polecat were in the unfamiliar position of being in the lead of their division and they were determined to stay there. The stroke rate was steady while they navigated down the winding, long and isolated sections of the lower Guadalupe river.

The Cowboys were several hours ahead of the USCA C-2 competition but were a couple of hours behind the multi man team in front of them. Strange looking creatures were starting to appear in the trees and along the bank. The colorful creatures would appear out of nowhere and stare at you with fire flaming out of their mouths and eyes. Large cartoon characters were smiling and waving from the river bank. Snakes were hanging from the lower tree limbs and were waiting to drop into the boat. Bridges and large trees blocking the river that are not really there. Critters running around in the boat trying to climb up on you. The list goes on and on. Polecat has learned from experience to just smile and enjoy the show and keep paddling. "Take a no doze pill and keep paddling", is Tom's good advice.

It is not unusual to have equipment problems that have to be dealt with in a hurry. The bow light suddenly went out and the Cowboys were heading down river in the total darkness. This potential problem was planned for ahead of time and Polecat was able to quickly turn on the head light that was strapped to his expensive cowboy hat. The backup head light was good enough to see down river but it was a lot weaker than the bow light.

The army of bugs that were zeroing in on the light was just something that Polecat would have to deal with. There were hundreds of bugs making a suicide bombing run into Polecat's face. No insect repellent was available and the only protection would be to stop and rub river mud all over his face. There was no way the Cowboys could waste time doing that.

The log jam cuts were mostly open because of the moderate river flow and the Cowboys were able to paddle around the mile long log jam without portaging. Alligator lake was next in line and the red eyes were glaring at the Cowboys from both sides of the cut as they cautiously paddled into the lake.

That was not a hallucination and the red eyes were scouting out their next meal opportunity.

The sun was starting to make it's glorious appearance on Monday morning and the Cowboys were approaching the salt water barrier dam. There was no public access to this area and no one was there to greet them. The Cowboys cleared the dam and headed for the Tivoli checkpoint.

Three Dots and the party crew were anxiously waiting for them when the Cowboys paddled into the boat ramp at Tivoli for the last water hand off. Three Dots told them that the bay was choppy with two to three foot waves. They needed to discard any unnecessary weight in order to lighten the load. Lone Wolf lifted the lid on his Styrofoam ice chest to reveal that it was still half full of his mothers home cooked meals.

Polecat could not hold back his disappointment and just shook his head in disbelief. The Cowboys had just carried all of that non-essential extra weight for 250 miles. The thought of telling him, "I told you that was way too much food for one person" came to mind but Polecat refrained from any negative comments and just said that the ice chest needed to go. Lone Wolf reluctantly agreed to take the unnecessary weight out of the boat only after downing a couple of the meal packs.

The spray skirt was snapped on and the Cowboys headed straight for Seadrift cut and San Antonio bay. The only necessary items left on board were a couple of water jugs, flares, a spare paddle and two life jackets.

The weight reduction was a good decision because the bay was rougher than what was expected and the waves were constantly crashing over the bow. Lone Wolf and Polecat were pushing on the foot pumps as fast and as hard as they could. They were frantically trying to keep the water that was leaking in through the spray skirt from accumulating in large amounts on the bottom of the boat. The finish line was within sight as they rounded the point and headed for home.

The Cowboys were so focused on keeping the boat upright and headed in the right direction that they were not thinking about what they were about to accomplish.

Lone Wolf and Polecat paddled into the finish line with an official finishing time of 50 hours and 36 minutes. A large crowd was gathered at the sea wall applauding and cheering. The Cowboys finished in sixth place overall and were the first USCA C-2 to make it to the finish line. They were also the first tandem boat to the finish line with five multi man teams finishing ahead of them.

This was a major accomplishment for Lone Wolf and Polecat. They awkwardly tried to climb up the steps at the finish line. There were no tears or sad looks of disappointment, just a lot of smiles and hugs with the bank crew. What had just happened did not really sink in until the next day at the finishers banquet. After seven straight finishes in the water safari and with very mixed results, Polecat was finally part of a team that had the breakout race that they were both hoping for.

John Bugge, Jerry Cochran and Mike Shively won the race with 28 teams finishing. The 1990 Texas Water Safari still stands out as one of the best races that Polecat was ever a part of. The best way this race can be described is, "I had a good run".

Darla gave birth to Jordan in September and he is a blessing from the Lord. The birth of a healthy third son, finishing the Houston marathon for the first time and winning the USCA C-2 division in the "World's Toughest Boat Race" made 1990 a very memorable year. Thank you Jesus.

Polecat and Lone Wolf navigate over Rio Vista dam

CHAPTER 13

The 1991 Houston Marathon

The next several months were a very busy and life changing time in our family with a new baby and two young sons to raise. Darla is a great mother and Polecat gives her all of the credit for being able to manage such a chaotic situation. She basically had to raise three young sons by herself most of the time because Polecat was working offshore in the GOM on a man made island and was working a seven day on and seven day off schedule.

A very funny story during this time happened after finishing a seven day hitch offshore. Polecat was heading home to see his family and stopped briefly to buy flowers for Darla. Polecat drove up to Floodplain ranch and was immediately greeted by an excited pack of river dogs. Polecat then proudly proceeded to enter the front door with a vase of fresh flowers. Darla greeted him at the door and she exchanged the flowers in his hand with a crying baby. Two young boys could be heard arguing and shouting at each other in the bedroom. She looked at Polecat and said, " you wanted him so here he is, take care of him". Darla put the vase of flowers on the cabinet and headed out the front door. "I'm headed to town to do some shopping and I won't be back until supper time". She desperately needed some quiet time to herself after a long and difficult week of raising three boys with no help.

Polecat understood this and it was pretty obvious to him that it was time to step up and take over his responsibility as a part time parent. This was a crazy time in our marriage and Polecat gives all the credit to the Lord for helping us get through it together. Family and work were dominating most of Polecat's time and the water safari was not talked about very much around the house for the next several months. The very limited amount of free time Polecat had on his days off at home were spent working on the house, taking care of animals and running.

The Thomaston running man was still frequently seen running the back roads around the area early in the morning with his river dogs following close behind. This running for no reason mentality would usually dominate his limited free time at home when he wasn't helping Darla with the boys. The secret thoughts of entering the Houston marathon for a second time were hiding in the back of his mind. Polecat would spend a lot of time in the weight room lifting weights after his shift was over at work in order to keep the upper body in shape. This was how Polecat tried to stay in shape during the Texas Water Safari off season.

1991 came around very quickly and the Thomaston running man had to break the ice and ask Darla for her approval for him to enter the Houston marathon for a second time. It was still a little early to talk about the water safari and there was no reason to push the envelope and start that difficult discussion until the Houston marathon was over. The Houston marathon was just a one day event and she gave her approval to the request after the Running man reserved a room for them at a five star hotel in downtown Houston for Saturday night. Darla's parents agreed to keep the boys that weekend so she could enjoy a couple of days without having to deal with rowdy kids.

Lone Wolf wanted to watch the race and he volunteered to team up with Darla and follow the Running man down the race course. The plan was to not start out extremely fast but keep a good steady pace going and try to finish somewhere around three hours and thirty minute mark. This would beat the finishing time from last year by seven minutes. The goal would be to try and maintain somewhere close to an eight minute per mile running pace for 26.2 miles.

The Running man's confidence level was pretty good after finishing his first race last year and after some long distance training over the last several months. The weather on that Sunday morning in down town Houston in the middle of January was very mild with cool temperatures. More than four thousand runners were lined up for the start of the Houston Tenneco marathon.

Marathon running is an endurance event and the Running man learned the hard way from last year's race to not line up right behind the world class runners. The Running man was almost knocked down and ran over by the faster runners that starting behind him. The world class runners start out like they are shot out of a cannon and they do not slow down for the entire 26.2 miles. The Running man made the wise decision to line up in his projected finishing time group and then try to hang with them for the entire race. There were several Texas Water Safari veterans entered in the Houston marathon that year and this gave the Running man a lot more incentive and determination to beat them to the finish line.

The pre race instructions were being announced and the Running man bowed his head in prayer and thanked the almighty God for his many undeserved blessings. The Running man specifically asked the Lord Jesus to please help everyone in the race make it to the finish line safely. "Amen"

The starting gun went off and it took a couple of minutes for the Running man's group to make it up to the starting line. There are numerous bottle necks in the first couple of miles of this race because of the overpass bridges that have to be crossed before the race course opens up and winds its way towards Rice University. Many runners get knocked down or accidentally bumped into as the large starting field bunches up on the overpasses. The plan early on in the race is to remain focused and do not allow yourself to get trapped in a large group of runners with no escape route when crossing over the bridges.

The group that the Running man was trying to hang with was moving along just over an eight minute per mile pace. The group passed Rice University and made the gradual turn back towards memorial park and buffalo bayou. Large crowds were lined up along the side walks and were cheering and applauding as the marathon runners passed by. There were several band's playing loud music and an occasional solo singer that would be singing popular songs. They were there to entertain the runners and the large crowd. Rice University was next in line.

The Running man felt pretty good with the steady pace. The group he was running with started getting smaller and smaller because some of the runners were slowing down as the miles were adding up. Mile twenty was just around the next bend in the road. The belly dancers at mile twenty were getting closer and the Running man could see the young ladies dancing in the middle of the street. The small group of runners started slowing down at the water station in order to grab a cup of water. The Running man did not slow down and ran straight through the water station and started to slap hands and high five several of the young dancers. The Running man had a big smile on his face.

Mile twenty in a marathon is kind of like mile 200 in the Texas Water Safari because this is a big hurdle to overcome. The physical and mental challenges are very intense and it is hard to stay focused and not dwell on the pain as you enter into the last sections of the race course. Many marathon runners start to struggle and have difficulty keeping the pace going at this point. That is very similar to what water safari racers experience below the mile 200 checkpoint. These races are very different events and require different training routines. They are similar in the fact that you always end up pushing yourself past your self imposed physical limits and this requires a mental toughness and focus that is hard to explain to someone that has never experienced this before.

The goal of finishing the race somewhere around three hours and thirty minutes was fading fast when the Running man entered downtown Houston and crossed mile 23. There were several runners limping along or were laid out on the sidewalk with leg cramps while the Running man passed by them. The first aid tents that were located along the last six miles of the race coarse were full of runners that were suffering from dehydration or leg injuries.

The Running man was struggling but was motivated to finish strong when he made the final turn towards the finish line. The large crowd was cheering and encouraging all of the runners when the Running man crossed the finish line with a finishing time of three hours and forty one minutes. This was four minutes slower than the finishing time from last years race.

That was a little disappointing but the positive take away from this race was that the Running man was in much better shape at the finish line. It was nice to have the strength and ability to be able to walk out of the cool down area on his own and with no assistance. The convention center was full of people and he needed to make the rounds to gather up all of the free stuff that was handed out to the finishers. The Running man had missed out on all of the free stuff last year because Darla and crazy cousin Jerry had to pick him up off the floor and carry him out of the convention center.

Darla was patiently waiting and the Thomaston running man headed straight over to his lovely wife and gave her a big hug. Lone Wolf was standing next to her but he had to settle for a handshake. The Running man once again managed to beat almost all of the Texas Water Safari racers that were entered in the Houston marathon that year. Several of them were consistently beating the Cowboys to the finish line in the Texas Water Safari but for some unknown reason the Running man was able to out run them for 26.2 miles and that put a big smile on his face.

It would usually take a couple of weeks before my legs started to feel normal again after running a marathon. The soreness and muscle tightness would take several days to finally go away, but the family and my offshore work schedule would not give me very much time for that healing process to happen.

CHAPTER 14

The 1991 Texas Water Safari and the "One eyed Polecat"

Lone Wolf and Polecat decided to team up again for the 1991 Texas Water Safari and defend their USCA C-2 win. The river training started in March and that meant that Polecat would have to dedicate at least one of his off days to paddling. Darla was not excited about the decision but eventually came on board with the plan because she understood that canoeing and running for no reason were the only hobbies Polecat had. The events themselves were not the problem, it was all of the training that was required to be physically ready.

Lone Wolf was living and working in Houston and that made training runs a little more difficult to coordinate. A year of experience in the boat together and they were very comfortable with Polecat in the bow and Lone Wolf in the stern. The USCA C-2 Polecat had was a we no nah model and it was several years old but it still had a few races left in. The forty mile prelim race was held in early May and the Cowboys did pretty well, finishing in the top ten and first in the USCA C-2 division.

The water safari training was finally over in late May and Polecat headed back to work for his scheduled seven day hitch offshore. This would be his last week offshore before taking off for some much needed vacation time. The vacation would include the Texas Water Safari and the sometimes annual family camping trip immediately after the race. Things were moving along as planned and then an unbelievable sequence of events happened that almost changed the big plans.

Polecat was in the process of repairing a chemical injection pump that was not working properly at the end of a very busy day at work. The discharge pressure on the tubing downstream from the pump had been bled off and Polecat was in the process of disconnecting the pump from the discharge line when he was accidently sprayed directly into his face with a very caustic chemical.

Polecat had safety glasses on but the chemical spray covered his face and dripped into his eyes before he could step back out of the line of fire. Polecat's eyes were burning very intensely and he rushed over to the emergency eye wash station that was located close by. Polecat started washing his face and eyes with fresh water in order to prevent the caustic chemical from burning his skin or damaging his eyes.

Polecat tried to focus on the emergency eyewash station directly in front of him but everything was blurry. The management team had to make the decision to put him on the field helicopter and fly him straight in to the nearest hospital for emergency treatment. The emergency room doctor basically washed his eyes out with a high pressure water solution.

Polecat tensed up and tried to deal with the very painful procedure. Darla drove to the hospital in order to pick the blind man up and take him home. The ER doctor placed patches over both eyes and told him to make an appointment with an eye specialist as soon as possible. Darla had to lead the blind man out of the hospital and help him get into the vehicle for the ride home.

Polecat was temporarily blind and was having to depend on others for assistance. This was something that he had never experienced before and hopefully will never have to deal with again. The eye specialist gave him the bad news the next day. The right eye would probably fully recover in the next few weeks, but the left eye was going to require surgery in order to remove a cyst that had suddenly appeared because of the chemical burn.

The 29th Texas Water Safari was only a week away and it was looking very doubtful that Polecat would be able to start the race. The eye surgery to remove the cyst was done the next day and the blind man was instructed by the doctor to leave the patch on the left eye for the next two weeks.

Polecat was able to see out of his right eye on a very limited basis, but everything was hazy and it was kind of like staring into a thick fog. The funny story from this terrible experience was when Polecat's offshore supervisor called and asked if he would consider coming back to work for the last day of the hitch so they wouldn't have to show the injury as a lost time accident. The way he explained it was that they could write the injury up as a first aid injury with no lost time, if the blind Polecat could just show up for at least one day at the end of the hitch.

Darla was not happy with the decision. She would have to drive the blind Polecat to the heliport in Port O' Conner early the next morning with Wade and Brandon tagging along. Jordan was dropped of at her mothers house on the way through Victoria. The blind Polecat and his family arrived at the heliport and the helicopter pilot was patiently waiting for them.

The blind Polecat and the helicopter pilot were good friends and the pilot was introduced to the family before they headed offshore. The helicopter pilot offered to take them on a joy ride around Matagorda bay if they were willing to wait for him to return after dropping the blind Polecat off at the offshore production platform.

They were very excited with this offer and Darla agreed to wait for him to return. The blind Polecat thanked the pilot for offering to do that. Several co-workers were waiting on the heliport to help the blind Polecat get down the stairs safely and into the quarters building. The blind Polecat called Darla that night and she told him about how much fun they had with the helicopter tour of the area and that Wade and Brandon really enjoyed the adventure. That was one of the few positive things that happened during that very difficult time.

The decision had to be made pretty quickly on whether or not the blind Polecat was going to be able to get in the boat and start the Texas Water Safari because it was scheduled to start in four days.

The vision in the right eye was getting a little better but the left eye was bandaged up and was in the healing process. Lone Wolf was very nervous and had resigned himself to the fact that the blind Polecat would probably be a no show and would not be able to start the race.

Friday came around and the blind Polecat told Darla that he was going to show up on Saturday morning for the start of the race and try to give it a shot. Darla looked over at him and shook her head in disbelief. "That is the dumbest thing I have ever heard". "You are willing to put yourself and Lone Wolf into a very bad situation that will probably not end very well". Darla was on a roll and the tongue lashing continued, "You can't even see me standing right in front of you and you think you can do the water safari"? "Good luck with that". The blind Polecat could not see the anger and frustration in Darla's facial expressions, but he definitely could feel her anger through her words.

Darla and the blind Polecat loaded up and headed out for San Marcos very early on Saturday morning to meet up with Lone Wolf and try to finish rigging out the boat. The right eye was starting to get much better and Polecat could now see hazy objects out of that eye on a very limited basis.

Race day was here and the Cowboys climbed into their USCA C-2 for a quick warm up paddle through Aquarena Spring lake. It was obvious that the one eyed Polecat was going to have a very difficult time picking out the right line to take through all of the rapids and hazards that you have to paddle through on the upper San Marcos river with just one functioning eye. Tom was going over the last minute race announcements when the one eyed Polecat reached up and ripped off the patch that was covering his left eye. That was probably not a smart thing to do but the one eyed Polecat was determined to be at his best through the rock infested upper sections of the race course.

Everything was very blurry when he first took the patch off but both eyes would give him the depth perception that is so desperately needed in order to make the right decisions. Trying to navigate through the many hazards that were waiting down river would require quick reaction time and good judgment. Tom led everyone in prayer and the one eyed Polecat personally thanked the Lord Jesus for his many undeserved blessings and for giving him the ability to see again. "Amen"

The Cowboys started on the second row when the starting gun was fired off with 39 teams starting the race. The one eyed Polecat tried to glance over to the observation deck in order to see if Ralph the swimming pig was there for the start. Everything on the left side of his face was so blurry and out of focus that the one eyed Polecat could not tell if his grunting friend was standing there.

Aquarena spring lake was going through some major remodeling during this time and Ralph would be forced into early retirement. It was a very sad moment to not be able to see him standing proudly on his platform grunting in excitement as the canoe racers paddled by. A long Texas Water Safari tradition was ending and all that was left were the funny memories.

Lone Wolf and the one eyed Polecat made it through the first portage with no problems even though they were very cautious because of the limited vision. The Cowboys quickly dragged their racing canoe over the island portage.

Rio Vista dam was next and they were determined to paddle over the dam without portaging. The crowd was yelling in excitement when the Cowboys cleared the dam upright even though they had taken on a significant amount of water in the process. Darla and the boys were there but the one eyed Polecat never saw them. The Cowboys cleared the dam and rapid and started pumping out the excess water that was in the boat with the foot pumps. The next portage at Thompson's island would give them the opportunity to get out of the boat and dump water.

Lone Wolf was yelling out instructions as they navigated through all the hard turns that are located in that area. Lone Wolf would yell out orders to the one eyed Polecat before the Cowboys closed in on the hard turns because a lot of maneuvering would be required to get through the river bends and rock infested rapids. Lone Wolf was doing a good job in the duel position of driver and lead scout. The Cowboys success-fully made their way through the numerous rock infested rapids and then cleared cotton seed rapid with just a couple of near misses with the large rocks.

Allen and Russ were the fastest team in the USCA C-2 division early in the race and they were moving along at a very fast stroke rate. They had a big lead on the Cowboys when they cleared the Luling dam and headed towards the Palmetto state park checkpoint.

The city of Luling was offering prize money for every first place team in each division at the checkpoint. The Cowboys were not fast enough and they missed out on the two hundred and fifty dollar payoff. The thinking was that they had to run a more conservative race, stay within their physical limits and let the chips fall where they may. The moderate river levels were creating a fast race and the Cowboys were confident that they could make a run at them on the lower sections of the race coarse. The last report Three Dots gave them was that they were almost an hour behind Allen and Russ at the Palmetto checkpoint. The good news was that the Cowboys with the big hats had made it through all of the hazards on the upper San Marcos river with just a few minor problems and minimal damage. The one eyed Polecat was doing the best he could with the extremely limited vision he was having to deal with up in the bow.

Three Dots and the party bunch were excited to see them when they reached the Gonzales gravel bar checkpoint around midnight. The Cowboys were in shock and disbelief when Three Dots gave them the news that Allen and Russ had just dropped out of the race and they were now the first USCA C-2. This was very unexpected. Three Dots explained that Russ was having a lot of physical problems and that they had officially pulled out of the race just before the Cowboys got there.

The one eyed Polecat felt badly for Allen and Russ because they were good friends and great competition. The Cowboys were looking forward to a big battle with them on the lower sections of the race course. There was no time for a celebration because they were looking at a long night ahead of them on their way to Hochheim. Three Dots also told them that a solo paddler was not very far in front of them. Taking over first place in their division was good news but the Cowboys would have preferred to pass Allen and Russ on the race course instead of them pulling out of the race.

The bow light the Cowboys had was not very good but it really didn't matter much in the overall scheme of things because the one eyed Polecat couldn't see very well anyway. The Cowboys eventually caught up with an interesting solo paddler named Zoltan. Lone Wolf and Polecat did not know him very well then, but they would all become good friends later on. Zoltan picked up his stroke rate and started drafting behind them. The Cowboys were enjoying the back and forth conversation with Zoltan and that motivated everyone to stay close together for a while.

The Cowboys suddenly entered into a very turbulent tight spot on the left side of the river. There was a downed tree on the left side of the river and a gravel bar on the other. The one eyed Polecat's vision was not very good and he over corrected the entry line while trying to avoid the downed tree. The Cowboys slammed hard into the gravel bar and this caused them to dip a gunnel and take on a lot of water. The Cowboys were barely able to avoid a wipeout and Zoltan took the same line.

Zoltan ended up right next to them with both boats grinding to a complete stop on top of the partially submerged gravel bar. Zoltan shook his head in disbelief at the near miss and everyone had to start bailing water out. Zoltan yelled out to the Cowboys to start following him because his bow light was much better than theirs was. Lone Wolf thought this was a good idea, so the Cowboys started following him for a while. The first night of the Texas Water Safari can be a very difficult time to stay focused and alert after a hard day of canoe racing through all of the hazards and portages on the San Marcos river. The Gonzales to Hochheim stretch of river can be very boring at times. Maintaining a fast stroke rate and staying mentally alert can be a big challenge but is very important.

Lone Wolf can't sing as well as Three Dots can but he is very good at telling interesting water safari stories from his previous races. The one eyed Polecat was not saying much because he was trying very hard to focus in on what was directly in front of them.

The long first night always seems to drag on with no end. The one eyed Polecat eventually started singing his favorite Willie Nelson songs in order to keep everyone alert. Zoltan unexpectedly pulled over for a quick pit stop and the Cowboys did not see him again until the finishers banquet. The one eyed Polecat just figured that he pulled over because he did not like the singing very much.

The sun was starting to make its glorious appearance and the Hochheim checkpoint was getting closer. The Cowboys pulled into the checkpoint not long after daylight and noticed that a tandem unlimited team was pulled up on the bank. They were both laid out on the river bank taking a break, so the Cowboys were very quiet while Three Dots changed out the water jugs. Three Dots quietly informed them that they were now in eighth place overall. There were six multi man teams and one tandem team still ahead of them.

The one eyed Polecat humbly lowered his head in prayer and thanked the Lord Jesus for his many blessings and for helping him overcome the vision problems. The long prayer finally ended when he asked the Lord to please watch over all of the racers and their bank crews while everyone tried to safely make their way down the race course to the finish line in Seadrift. "Amen"

The second day was not very exciting because the Cowboys were paddling by themselves and they were trying to focus on catching up with the tandem team that was directly in front of them.

A funny story happened at the Cheapside checkpoint when they quickly pulled over for the water jug hand off.

The race official was standing in the knee deep water next to Three Dots when the Cowboys paddled over to the bank for the hand off. Roy was standing right next to the one eyed Polecat and was drinking an ice cold bottle of coke that had condensation dripping off it. The one eyed Polecat was mesmerized by the sight of this coke and could not do anything but stare at it. The temptation and bad thoughts of snatching it out of Roy's hand was dominating his thinking. Lone Wolf and Three

Dots were talking to each other but Polecat's one good eye was focused on stealing Roy's coke.

The water jug exchange quickly ended and Lone Wolf started paddling again. The one eyed Polecat suddenly reached up to grab the coke out of Roy's hand, but it was out of his reach and he missed out on his only chance. The lingering sight of an ice cold coke right next to his face dominated his thinking for the next several miles. The pleasant thought of a team captain handing the one eyed Polecat an ice cold soda was just a dream that would never happen in this race without an instant disqualification under the Texas Water Safari rule book.

Three Dots was calling the Peacocks and was doing his Pat Kelly impersonation when the Cowboys paddled into the Cuero highway 72 bridge. Dad, Jack and Connie were sitting in their lawn chairs along with several other friends and they were enthusiastically cheering the Cowboys on. The Peacocks finally started answering back to Three Dots and everyone was enjoying listening to the loud squawking noises. Mr. Harras was busy taking pictures of the Cowboys while they quickly paddled by and headed for the Cuero checkpoint and then on to Floodplain Ranch.

Polecat rapid is located about two and a half miles above Floodplain Ranch and a mile below River Haven. The rock infested rapid can sometimes be a difficult area to get through at higher water levels. Large trees that are floating down river during a flood will sometimes get lodged at the bottom of this rapid and can cause it to be a very challenging place to maneuver through. It is also a good fishing spot and Polecat has spent a lot of quality time in that area over the years fishing for catfish.

It started out as a joke when he named it Polecat rapid to friends and family but they seemed to like the idea and it has taken off. Several water safari veterans call the place Polecat rapid, so maybe it will catch on someday and become the official name of the rapid during the race. That would be an honor that is not deserved, but it would definitely be appreciated.

The sight of the one eyed Polecat's bedroom window was within view when the Cowboys approached Floodplain Ranch. The sun was beating down on them and it was close to 100 degrees on that Sunday afternoon in June. Three Dots was patiently waiting for a quick water hand off at the primitive boat ramp along with Polecat's mother and Darla and the boys. Darla was holding Jordan because he was only nine months old and could not walk yet. The Cowboys were leading the USCA C-2 division and were running a fast race, so there was very little time allowed for conversation with the family. They were all very excited to see the Cowboys doing so well in the race and they were looking forward to following them all the way down to the finish line. The conversation with Wade and Brandon was awkward and the one eyed Polecat had just enough time to tell them how much he loved them before heading on down river. The last request was for them to be nice to everyone and to take good care of their Mom.

Large Cowboy hats can come in handy during the scorching after-noon heat when you take them off and dip them into the water before placing the hat back on your head and letting the cool river water run down over your neck and shoulder area. Lone Wolf and the one eyed Polecat would alternate this maneuver at least once or twice an hour in order to help keep the body temperatures in the normal range during these very hot and humid conditions. The stroke rate was good and was holding around fifty five strokes per minute. The Cowboys were trying to maintain a good boat speed in the late afternoon heat and catch up with the tandem team that was still in front of them.

The Victoria riverside park checkpoint was next after they success-fully made it through the Nursery rapids with no major problems. The Cowboys arrived at the Victoria river side boat ramp and Texas Water Safari mile marker 200 about an hour before dark. Three Dots gave them the good news that they had gained some time on John and Mike and they were now only about thirty minutes behind them. This was encouraging news and it gave the Cowboys with the big hats a much needed confidence boost. They could catch them if they just kept the stroke rate up and did not waste any time at the check points. The sun was starting to make its glorious descent on the western horizon and it was lighting up the sky with amazing colors.

The lower river logjams and hallucination alley were next in line as they headed towards the swinging bridge checkpoint. The conversation was minimal because they were concentrating on the stroke rate and the race course directly in front of them. The bow light was not helping very much so the one eyed Polecat would occasionally turn on the head light that was strapped around his expensive cowboy hat in order to help illuminate any potential obstructions in front of them. The limited vision that he was suffering from for the entire race was not getting any better. The one eyed Polecat had learned how to deal with it and just let Lone Wolf make the call when they were getting close to a potential hazard. The hallucinations were not as intense and distracting as usual because the one eyed Polecat could not see things very clearly anyway.

The Cowboys made it into the swinging bridge checkpoint around one o'clock on Monday morning. Three Dots was smiling while he patiently waited with fresh water jugs before telling them the good news that they were only about ten minutes behind John and Mike. The checkpoint was very quiet because they had a big lead on the next boat that was behind them. It was time to kick it up into a higher gear and try to pass the tandem team they had been chasing all day.

The logjam cut was partially open and had to be carefully navigated through because of the low hanging tree limbs and numerous obstacles. The scary thought of a water moccasin dropping into your lap as you crash through all of the low hanging tree limbs is always in the back of your mind. The one eyed Polecat was trying very hard to not let that kind of negative thinking slow him down.

The bow person will end up taking most of the abuse during these situations and they are sometimes used as the gauge on whether or not you can make it through the obstacle. If you come to a complete stop and the bow person is pinned down in their seat with thorn bushes or a tree limb laying on top of them, the stern paddler will have to paddle in reverse and back out of the hazard. Paddle backwards until you are clear of the obstacle and then paddle forward again to try a different angle and hopefully have better results. It is very common for this procedure to be performed numerous times while you try and make your way through the very narrow cut. Red eyes are usually glaring at you from the bank. Large alligators are focused in on a potential meal opportunity.

The Cowboys successfully made their way through the logjam cut after several of these maneuvers had to be performed and they did not have to portage. The expensive Cowboy hat on the one eyed Polecat's head took a severe beating and blood was streaming out of the many deep scratches on his arms. That is just one of the many reasons why they call this race the "Worlds Toughest Boat Race" and you have to ignore it and focus on what is next.

Alligator Lake was next in line and it was deep enough to paddle through because of the moderate river level. The lake has to be avoided when the river levels are lower because it is shallow and will end up taking to much valuable time to get through.

Lone Wolf noticed a bow light not very far in front of them when they entered the lake. John and Mike were taking the long route across the northern edge of the lake and were following the shoreline that is located next to the river. Lone Wolf and the one eyed Polecat have trained on this section of the race course many times over the years and they knew where the fastest route across the lake is located. The problem is that the lake level constantly changes when the river level changes and it will look different and can cause confusion on where the most direct route across is located.

This appeared to be happening with John and Mike and the Cowboys were determined to make the right decision and pass them. They are good friends but friendly conversations and story telling can wait until the finish line. The one eyed Polecat knew Mike from previous water safari races because Mike had beaten him in the solo division once. He did not know John very well then but that would soon change. John played the part of a Mexican soldier in the famous Alamo movie that starred Billy Bob Thornton a few years later. Polecat would jokingly call him the famous movie star because of his limited role in that movie. Those kind of conversations would have to wait until the finishers banquet on Tuesday.

The Cowboys turned the headlight off so they would not notice when they passed them on the way to the lake exit. The lake exit cut can sometimes be hard to find and it is the only legal entry point back into the river. Lone Wolf and the one eyed Polecat knew where this exit cut was located and they quietly headed in that general direction. It was a dark night and there was just barely enough sky light to help them find the exit. The bow light was turned back on and they quickly paddled back into the river and headed for Tivoli. The home stretch was just ahead and it looked like there would be a calm bay waiting for them because of the light winds. The sun was starting to make its glorious appearance when they paddled in to the Tivoli bridge checkpoint.

Three Dots was there to give them fresh water jugs along with the great news that they were now in seventh place overall and the first tandem team. Lone Wolf had once again brought way to much food with him and he had to discard several of the home cooked meals that his mother had made for him. The one eyed Polecat's food supply of peanut butter and honey sandwiches, breakfast tacos, jalapeno dried sausage, canned peaches, peanuts, corn chips, powdered gatorade, three cans of coke and a large bag of power jells were long gone and the food bag was empty. This ended up being a very fast pit stop because of the tandem team right behind them. The bay crossing was next in line and they were in a hurry to get across San Antonio bay as fast as they could before the winds started picking up.

The spray skirt was snapped on at the mouth of Seadrift cut because of the slight chop in San Antonio bay and because of the threat of the south easterly winds picking up very soon. The bay crossing was pretty uneventful and the Cowboys sprinted into the finish line with family and friends waiting there to help them celebrate.

The one eyed Polecat and Lone Wolf finished in seventh place overall with a finishing time of 48 hours and 22 minutes. This was the second straight year they were the first tandem team and the first USCA C-2 to the finish line. There were six very fast multi-man teams that finished ahead of them. John Bugge, Jerry Cochran and Mike Shively won the race with twenty nine teams making it to the finish line in Seadrift. The Cowboys new friend, Zoltan, won the solo division. This was another great finish for the Cowboys and it was time to celebrate. The best way their race can be summarized is that they had a good run. That is Polecat's favorite saying and it accurately describes a very good water safari finish. This can also describe a successful ending when you have to navigate through the many hazards, obstacles and challenges that life can sometimes throw at you.

The left eye healed up a few weeks later and Polecat was able to regain normal vision in that eye.

Mike Spencer, the race director at the time approached Polecat before the banquet started and asked if he would do the opening prayer at the official start of the festivities. This request caught Polecat by surprise and he humbly replied that it would be an honor and privilege. Polecat did not have much time to prepare and he quietly asked for the Lord's guidance.

The prayer started and Polecat thanked the Lord Jesus for helping everyone get to Seadrift safely. Polecat thanked the Lord for all of the race officials and volunteers who donate so much of their time and effort into this great race. Polecat then emotionally prayed for those that were still on the race course and were struggling to get to the finish line. "Amen". This was the first time Polecat had been asked to do the prayer and it was the biggest honor and privilege that he ever had during his many years of competing in the " World's Toughest Boat Race". It was time to hang the Texas Water Safari plaque up on the wall and return his undivided attention back on his beautiful family.

The Thomaston running man and his gang of river dogs made their return to the country roads close to home. The Houston marathon training season intensified in the fall of 1991. The running for no particular reason was starting to dominate the Running man's limited time off from work when 1991 was coming to an end.

Things dramatically changed in December of 1991 when a big rain event occurred in central Texas just a few days before Christmas. The long range forecast was predicting a major river flood for the lower Guadalupe and that forced Polecat to start making evacuation plans for the family. Moving family, furniture and personal items out of harms way ended up being the main focus and objective during the days leading up to Christmas.

Darla and Polecat had experienced major flood damage to their home in 1981 and 1987, but this one was different because of the time of year. Flood waters entered their home on Christmas eve and the river level crested with about one foot of muddy water in the house. There were no tears allowed because of the bad situation they found themselves in because it was time to celebrate the Lord's birthday at Darla's parents house on Christmas morning. The flood was not talked about very much while they celebrated Christmas with the extended family.

The flood was just a minor setback that could be overcome in time and it was just a bump in the road to an other wise great year. Polecat was in a good mood when he paddled out to the flooded house on Christmas day after the family celebration was over. His mother was determined to go see the damage and help with the cleanup, so Polecat agreed to put her in the bow of the canoe and bring her along to help with the mud removal.

Mom is an independent and hard working woman who has had a lot of positive influence on Polecat and his sister. Mom taught them how to become successful in life through hard work and perseverance in everything they attempt to do. Mom was the one who dished out the discipline in the family and she had the arm strength of a major league pitcher. She could quickly take off her shoe and hurl it several yards and accurately nail a young boy in the back when he was trying to run away from his bad behavior. The running boy knew what this meant and he would quickly stop and return to face the music after being nailed in the back with her shoe. That is just one of the great memories that Polecat has of his mother. Thank you Lord Jesus for giving me a loving and caring mother who had such a positive influence on me and everyone that knew her. "Amen"

The mud needed to be swept out of the house with a broom before it could start drying. An empty five gallon bucket was used to dip into the river and then dump the river water onto the floor in order to help wash all of the mud and sand out. There was also some carpet that had to be pulled up so the wood flooring under it could start drying out. Thankfully, the furniture had been moved upstairs before the flood and there was only flooring and wall damage to deal with.

The funny thing Polecat remembers most about this Christmas day flood clean up was when they started playing Christmas music on the radio. The river mud was being swept out the front door and there was no pity party or depressed feelings, only cheerful and joyful Christmas music being played on the radio while the dirty work continued.

Top canoeists

Former Victoria resident John Mark Harras of Houston, left, and Bill Stafford of Thomaston were presented the first-place trophy Tuesday in Seadrift in the U.S. Canoe Association's C2 division in the 29th annual Texas Water Safari on the Guadalupe River. Harras has his arm in a sling because he said his shoulder was sore from 48 hours of continuous paddling in the race, which officially ends at 1 p.m. Wednesday.

Lone Wolf and the one eyed Polecat showing off the first place USCA
C-2 trophy after the finishers banquet

CHAPTER 15

1992 Houston Marathon

1992 came around very quickly and the family was finally able to move back in to the river house after the damaged flooring and walls were repaired. The marathon training had abruptly come to an end because of the flood and the several weeks of repair work that followed. The Houston marathon was scheduled for the third Sunday in January and the Thomaston Running man had not had the time to do any serious training for over a month. The Running man needed a break from work and the on going flood repairs so Darla gave him her permission to enter his third straight marathon.

Darla was looking forward to the weekend getaway because of the rare opportunity to stay at a five star hotel in down town Houston and dining at a famous restaurant. Darla would have the rare opportunity to be entertained by watching the Running man push himself to his physical limits in a 26.2 mile marathon.

The 1992 Houston marathon started on a cold Sunday morning in January with well over four thousand runners jammed together at the starting line next to the George Brown convention center. The personal goal once again was to beat the finishing time from the 1990 race. The Running man was entered in the thirty five to thirty nine year old male division and also in the over two hundred pound category. The finishers card that was mailed to you after the race was over would show how well you finished in your respective division.

The over two hundred pound division was very unique in marathon running because there were not that many runners who could fit into that category. The vast majority of marathon runners are small framed people and big men like myself are obviously at a disadvantage because of having to carry more baggage around the race course. The race started and the Running man quickly fell in line with the eight minute per mile group because he was determined to hang with them and finish the race under three and a half hours. This group of runners is usually very consistent and locked in to that pace for the entire race.

The race was moving along without any major problems and the Running man was hanging in there with his group as they approached the young belly dancers at mile twenty. The tightness and fatigue in his legs were starting to slow him down some and the pain was getting worse. The Running man enthusiastically slapped hands with the scantily dressed young ladies on the way through the water station. The marathon experience that he had learned the hard way during his previous races had prepared him for the difficult push to the finish line.

This race was shaping up a little differently because the Running man had pushed himself a lot harder for the first twenty miles because he was trying to make it to the finish line in three and a half hours or less. The legs were cramping and the pain was getting worse at mile twenty three.

The better strategy would have been to slow down much sooner and stay closer to the pace per mile time he had trained for. The water safari mentality of pushing yourself beyond your self imposed limits had kicked in and taken over the Running man's thought process. This pace was just to fast for what he had trained for and it was starting to catch up with him in a hurry.

The Running man was starting to slow down and there was nothing he could do about it. The personal goal of beating his previous best marathon time was not going to happen. The Running man started focusing on trying to make it to the finish line without having to stop and stretch out his aching leg muscles. Several runners started passing by. The Running man was trying to re-focus his attention on finishing the race instead of all the severe leg pain he was experiencing.

The funny part of this story is that there was a young marathon runner that was completely dressed out in a clown outfit not very far behind. This young man was a good marathon runner and he would always run this race in a brightly colored clown outfit. If the clown was able to beat the Running man to the finish line in this race that would be the last nail in the coffin. It would be the sign needed to retire from marathon running and throw the running shoes into the nearest trash can.

The muscle cramps and fatigue were getting much worse. The Thomaston Running man made the last turn and staggered towards the finish line. The terrible thought of maybe having to crawl on his hands and knees over the last one hundred yards started going through his mind.

The Thomaston Running man was able to stumble across the finish line with an official finishing time of three hours and forty eight minutes. This was eleven minutes slower than his previous best time. The debilitating leg cramps were very painful but he made it without stopping and without having to crawl in to the finish line. The clown ended up finishing several minutes behind him.

The legs were not functioning properly and he had to lay down in the reception area and do a lot of leg stretching. It was time to get up and make the rounds and get all of the free stuff that is offered to the finishers. The finishing time was a little disappointing but the Thomaston Running man was able to limp in and finish his third straight Houston marathon.

Darla was ready to load up and head for home. The orders were issued to hurry up and finish making the rounds through the convention center. The marathon was over and it was time to head home and pick up our three sons. Darla had to help the Thomaston Running man into the vehicle and she drove back home because he could barely walk after all the leg muscles started seizing up. It was going to take a few days of rest to get back to semi-normal again.

CHAPTER 16

1992: A flooded race course and a crazy finish

The 1992 Texas Water Safari training season started in March after only getting a few weeks of recovery time from the Houston marathon. It was an easy decision for Lone Wolf and the Polecat to team up again and defend their USCA C-2 winning streak in the last two races. Lone Wolf and Polecat felt pretty good about being the first tandem canoe to the finish line for the last two years and they wanted to repeat that performance one more time. A picture of the Cowboys with the big hats navigating their canoe through cotton seed rapid during the 1991 race was on the cover of the official Texas Water Safari brochure in 1992. This put a lot more pressure on the Cowboys to team up again and defend the USCA C-2 title. The brochure cover picture was an undeserved honor that was probably put there because of the very nice cowboy hats that they wore. The picture was taken early in the race and the hats were still in pretty good shape. Lone Wolf and the Polecat had never been serious contenders for the Argosy cup but they had finished pretty well in the last two races.

There were a lot of big rain events in the spring of 1992 and that was causing the river levels to stay very high as the start of the thirtieth annual Texas Water Safari inched closer. The very wet conditions had started back in December. Polecat and his beautiful family celebrated the holidays with a foot of river water in the house on Christmas Eve.

The river levels all along the race course were at or near flood stage and race day was almost here. Lone Wolf and Polecat had to limit their training runs to the lower Guadalupe because of the high water levels on the San Marcos river. The common opinion of most water safari veterans a week before the start was that the race would be postponed until July. The check in on Friday was held as scheduled and Tom announced to everyone that no decision on a postponement would be made until just before the start on Saturday morning.

The river levels along the upper San Marcos river were starting to fall just below flood stage and there was still a slim chance that the race would start as scheduled. Several sections of the lower Guadalupe river were well above flood stage levels but the water safari board was not concerned with that. There was no insurance policy covering the race during this time and the board was making a hard decision on their own. Tom had previously made it clear to everyone that any law suits filed against the Texas Water Safari would be challenged in court by several of his lawyer friends and they would volunteer their time and expenses. In other words, you were entering the " World's Toughest Boat Race " and you are accepting full responsibility for all of the bad things that can happen to you and your team. The personal responsibility waiver was signed at the check in by everyone who entered the race and was never challenged in the previous twenty nine races.

The thirtieth anniversary of the Texas Water Safari was being celebrated at the check in with several safari veterans from past races being introduced to the cheering crowd. The opportunity to meet some of them and listen to their interesting stories was the highlight of the evening. A reporter from the Victoria advocate newspaper contacted Polecat several days before the water safari and asked if he could interview him before the race. The reporter wanted to follow the Cowboys down the race course and take pictures and write newspaper articles on their progress. This was an unexpected request, so Lone Wolf and Polecat talked it over and agreed to do the interview. The Victoria advocate was showing some interest in their team and the Texas Water Safari so they looked at it as an opportunity to promote the "World's Toughest Boat Race" to the crossroads area. Tim and Frank would end up following the race all the way down to Seadrift.

Race day arrived on a beautiful Saturday morning in early June with everyone anxiously waiting for the official decision to be made if the race was a go or not. Tom finally made the announcement about an hour before the scheduled start that the 1992 Texas Water Safari would start as planned and it would not be postponed. This was very good news and the Cowboys finished up their last minute boat rigging and launched into Aquarena Spring lake. There is no way this race would have started as scheduled in today's environment because most of the lower race course was at flood stage levels.

This was going to be a very interesting first day because the first fifty miles or so was basically going to be a white water race in a very swift, turbulent river. The biggest test would be if your team could manage to keep the boat upright and damage free.

Racing canoe's are not made for white water paddling. They are built for speed and are made of lightweight materials that can be easily damaged. A long and narrow racing canoe can be very unstable in turbulent water and it will usually end up plowing through the waves instead of going over them. This will significantly increase the chance of a bad wipe out. Paddling through intense rapids is something Polecat really looks forward to and enjoys doing but not while paddling a Kevlar racing canoe that was made for lake and open water racing.

Tom led everyone in prayer before the race started. Polecat lowered his head and personally thanked the Lord Jesus for his many undeserved blessings and then he humbly asked the Lord to please watch over his beautiful family and help everyone get to Seadrift safely. "Amen"

Lone Wolf and Polecat started on the second row when the starting gun went off with 48 teams lined up in rows of six. The reality of the situation started sinking in when they cleared the island portage at the end of spring lake and approached Rio Vista dam. It was very obvious that they were going to have to portage around the dam because of the high water level and the very large standing waves that were lined up at the bottom of the drop. Polecat's thought process and tendency is to go for it and paddle over these potential hazards, but this was the highest water level he had ever seen at this spot. The smart decision was made to portage the dam on the left side and to quickly jump out and carry the boat through the crowd that was gathered there to watch the show.

This was just the beginning of a long day of portaging around some very turbulent rapids and flooded dams. The upper San Marcos river can be very challenging to navigate through at higher water levels and this was shaping up to be a test of survival. Lone Wolf and Polecat were focused on trying to keep the boat damage free while they paddled down the swollen river.

The dam portages gave them the opportunity to quickly dump water because the bilge pumps could hardly keep up with all the water that was splashing into the boat. Lone Wolf and Polecat amazingly made it through the many obstacles above Martindale with just a few minor problems and several close calls. There were no stops made except for the necessary portages and a couple of unscheduled pit stops to dump water.

Cotton seed rapid was next in line and the race plan was to run it until they had personally experienced how difficult the upper river was to maneuver through. Lone Wolf and Polecat decided to portage the rapid and not take any unnecessary chances. This was a very hard decision to make because they normally looked forward to the excitement of paddling through this rapid. There was a long race course ahead of them and this flooded rapid had the potential to abruptly end the plans of a third straight USCA C-2 win if they couldn't make it through upright.

It turned out to be a good decision. Lone Wolf and Polecat jumped out of the boat upstream of the rapid on the right side and started climbing over what was left of the old cotton mill dam. After clearing the dam they started carrying the boat as fast as they could along the right bank. There was a big crowd gathered on the left bank and they were patiently waiting to be entertained with the next victim to come paddling through the large standing waves.

The rapid was far worse than what they expected to see and they would have had a hard time getting through it without swamping out and capsizing. Two tandem teams had wiped out just in front of them and were upside down in the rapid. One of the boats was pinned up against a large rock and the other was floating down river with two paddlers swimming behind it in hot pursuit. Lone Wolf and Polecat have made a lot of bad decisions in this race over the years but this was not one of them. The crowd was disappointed that the Cowboys did not provide them with any picture taking opportunities. This was going to be a long race and there would be many more chances for that.

Polecat took the time to wave at his lovely wife and young sons while the Cowboys with the big hats loaded back into the boat and headed down river to the next obstacle. Wade and Brandon were yelling " go Polecat go " while they paddled out of sight. Lone Wolf had introduced his new girl friend to Polecat before the race and she was standing on the bank watching the action. Mary grew up in Ireland and was now working at a laboratory in the Houston area. She was planning on hanging out with the bank crew and following the race all the way to the finish line.

Mary seemed to have a very nice personality and Polecat was hoping that their very loud and partying bank crew would not scare her off or give her a bad impression. She was definitely a big step forward in the right direction for Lone Wolf and it would be good for him if things worked out between them. Three Dots and the party bunch were well known throughout the water safari as the entertainers and the people to hang out with at the check points.

The high water levels had created a lot of dangerous conditions at the dams and low water bridges along the upper San Marcos river. There were several mandatory portages that required everyone to take out several yards upstream of the flooded obstacle and then put back in well below the hazard in order to avoid the intense water conditions. Lone Wolf and Polecat were flying down river at a very fast stroke rate and were able to successfully navigate through the many hazards and stay upright. The fast pace was keeping the Cowboys motivated and focused on what was waiting around the next bend. Lone Wolf and Polecat had never seen the San Marcos river at this level before in the water safari and they were focused on getting down river as fast as they could. The bigger problem was that their main competition in the USCA C-2 class was moving along at a faster pace than they were.

Art and Jon were slightly ahead of the Cowboys but they were not that concerned at this point. Lone Wolf and Polecat normally can make up time and do much better on the lower sections of the race course. This race was shaping up much differently from previous years due to the high water levels and fast times. Lone Wolf and Polecat made it to the Luling dam in record time for them as teammates in the USCA C-2 division. That meant there was only two more dams and a lot of open water ahead of them. The Palmetto state park low water bridge was completely submerged and they paddled right over it without even slowing down. The water jug handoffs had to be done a little differently in this race because the normal pit stops were either under water or too swift to stop at. The Cowboys were pumped up with excitement when they made it to the Guadalupe river and the Gonzales dam portage before the sun had disappeared on the western horizon.

Polecat had made it to the Gonzales dam once before in the daylight during his first water safari finish in 1984. The difference was that it was almost twelve hours later on Sunday morning.

The sight of the Gonzales dam completely under water was amazing. The Cowboys were forced to do the long portage along the right bank in order to avoid the large standing waves and the turbulent cross currents below the dam. Three Dots was patiently waiting at the gravel bar checkpoint and he gave them the news that they were in the top twelve and that Art and Jon were about thirty minutes ahead of them. Three Dots quickly changed out the water jugs and Polecat waved to the party bunch. Mary was standing on the bank with Darla and they seemed to be having a good time following the race. Tim and Frank, the Victoria advocate reporter and photographer were there taking pictures and asking questions that the Cowboys did not have the time to answer.

The stroke rate picked up a little and they headed down river for Hochheim with nothing but a flooded race course in front of them. The Cowboys had made it all the way down the San Marcos river with just a few minor problems and many close calls. The more open sections of the race course were in front of them and it was time to kick it into high gear and put some heat on the competition.

The river below Gonzales was wide open and flooded and you had to stay clear of the cross currents and the large turbulent eddies along the river bank. The large eddies could abruptly change the direction of the boat and turn you over. Staying in the main current and keeping up a fast stroke rate was very important in these conditions and that is what the Cowboys were focused on.

Lone Wolf and Polecat made it to the Hochheim checkpoint in record time for them as teammates and that was motivating the Cowboys to push even harder. Art and Jon were still in the lead but they were gradually making up time. The Cowboys made it past the halfway mark at the Cheapside check point and were in the Cuero area before the sun started making it's glorious appearance on Sunday morning. The beautiful sunrise was helping to bring them out of the mental fatigue they were experiencing and Polecat led the prayer to thank the Lord for his many blessings.

"Thank you Lord Jesus for this beautiful day and for giving us the ability to compete in this great race. We humble ourselves today before you because we know that you are in control and we pray for safety for all of the racers and their bank crews while everyone makes their way to the finish line in Seadrift. We know that you care about personal relationships. Our prayer today is that this canoe race will bring everyone involved in it a lot closer to you and that your name will be honored and glorified. In the name of Jesus we pray, Amen."

This was a great way to start Sunday morning while they paddled down the flooded river towards Floodplain ranch. Polecat's beautiful family would be waiting there to cheer them on.

A big smile came across Polecat's face when he thought about his first water safari finish in 1984. The sun was rising around the same area of the race course twenty four hours later due the extremely low river levels. The record low river levels eight years earlier had turned that race into an ultra endurance event that ended up with very few boats making it to the finish line. The 1992 water safari was completely the opposite and was turning into a sprint race with everyone flying down the race course in personal record setting times.

Lone Wolf and Polecat were doing their best with no major mistakes and wasted time so far. They were consistently maintaining a steady stroke rate of around fifty five strokes per minute with the high expectation of eventually catching up with the competition.

Floodplain ranch was within sight and Polecat could see Darla holding Jordan. Wade and Brandon were running along the river bank yelling out encouragement. This was not going to be a good water hand off spot because the river was to high and swift at the primitive boat dock. All the Cowboys could do was slow down a little and try to thank everyone there for their support and encouragement. Tom's good advice was still fresh in Polecat's thinking that there would be plenty of time for conversation and story telling at the finish line.

The Victoria riverside park boat ramp checkpoint at mile two hundred was packed with spectators. The Cowboys with the big hats paddled up for a water hand off early Sunday afternoon.

Tim published a lengthy article along with several pictures in the Sunday advocate news paper about the Cowboys first day race progress. There were very few water safari racers from the Victoria area during this time and they were stirring up some interest from the local community in "The Worlds Toughest Boat Race." Lone Wolf and Polecat would not normally be looked at as anything special within the small circle of water safari veterans and definitely were not worthy of a front page picture in the Sunday morning paper. The best way to look at it was that they were promoting a very unique canoe race that went straight through the crossroads area.

Three Dots gave them the good news that the Cowboys with the big hats had made up some time on Art and Jon and they were just a few minutes behind them. That positive development gave them a burst of energy and some much needed confidence that they were catching up to the main competition in their division. Lone Wolf and Polecat did not focus their attention on anyone except for Three Dots in the large crowd that was gathered at the checkpoint because every minute was important and there was no time to waste with conversations. The south Texas 100 degree temperatures were making their ugly appearance on that Sunday afternoon while they changed out water jugs before heading down river. Sunday was quickly turning into an extremely hot and humid afternoon and they needed to use that to their advantage.

Polecat seemed to be able to handle the scorching heat better than some of the competition could. The long and extremely hot days working on an offshore oil and gas production platform in the Gulf of Mexico helped prepare him for these situations. Lone Wolf was an office worker for an oil company in down town Houston, but he ran a lot during the off season and was able to handle the one hundred degree days pretty well. The stroke rate started picking up even more and they focused on catching up to Art and Jon.

Three dots was at the highway 59 bridge and was patiently waiting on them with fresh water jugs. Three Dots told them that Art and Jon had picked up their pace after hearing that the Cowboys were right behind them and they were now about ten minutes ahead.

It was an extremely hot afternoon and the Cowboys would occasionally dip their expensive cowboy hats into the river to cool their heads and bodies off with river water. The cool river water felt pretty good as it trickled down over their over heated bodies. There were no ice packs allowed back in those days so this was the next best option. Lone Wolf and Polecat would occasionally splash water on each other with the paddles. This was done while switching sides after a hut was called and did not usually interfere with the intense stroke rate.

Polecat noticed another canoe not to far ahead around the next gradual bend in the river. Lone Wolf and Polecat quietly made a plan to pick up the pace even more and quickly pass by them to try and give the impression that there was no way they could hang with them. The Cowboys pulled up next to Art and Jon and started a conversation. Polecat yelled out that it was a beautiful Lord's day and that it was kind of like being in a steam bath. Jon quickly answered back that the heat and humidity was the worst he had ever experienced. Polecat responded that it was going to probably get much worse. There was no reply in return while the Cowboys paddled by them and headed down river for the swinging bridge checkpoint.

Lone Wolf and Polecat did not know Art and Jon very well but they seemed to be nice guys. There would be plenty of time to trade stories and get to know them better at the finishers banquet.

Three Dots and the party bunch were cheering with excitement and enthusiasm when the Cowboys paddled up to the boat ramp at the swinging bridge checkpoint. It ended up taking over two hundred and twenty miles of hard paddling but they had finally passed their main competition and were now in first place in the USCA C-2 division.

The party bunch was very excited to see them in first place. Dad, Jack and Connie were making plans to head for Seadrift and enjoy a long night of partying. There was a lot of self inflicted pressure on the Cowboys to keep the party going. Three Dots informed them that their friend Zoltan and his partner Kevin were not that far ahead and were next in line. That was good news. The Cowboys started to realize that there was a slim chance for them to possibly get to the finish line in under forty hours. That would be an amazing accomplishment that neither one of them had ever come close to before. Lone Wolf and Polecat briefly talked about this possibility and then headed down river for the log jam cut and alligator lake.

The late afternoon sun was still shining bright on the western horizon and they made it through the log jam cut without having to portage. Alligator lake was at the highest level either one of them had ever seen before in the race and it was kind of like paddling across a large man made reservoir.

The sprint across alligator lake was uneventful and went pretty quickly because of the high water level and lack of any obstacles. Lone Wolf and Polecat were back into the river again and there was still some daylight left. The sun was starting to set on the western horizon when they paddled over the submerged salt water barrier dam without slowing down.

This was not an accessible location for team captains or race officials back then and no one was there. Darkness started setting in when they paddled up to the Tivoli checkpoint at the boat ramp located just below the highway 35 bridge. Three Dots was patiently waiting and gave them the good news that they had closed the gap on Zoltan and Kevin and that they were within their reach. The bad news was that the bay was rough and that could possibly give them some trouble. Lone Wolf and Polecat were focused on catching the next boat in front of them and possibly even finishing under forty hours. The Cowboys did not let the bad news of a rough bay bother them. Lone Wolf and Polecat were still paddling at a very high stroke rate and were motivated to finish strong.

The Cowboys had a lot of extra food still stashed away in the food bags because of the very fast race times up to this point. This was the first time that Polecat had ever discarded unused food and supplies at the last checkpoint. It was usually the other way around and Polecat would be running short of almost everything at this point in the race.

The problem with a rough bay was that the spray skirt they had for this boat only covered about two thirds of the canoe and the stern paddler did not have any protection over his legs or upper body. This had not been a major problem in the previous races with this boat. The bay would be a lot rougher this time around and they were about to ex-perience a wild ride across San Antonio bay. Polecat should have asked Paula to upgrade the spray skirt several years ago but hindsight is always twenty twenty vision.

Lone Wolf and Polecat paddled into Seadrift cut and briefly pulled over to snap on the spray skirt before heading into a very turbulent San Antonio bay. The Cowboys still had a chance to finish this race in under forty hours if they could just make a fast and clean bay crossing.

The large waves were crashing over the bow and pounding into Polecat's chest. The Cowboys paddled straight through the three to four foot waves and slowly made their way towards the point. Lone Wolf and Polecat were gradually angling towards the barge canal point and the bilge pumps were barely able to keep up with the water that was splashing into the boat. Lone Wolf was giving Polecat constant updates on the increasing water levels that were accumulating under him. There was no shoreline close enough to paddle over to and dump water. The Cowboys had no choice but to keep the semi submerged boat headed towards the point. The only positive thing to dwell on was that even though they were making slow progress, they were still upright and going in the right direction.

The waves started getting much bigger. The point was not very far away but the bilge pumps were not able to keep up with all of the water that was splashing in. Lone Wolf started shouting out that they were sinking and that they would soon be going under. The decision was made to head straight into the shoreline and try to make it into shallower water before the boat completely swamped out. The stroke rate was very intense at this moment and they were putting everything they had left into trying to reach shallow water before the boat went completely under.

The forward movement suddenly stopped and Lone Wolf yelled that the stern of the boat had sunk. The boat was very unstable at this point and that caused them to lose their balance and roll over into a very rough and turbulent San Antonio bay. Lone Wolf was able to get out of the boat pretty quickly but Polecat was pinned in the bow seat upside down. Polecat was completely under water and was pinned in the boat because the spray skirt was tied around his waist. Polecat was frantically trying to loosen the spray skirt so he could get out of the submerged boat and breath again.

The bad situation Polecat was in seemed to be getting worse. Polecat was swallowing large amounts of bay water before he was finally able to loosen the spray skirt and crawl out of the boat. Polecat's head finally emerged above the water line and he started to violently throw up large amounts of sea water that he had breathed in and swallowed while under water. This was a close call and Polecat was thanking Jesus for helping him escape the near fatal drowning experience.

The boat was upside down and Lone Wolf was hanging on to the stern. Polecat started breathing normally again and then looked around to survey the bad situation. The large waves were constantly crashing over their heads. Polecat would have to take a deep breath in between the waves and then hold it as the next wave rolled over him. Polecat was able to barely touch bottom in between the large waves.

The strong south wind the Cowboys had been paddling straight into was trying to push them back across the bay to where they had started. Polecat was finally able to take a deep breath again and firmly plant his feet into the muddy bottom. Polecat started pushing himself towards the shoreline with the submerged boat in his grasp behind him. The beach was over one hundred yards away.

This was going to be a slow process. Large waves were constantly crashing over them and this was slowing down the limited progress. Lone Wolf was not able to touch bottom so he hung on to the stern and tried to push the boat forward by kicking his feet in a swimming motion as hard as he could. The swimming Cowboys were making some limited progress and it looked like the shoreline was getting a little closer but this was taking a lot of valuable time.

This would probably end up costing them the lead in the USCA C-2 division. Polecat's competitive nature started to dominate his emotions. Polecat yelled out to Lone Wolf that it would be a much faster process if he would just let go of the boat and let him try to walk the boat into the shoreline by himself. Lone Wolf did not respond when Polecat continued, "I will dump the water out of the boat and then paddle back out to get you." This sounded like a good plan to Polecat and he was pretty confident that it would save them a lot of time.

The problem with that thinking and something his sleep deprived mind had not considered was that it was a very dark night and the south wind would probably push Lone Wolf back out into the middle of the bay and make it very unlikely that he would be able to find him again.

The silence was deafening as Polecat patiently waited for Lone Wolf's response to the plan. There had been several times in past races that Polecat had momentarily thought about dumping his good friend and former partner Three Dots, but he had never had those same negative thoughts about Lone Wolf until now.

Lone Wolf finally yelled back that he did not think that was a good idea and he was not going to let go of the boat. "We are in this race together and we just need to keep pushing towards the shoreline and get ourselves out of this bad situation." That was a great answer and those bad thoughts that Polecat briefly had started to disappear. They were replaced with a more focused attitude towards getting the boat to the shoreline as fast as possible.

The Running man made his return and Polecat started running with the submerged boat in tow behind him. Polecat would hold his breath when a wave rolled over his head and then start running again before the next wave came crashing into them. The very rough bay was starting to get a little shallower and Polecat was able to pick up the running pace a little more. Lone Wolf was finally able to touch bottom and he started running behind the stern and pushing the submerged boat forward.

Running while your body is submerged in water is hard work but the jogging pace was getting the job done and they finally made it into waist deep water with the shoreline only a few yards away.

Lone Wolf and Polecat were filled with excitement when they finally reached the shoreline and pulled the boat up onto dry land. This ended up being a very long process and it took a lot out of them physically. They managed to get through it and now they were back in the race. It was time to lick their wounds, dump water and get to the finish line as fast as they could before another boat passed by.

The swimming Cowboys never saw a headlight pass by during this extended ordeal but someone could have snuck by without being noticed.

The barge canal point was within sight. Lone Wolf and Polecat quickly dumped the water out and got back into the boat. The stroke rate gradually increased to racing speed and they finally reached the point and turned the boat towards Seadrift. The bow was pointed at a slight angle while they cautiously paddled over the large waves. This was the normal route that most teams take and they were very familiar with it. The Cowboys did not know it then but this would end up being another critical mistake that would cost them valuable time.

Lone Wolf and Polecat suddenly came to a complete stop for no apparent reason. This was a very confusing situation because they were over fifty yards away from the shoreline and this area is normally several feet deep. Polecat turned the light on that was strapped to his badly damaged cowboy hat and looked straight down into the turbulent bay water. He noticed that they had just paddled into some muddy shallow water. The Cowboys could not figure out what had just happened because this was not normal and was unexpected.

Lone Wolf and Polecat both jumped out of the canoe and were immediately buried and engulfed with mud and sludge. Polecat went down into the muck and slime all the way up to his neck area before stopping. There had been some recent dredging activity along the barge canal and they were now stranded neck deep in a mud and sludge pit. The mud and sludge had been dredged out of the main channel and was piled up along the outer perimeter.

Polecat started to drift into panic mode again while he tried to figure out what to do next. It was kind of like being stuck in a quick sand pit with no bottom and there was nothing to stand on. Polecat was finally able to pull his body out of the mud and sludge after struggling for several minutes. Polecat was completely covered with mud and slime but was finally able to start moving forward again by swimming with one arm and pulling the boat behind him with the other.

Lone Wolf started doing the same thing from behind the boat and was pushed the boat forward by kicking his feet in the sludge pit while staying on his stomach in a swimming position. This comical scene was kind of like like two wild hogs playing in a mud pit. Thank the Lord that no one was there to film it.

Polecat finally figured out that squirming like a worm while pulling the boat behind him was a faster and more efficient way to proceed.

Polecat yelled out to Lone Wolf that it would be better if he would just squirm like a worm in a sand pit and keep trying to push the boat forward. The worm in a sand pit strategy seemed to be working and they were making some progress moving the boat forward. It sure seemed like a lot of valuable time had been wasted playing in the mud before they finally reached deeper water again.

This was probably the second most bizarre sequence of events that Polecat had ever experienced in the water safari. It was just behind the 1989 race when Three Dots and Polecat were very busy putting metal art together instead of racing. Lone Wolf and Polecat were both in good physical shape and had just enough energy left to successfully climb back into the boat and continue the journey across the barge canal point. Polecat was covered from head to toe in mud and slime but that was not very important because the flashing yellow light at the finish line was now within sight. The wasted time was very depressing because they figured that their lead was gone and that they had lost the race due to terrible decision making at the end.

The swamp and swim incident could have been avoided if they would have just paddled straight across the open water sooner and the worm crawling incident could have been avoided if they just would have gone a little further out before cutting across the barge canal point. Two major mistakes were made at the end of an otherwise problem free race and that bad decision making had probably cost them dearly. Thank the Lord that they were finally back to paddling instead of swimming and crawling on their bellies.

The flashing light at the finish line was within sight while they plowed ahead and tried very hard to keep the bow pointed in to the waves in order to maintain stability. Polecat could barely see the start of the sea wall which officially marks the last one hundred yards of the race course because of all the mud and sludge that was caked up on his face. The boat was gradually filling up with water again and they would soon be swimming if they did not change course and head to the shoreline pretty quickly. The decision was made to head straight for the seawall and walk the boat in to the finish line just before they almost went completely under.

The completely submerged boat violently slammed into the shoreline and they were able to jump out of the boat before it went bottoms up. The slime covered Cowboys slowly started dumping water and then pulled the boat up onto the top of the seawall. Tim, the advocate reporter was standing there watching the action while they quietly picked the boat up and started carrying it towards the flag pole.

Polecat had his head down and was in a deeply depressed state of mind when he stopped and asked Tim how many boats had passed them since the last check point at Tivoli. Tim answered back in a loud voice that no one had passed them but there was a boat light directly behind them. Lone Wolf and Polecat both looked at each other in disbelief at his comment and they asked him to please repeat what he had just said. The slime covered Cowboys looked back to see a bow light shining brightly just a few yards behind them. There was no reason for a team meeting to formulate a game plan at this point.

There was no discussion or hesitation while they quickly picked the boat up and placed it on top of their shoulders. The slime covered Cowboys started running as fast as they could down the seawall towards the flag pole. This sudden burst of energy came out of nowhere because they were both physically drained after the swimming and worm squirming incidents.

Lone Wolf and Polecat were running as fast as they could with a long racing canoe on their shoulders and the crowd that was gathered at the finish line was cheering and applauding. The Cowboys reached the official finish line and stopped to lower the boat from their shoulders and then bumped the bow into the flag pole.

The bow light that had been right next to them just a few minutes earlier was now several yards behind and had not made it to the finish line yet. Polecat and Lone Wolf finished the 30th Texas Water Safari with the official time of 41 hours and 43 minutes and they were the first USCA C-2 to the finish line. Art and Jon ended up finishing ten minutes behind them and were the second C-2. The crowd that was gathered around watching the show were entertained with the crazy finish.

Polecat turned around to shake his team mates hand. Lone Wolf had suddenly disappeared and was laid out motionless in the grass next to the boat. This was very confusing to Polecat because they had just ran over a hundred yards as fast as they could with a canoe on their shoulders and now his partner could not even stand up and shake his hand. Polecat started to walk over to him to see what was wrong when all of a sudden Mary emerged out of the crowd and leaned down over him. This strange sequence of events started making some sense and it finally dawned on Polecat what Lone Wolf was attempting to do with this sudden collapse. Lone Wolf was seeking attention from his new girl friend and the celebration with Polecat and their bank crew would just have to wait until later.

Seeking attention like that in a dramatic way is something Polecat always wanted to do but his lovely wife Darla did not feel sorry for him in these situations. Darla always looked at it as "self inflicted pain and suffering" and it did not deserve much sympathy.

Darla was very reluctant to give the foul smelling Polecat a hug because of the mud and slime that was covering his face and body.

Three Dots and the party bunch were standing close by and were celebrating with Polecat on a third straight USCA C-2 win and a top ten finish. This was a crazy ending to a very fast race and it was the best finishing time that either one of them had ever accomplished up to this point. The only disappointment was that they were not able to finish under 40 hours due to the wasted time lost in the bay crossing and they were beaten to the finish line by four tandem teams in different divisions.

The four man team of Joe Burns, Brian Mynar, Fred Mynar and Joe Mynar won the race and received the Argosy cup at the finishers banquet on Tuesday.

Lone Wolf and Polecat were called up to the stage to receive the USCA C-2 trophy and Polecat was handed the microphone in order to tell a story. The small crowd at the banquet seemed to really like the story about how they had to wiggle like worms in a quick sand pit in order to get through the mud and sludge that was piled up along the outer edge of the barge canal.

The awards banquet was over and the 30th annual Texas Water Safari came to an end. Tim and Frank had followed them for the entire race and were still there after the banquet was over. They were interviewing the top teams and were taking pictures while several water safari veterans walked around the other boats checking out the rigging and exchanging water safari stories.

Lone Wolf and Polecat racing down the flooded San Marcos river in
1992

Polecat and Lone Wolf pull in for a quick water handoff from Three
Dots at the flooded Victoria Riverside park checkpoint in 1992

CHAPTER 17

The Corpus Christi Adventure

John Dunn walked up to Polecat after the banquet was officially over and started a long discussion about the race. John had just finished in third place overall on a three man team with Phil and Roger. John is a young man who had several impressive water safari finishes over the past few years and his name was becoming well known throughout the small circle of water safari veterans. John and his wife Ginsie are good friends with Darla and Polecat. It was always fun to hang out with them at the various canoe racing events and short races that were held during the year. Ginsie is a Louisiana girl with a good sense of humor and she would soon become a very good Texas Water Safari racer herself a few years later.

John and Polecat had previously talked about paddling the original Texas Water Safari race course that ended at Emerald beach on shoreline drive in Corpus Christi. This discussion was usually not very serious. The extreme difficulty and what it must have been like for the very few teams that ever made it to the finish line in Corpus Christi back when the race first started in 1963 impressed them. John and Polecat were both very interested in Texas Water Safari history and that kind of topic would usually come up when they were together. This was the 30th anniversary of the Texas Water Safari and the history conversation started again.

The discussion eventually shifted to the possibility of retracing that last 80 miles from Seadrift to Corpus Christi. Darla and Ginsie were not paying much attention to them and it got more serious and intense. John and Polecat started making a tentative plan and going over the details. John did not have any plans for the next few days and Polecat still had a few more days scheduled off before having to go back offshore. The plan started to come together and the next step was to figure out what boat they were going to use for the Corpus Christi adventure.

Lone Wolf walked up during the planning discussion and was listening to the conversation. Lone Wolf abruptly turned around and said, "don't count me in" when everything started to get serious. It looked like they would be on our own, so Polecat suggested that they use the USCA C-2. This would also have to include a prayer for calm winds because the spray skirt had been severely damaged during the extended bay crossing. The damaged spray skirt would definitely be a liability if the four different bays along that extended course were choppy.

This sounded like a good idea. John and Polecat started to plan out the meals and other minor details. Darla and Ginsie joined in to the discussion but they did not have the same enthusiasm that they did. They were not very excited about the idea of having to follow them for another 80 miles to Corpus Christi. There were some intense negotiations and compromise before they finally agreed to give them their permission. They both reluctantly agreed to the plan, but they were going to Polecat's house first in order to clean up and get some much needed rest. They would come back tomorrow and try to find them somewhere around the Ingleside area.

Wireless cell phones were a luxury that they did not have back then. The reality of the situation was that it would be very unlikely they would find them because they did not know how long it was going to take to paddle 80 miles across four open bays. Tim and Frank from the Victoria advocate newspaper were still there interviewing water safari finishers and taking pictures of several teams at the finish line. They walked over to say goodbye and got there just in time to listen in to the back and forth discussion about the Corpus Christi plan. The trip was coming together and they enthusiastically asked if they could follow them and do a story on the Corpus Christi adventure. They even volunteered to keep Darla and Ginsie up to date on the progress and this would give them the information they needed to come join the fun whenever they wanted to.

The last minute plan to retrace the route of the first Texas Water Safari in 1963 was finally starting to come together and it seemed to be gaining some limited support from their wives. Three Dots said that he could not hang around and participate in the fun because he had to load up and start heading back to Levelland. There was plenty of water safari food left over from the race because of the fast finishing times and it did not take long to accumulate what was left and throw what was still good into the food bags. Everything else went straight into the nearest garbage can.

There were several water safari racers listening in to the conversation and they offered to give them some of their left over food. This was a very nice offer but a lot of this food had been smashed and con-taminated with river water during the race. John and Polecat politely thanked them and respectfully declined. The biggest problem for Pole-cat was going to be getting back into the racing clothes that he wore during the water safari because they were covered in mud and smelled very bad. Polecat looked them over and quickly discarded them into the nearest garbage can. The brand new Texas Water Safari tee shirt that was presented to the racers and a pair of clean shorts would have to work. It was getting late and they needed to get the show started.

John and Polecat launched the well used USCA C-2 back into San Antonio bay at the water safari finish line on Tuesday afternoon around five o'clock with a pretty good size crowd watching. Several water safari veterans were standing on the sea wall and were giving them a hard time because they figured that this was just a show and this adventure would not make it very far before it ended.

John and Polecat hugged their wives and waved goodbye to the crowd before slowly climbing into the boat. Lone Wolf was watching the show and he did not think this last minute team would make it very far. John and Polecat started paddling and a large wave came crashing over the bow and rolled them over. This was a very embarrassing moment for the new adventure team because they had to walk the submerged boat back into shallow water in order to dump the water out.

John and Polecat could hear the water safari veterans laughing at them. They quickly dumped the water out of the boat and started to carefully crawl back into the damaged spray skirt. This was a bad start to the trip. They did not know it but the people laughing at them after the sudden wipeout were making John and Polecat more focused and determined to make it to Corpus Christi.

John and Polecat paddled out of sight and headed across the open bay towards the intra coastal canal. John was in the bow and Polecat was in the stern. Very large swells were crashing over the bow. John and Polecat were trying as hard as they could to hit them at an angle instead of straight on in order to keep the boat upright and water free. The rough San Antonio bay crossing was intense but finally eased up some as they approached the intra coastal canal. The tentative plan was then to follow the protected intra coastal canal until reaching Copano bay.

The route John and Polecat took up to this point was a little different than what the original race course looked like back in 1963. In the first Texas Water Safari in 1963 they paddled to Austwell instead of Seadrift. They were required to camp out on the beach front and wait until everyone that was still in the race made it there before the cut off time. They would then restart the race and do several bay legs before eventually making it to Emerald beach in Corpus Christi. The elapsed time of each team was stopped and officially recorded when they reached the checkpoint of each leg.

John and Polecat had already broken the rules that were followed in the 1963 race a couple of times. Staying in nice hotel rooms on Monday night and enjoying the food at the local restaurants in Seadrift after finishing the race on Sunday would have been grounds for disqualification in 1963.

The Texas Water Safari racers that competed in that first race in 1963 were required to camp out on the Austwell beach and they could not accept any assistance or supplies from anyone while waiting for all the other teams to get there. The stories that were told was that it was very common for the racers who were camped out to start fishing and gathering crabs so they could cook some fresh fish and crab on their campfire. This was done to supplement the food they had left during the wait. John and Polecat were fascinated with these old stories of how different the race was back then. In a much different way they were trying to personally experience what the 1963 racers had endured through during that first race twenty nine years earlier.

John and Polecat eventually made it in to calmer water. The intra coastal canal was within view and there had not been any more major wipe outs. The bilge pumps were able to keep up with the constant flow of water that was pouring in through the damaged spray skirt. This would give them some much needed time to figure out what the plan was going forward while they paddled towards Copano bay.

The sun was starting to disappear on the western horizon while they watched the magnificent colors. It was time to pick up the stroke rate and head down the intra coastal canal towards Rockport. The plan was to paddle without stopping until they reached Rockport and then make a decision on whether or not to stop for a while. The southeast wind they had been paddling into all afternoon was still blowing hard as darkness set in. A decision would have to be made pretty soon because Copano bay was a large and open body of water and the intra coastal canal went straight down the middle of it with no island barrier on either side. This would mean that they would have to cross a deep and rough bay at night with a damaged spray skirt. John and Polecat made the wise decision to pull over in the canal and wait for the wind to die down a little before trying to paddle across the wide open Copano bay.

It was around midnight when they finally had to pull over to the barrier island because there was a large convoy of barges coming down the canal towards them. The large waves that these barges create would probably swamp them out and sink the boat so this was a good opportunity to pull over and wait for better conditions before proceeding. The long convoy of barges were just about on top of them when they quickly paddled over to the canal shoreline. John and Polecat were very tired because of the long afternoon of paddling through the choppy San Antonio bay and from the lingering effects of a 265 mile canoe race that they had just finished two days earlier.

John and Polecat tried to eat some of the left over water safari food before dosing off. The boat was blocking most of the south wind and they laid out in the sand behind it. There were no sleeping bags or pads in the boat because of the last minute plans. The sandy canal shoreline would have to function as a bed roll for the next couple of hours.

The night time temperature was somewhere around 78 degrees and it felt cool because of the constant wind and high humidity. John was snoring a few yards away while they both tried to get some much needed rest before continuing on with the Corpus Christi adventure. The sun was starting to make its glorious appearance on Wednesday morning when Polecat suddenly woke up and observed several sand crabs and large bugs crawling next to his head and all over his body. The unusual sight of crabs crawling on your body will force you to quickly react and jump up and start swatting at them.

This was the wake up call that Polecat needed in order to start focusing again on getting across Copano bay before the south winds started picking up speed. John was getting up out of his sand pit bed about the same time and was staring at the open bay in front of them. Polecat's upper body muscles were tight and in knots due to all the physical abuse he had inflicted on himself over the last few days. John and Polecat both took some time to stretch out a little before getting started again on their journey to Emerald beach.

Polecat was craving for a strong cup of coffee but they did not bring any with them and there was no time to waste. The area forecast was for the south winds to pick up during the day to over twenty miles per hour and they needed to get across Copano bay before that happened.

John seemed to be in a good mood that morning and he started telling Polecat about his future plans of going back to school and becoming a paramedic. Darla was also a paramedic and this subject was very interesting. Polecat asked him numerous questions while trying to keep the conversation going.

The bay was calm and the wind was starting to pick up a little while they paddled into the open water and followed the canal markers towards Rockport. It was going to take several hours of hard paddling to get across this large bay so they started picking up the stroke rate in order to take advantage of the early morning calm winds. A can of warm coke and a couple of high calorie breakfast bars would end up being the breakfast meal. This adventure was not supposed to be a race but it sure seemed like it was because they were racing against time and the weather forecast.

The swells seemed to be getting much larger after a couple of hours of paddling at racing speed. The outline of Rockport was in the distance. This gave them a much needed boost of confidence because they were able to get across this large bay before the wind and waves became a factor. The spray skirt was still in decent condition where John was sitting in the bow but it was ripped and had large holes in it towards the middle of the boat. If the waves were big enough to start splashing over the gunnels they would take on a lot of water and the boat would sink. The bilge pump was working but it would not be able to keep up with a large volume of water splashing into the boat.

The shoreline of Rockport was getting a lot closer. The waves were getting bigger and they started splashing over the gunnels. The boat was slowly starting to fill up with bay water. John and Polecat were paddling at water safari speed. There was a cement boat ramp and bait house in the distance and the wind and waves were getting much stronger. John and Polecat were eventually able to make it back into a section of the intra coastal canal that was protected by a barrier island. It was a major accomplishment to get cross Copano bay upright and without having to swim in with a submerged canoe.

The boat ramp was a busy place where the locals would launch their fishing boats. This was early Wednesday afternoon and there were a couple of fishing boats tied up at the pier that was located just to the side of the boat ramp. The fishermen that were loading into their expensive fishing boats were staring at them. The weird sight of two guys paddling up to the pier in a long and narrow canoe was very unusual. The south winds were blowing pretty hard and that made their sudden arrival look even more out of place. John and Polecat quickly jumped out of the boat and started carrying it up the boat ramp, trying to find a spot to put it where it would be out of the way. The fishermen standing next to their boats just stared at them while they carried the boat past them. The fishermen probably figured that they were a couple of lost homeless folks that were looking for a handout.

The bait shop had a sign in front of the building that was advertising fresh bait and fishing supplies along with hamburgers and cold drinks. Polecat had brought some money and his first reaction to the sign was, "a burger and fries sound pretty good to me". John was quick to agree and they ventured over to the bait shop to find out what the lunch special was for that day. John and Polecat would have been disqualified for this in 1963.

The jalapeno burger, large fries and a cold bottle of coke went down very quickly. John and Polecat sat at the picnic table outside of the bait house and tried to figure out what the next step should be. The nice people running the bait house let them fill up their water jugs and Polecat purchased a bag of ice to help cool everything down a little. This would have been another violation of the 1963 rules because they had to start the race with everything they needed to make it all the way to Corpus Christi. They would purify river water for drinking during the first leg of the race from San Marcos to Austwell. Drinking water would then be provided for them by race officials at the start of the four bay legs.

The 1963 race was scheduled for twelve days and had 58 teams entered. Twenty teams made it to Austwell in time before the official start of leg two. Eighteen more teams dropped out over the next three bay legs because of high winds and strong tidal currents. John and Polecat were getting an up close and personal experience with what they had to endure and overcome during that first race.

There was a public pay phone at the bait shop and they decided to try and make contact with their wives to let them know where they were. Polecat called his home number and was very surprised when Darla answered. Darla seemed to be very happy to hear Polecat's voice. She then started telling him that everyone was worried about them because of the high winds and rough bay conditions. She reminded Polecat that this added on adventure was not a race and that they should make a smart decision to just call it off and wait for her and Ginsie to come pick them up. Polecat's response was not what she wanted to hear and the conversation between them started going down hill quickly.

John and Polecat were about half way into their 80 mile Corpus Christi adventure and there was no way they were going to quit now. Darla could not understand the thinking because the weather forecast for Thursday was going to be more of the same with high south winds and rough bays. John and Polecat had finished the Texas Water Safari several times over the last few years with different partners and the same mindset of never giving up after you start something was ingrained into their thinking. Darla was not happy with Polecat but she reluctantly agreed to try and contact some of their water safari friends that had shown some interest in what they were doing and let them know where they were located. Ginsie was staying with Darla, so John was able to take the phone and have a long conversation with her also.

The reality was that they were basically on their own for this extended adventure and would probably have to figure out a way to get back home if they were fortunate enough to make it to Emerald beach. There was no time to dwell on this negative stuff because Aransas bay was the next obstacle to cross and it was time to get moving in that direction.

It was a very hot and humid south Texas afternoon when they launched their boat back into the intra coastal canal and started heading for Aransas Pass. The canal winds its way through the open water between Rockport and Aransas Pass. The majority of the canal is located in open water and is not protected by land. John and Polecat did not talk about it but they were both expecting this next bay crossing to be very rough and difficult due to the high winds. John and Polecat did not know exactly what to expect because neither one of them had ever paddled through this area.

Aransas Pass was next in line and that started bringing back the wild memories from Polecat's teenage years. In the spring of 1974 when a young Polecat was seventeen years old, a large group of high school friends would load up off road motorcycles and spend the weekend at Port Aransas. The plan was to race their dirt bikes over and around the sand dunes. This was legal back in those days and after many hours of racing and crashing motorcycles into the sand dunes and the surf they would set up camp somewhere and party all night long. The motorcycles would not start on the second day because of all the salt water exposure and that is when the surf boards would get unloaded. The teenage partiers would then spend several hours awkwardly trying to surf the waves in the Gulf of Mexico.

The young Polecat was also a street racer during those wild teenage years. Auto racing was very popular with young men at that time and it was not hard to get into a street race while cruising around town if you were looking for competition. It escalated to the point to where the young Polecat eventually entered the drag races that were held on Sunday at a former airfield in Victoria. The only positive thing to come out of all this expensive auto racing was when the young Polecat won the stock class on a beautiful Sunday afternoon at the Aloe field quarter mile drag races in 1977. After celebrating the big win that night with friends at a local bar, the young Polecat crashed his beautiful Oldsmobile cutlass into a fence and flipped it over on its roof after failing to navigate a sharp turn. That was the last race for his cutlass. It was totaled out and had to be sent to the junk yard for scrap. The final tally for the young Polecat's auto racing career was fifteen vehicles during a seven year span that were either totaled out in a violent crash or the engine was ruined because of abuse. That is where all of the young Polecat's time and money was spent and he was very fortunate to have walked away from all of the bad crashes.

That was a crazy time in the young Polecat's life and all of the credit for still being here belongs to the Lord Jesus because he successfully navigated the young Polecat through all of those bad choices and near misses because he had a long range plan for him. The time would eventually come when Polecat would wake up and turn his life over to him. An important life lesson was learned a few years later. Canoe racing was more physically challenging and a heck of a lot cheaper than auto racing.

The boat started veering off in the wrong direction because Polecat was in a mental fog while he day dreamed about events that had happened years ago. The memories that Polecat remembered from back when he was a young man that was going in the wrong direction was putting a big smile on his face. John suddenly yelled out to him, "is everything ok back there". Polecat woke up and realized where he was. "Everything is good back here, thanks for asking".

It was time to refocus and start concentrating on the big job in front of them. John and Polecat started paddling into the open water of Aransas bay and were surprised that the waves were manageable. The open bay was choppy but Mustang island was apparently blocking some of the wind and turbulent water even though it was a couple of miles to the south of them.

The confidence level was starting to pick up and things appeared to be heading in the right direction. John and Polecat cautiously paddled over the top of the choppy waves and focused their attention on boat balance and staying upright. There were several large barges being pushed down the canal and they were heading straight for them. The only option was to get out of their way and skirt the edge of the canal in order to avoid the wave turbulence that the barges were creating.

The waves were spaced out just far enough to where they could paddle up and over them at a slight angle and this helped to avoid plowing straight through them and taking on large amounts of water. John was doing a good job in the bow and Polecat was focused on trying to correct the boat angle after each wave passed by. This procedure seemed to be working and they were slowly making their way across Aransas bay towards Ingleside. Thank the Lord that neither one of them was suffering from motion sickness because the swells were getting much bigger and they were constantly being forced up and over the large waves.

John and Polecat eventually got back into calmer water and entered into a section of the intra coastal canal that was protected on both sides. This gave them a much needed opportunity for a food and water break after several hours of non stop paddling. It was starting to get late in the afternoon and a decision would soon have to be made on whether or not they were going to camp out somewhere or keep going and take their chances at a night run across Corpus Christi bay.

The wind was still howling at over 20 miles per hour and that would definitely be a big factor in the decision making. John and Polecat plowed ahead and were discussing the pros and cons of doing a night run across a large open bay that they were not familiar with.

There was someone standing on the bank a few hundred yards in front of them. Two people were laughing and waving at them to get their attention. John and Polecat paddled over a little closer to the shoreline in order to see what these characters wanted. The loud laughing that was echoing down the canal sounded very familiar and it soon became obvious to Polecat that it was Three Dots doing his Pat Kelly impersonation. Polecat thought that Three Dots and Vowery had headed back home after the water safari banquet was over, but there they were standing on the canal shoreline.

Three Dots was laughing and explained that after watching them awkwardly start their 80 mile adventure at the water safari finish line in Seadrift the day before, he felt motivated to come back and help any way he could. Darla had been in contact with him and had passed on what little information she had on the slow progress. It was great to finally see someone they knew because the adventure paddlers were at a crossroads on what to do next and any suggestions on how to proceed would be greatly appreciated.

Three Dots told Polecat that John Dupont was also very interested in what they were trying to do. John Dupont called one of his business clients that owned an oil field supply company on the intra coastal canal very close to Ingleside. They had a small office and a large warehouse located there. Three Dots explained to Polecat that the business owner offered his small office as a shelter to spend the night in. This unexpected and generous offer sounded pretty good after a long day of paddling across two rough bays and it did not take long or any debate to accept the invitation. The sun was making it's glorious disappearance on the western horizon and there was still a ways to go down the intra coastal canal before reaching Ingleside.

The new plan was to get some much needed rest at the oil field business office and then restart the journey towards Emerald beach on Thursday morning before the strong southerly winds started to pick up again. Three Dots and Vowery were waiting for them with some food at the business office when they paddled up to the boat dock that was located nearby. John and Polecat were once again breaking the rules from 1963 by accepting food and shelter from someone. They did not give it a second thought and quickly downed the seafood plates that Three Dots had purchased at a local restaurant. It would be great if a water safari racer could get meals like this handed to them during the water safari and not get disqualified but that is just a dream that will probably never happen. The office was very small but it did have a well used couch that one of them could lay out on.

At this point in the 1963 race there were only four teams left. They were facing 30 to 40 mile per hour winds and strong tidal currents in the intra coastal canal while they made their way to Ingleside. Two teams could not make much progress while paddling and they were forced to drag and pull their boats down the edge of the canal when time expired. Roger is a good friend and well known water safari veteran and he was paddling solo in that race. Roger was one of those two teams that did not make it to the Ingleside checkpoint in time. Lynn and Jim of team 102 used oars to get their 17 foot Grumman canoe to the checkpoint with just a few moments to spare. Fred and Sam of team 163 were using a sail on their 17 foot Grumman canoe and were able to sail almost dead into the wind down the intra coastal canal and make it to the checkpoint before the cutoff.

Roger's description of what the 1963 race was like and what they had to overcome should be mandatory reading for anyone that is interested in the history of the Texas Water Safari. Roger's one page summary of the 1963 race can be read on the official Texas Water Safari web site. Polecat had the privilege to talk to Roger on several occasions at various water safari events over the years and would always enthusiastically listen to Roger's incredible stories from that first race.

Three Dots and Vowery hung around for a while and watched John and Polecat devour the donated seafood plates. John and Polecat tried to describe to them what they had just paddled through since leaving Seadrift on Tuesday afternoon. The stories were getting bigger and bigger when everyone realized that time was getting away from them and it was getting late.

There was a phone in the office and they were able to call home to check in with Darla and Ginsie. Darla was very worried about the last leg of their extended trip across Corpus Christi bay because the forecast was calling for 20 to 30 mile per hour winds on Thursday. She also told Polecat that his friends from the Victoria advocate had called her several times and they were trying to figure out where the adventure paddlers were located so they could come follow them into Corpus Christi. The good news was that Darla and Ginsie were planning on being at the Holiday Inn beach front on Thursday afternoon to watch them finish the extended adventure and give them a ride back home.

That all sounded good but the bigger problem was if they could get across the large Corpus Christi bay in a racing canoe with strong winds blowing in from the south. That was a big "if" that they did not want to dwell on at this point because it would be staring at them in the face soon enough. Three Dots and Vowery had to end all the story telling and say goodnight so they could go find a hotel room. John and Polecat thanked them for all of the help before they headed out the door.

They told them to be sure and lock the building on the way out in the morning.

It was time to get some much needed rest before restarting the adventure early in the morning. The task before them was going to be very difficult so the discussion ended and they did not talk about it anymore and risk staying up all night worrying. John let Polecat have the couch and he laid out on the floor in the small air conditioned office space. This was a lot better than laying in the sand on the intra coastal canal shoreline with sand crabs and bugs crawling all over you. John was up at the crack of dawn because he was eager to get started on the final leg of the Corpus Christi adventure. There was a coffee pot in the office and Polecat took advantage of that and made a pot of strong coffee. Corpus Christi bay would have to wait a few more minutes because Polecat is a coffee addict and really needed the caffeine boost. The winds were calm while John and Polecat wrote a thank you note to the business owner and locked the door on the way out.

The sun was starting to make its glorious appearance on the eastern horizon. John and Polecat shoved off and started paddling down the intra coastal canal towards the ship channel at Ingleside. It was a beautiful morning and they both knew that the winds were going to drastically increase very soon. It was a good time to pick up the pace and take advantage of the calm morning.

John and Polecat noticed a large fishing boat with twin outboard motors heading straight towards them from the opposite direction. It became obvious that the boat was heading towards them on purpose, so they slowed the stroke rate down to see what the passengers on the boat wanted. The fishing boat started slowing down as it got closer and then the driver shut down the outboard motors and they slowly drifted up next to them. Tim and Frank from the Victoria advocate had big smiles on their faces when they pulled up next to the adventure paddlers. Tim said that they had chartered the boat out of Ingleside and they had been trying to find them since Wednesday. They had planned on following Polecat and John to Emerald beach while taking pictures and writing an article about the adventure for the newspaper.

They had to shut down their search for them at sunset on Wednesday but started looking for them again at first light. Tim was on a mission and he did not waste much time with small talk before he started asking one question after the other about their experiences on the multiple bay crossings. John and Polecat took the time to talk about the many close calls they had managed to get through during the extended trip up to this point. The worst one was still waiting directly in front of them. Frank was busy taking pictures during the interview. The adventure paddlers politely tried to end the discussion in order to continue on with their journey to Emerald beach before the winds picked up. The chartered boat was going to keep following them at a distance and take pictures and make notes of the Corpus Christi bay crossing. It was time to get moving again and the ship channel at Ingleside was within sight.

This would be a very strange experience for everyone because the ship channel is a very busy place with large super tankers going in both directions. The tankers are moving in and out of the port of Corpus Christi. John and Polecat entered the ship channel very cautiously and tried to stay close to the shoreline just in case the very large swells coming off the super tankers rolled over the boat and swamped them.

The chartered boat with Tim and Frank on board was not very far behind when two large super tankers loaded with crude oil were passing each other going in opposite directions. John and Polecat were paddling along the shoreline just a few yards away and were right beside the tankers while they passed each other. Frank got a picture of the unique scene and it looked like the tankers and the racing canoe were all lined up passing each other. Two large super tankers and a tandem racing canoe were all in a row across the canal and were passing each other at the same time.

John and Polecat were focused on the large waves that were coming straight at them and the unique moment did not register with them at the time. The Corpus Christi adventure team was able to paddle over the large waves without capsizing even though John disappeared into the salt water as the bow of the boat plowed through the swells that were coming off the tankers. The boat was about half full of water at this point and the damaged spray skirt was letting water in by the bucket load. Polecat frantically leaned out to one side and braced with his paddle in order to keep the boat upright. This procedure was repeated several times before the waves started to slow down and they were able to paddle over to the shoreline and dump water.

The boat captain from one of the super tankers blew his horn at them while they passed by. Polecat's expensive and abused resistol cowboy hat disappeared into the channel and was never seen again after the wave crashing debacle. This was a very sad and depressing time for Polecat because that hat had made it all the way down from San Marcos and it was now buried at sea. There was no time for tears or a memorial service because the biggest obstacle of the adventure was staring at them in the face just around the next bend. The best way to look at this is that Polecat's favorite cowboy hat had served him well for the last six days and it went down to the bottom of the ship channel in glory.

The chartered boat with Tim and Frank on board were close behind and were taking pictures of all the action. John and Polecat did not know it then but a picture of them along side the super tankers would soon appear in several well known newspapers around the country. Frank sent several of the pictures that he took of them while passing the super tankers to the associated press and many major newspapers around the country picked it up and published it. The picture that was published was taken from behind and all you can see is the back of their heads while they paddled their racing canoe past two large super tankers. It is very hard to believe that two unknown canoe racers that were trying to retrace the first Texas Water Safari race coarse from 1963 would end up on the front page of several major newspapers around the country. The best way to look at that is they were advertising the "Worlds Toughest Boat Race" to the rest of the country.

John and Polecat made it to the open water of Corpus Christi bay just as the south winds started to drastically pick up. The open bay was getting very rough when they made the turn out of the protected ship channel and headed for Corpus Christi. The only land in front of them was a small island and they headed straight for it in order to dump water and figure out the line they needed to take across the bay. Tim and Frank pulled up next to the island and yelled out from a distance that they would not be able to keep following them across the bay. The boat captain had made the decision that it was going to be too rough and dangerous for them to continue.

John and Polecat did not want to hear that kind of bad news from a professional boat captain because they were in a small racing canoe and Tim and Frank were in a large motor propelled fishing boat. Polecat thanked them for all the time and effort they had spent trying to find them and for following the water safari. Tim would soon become the managing editor of the Victoria advocate and this would not be the last time he would show a lot of interest in the Texas Water Safari. They started heading back towards the protected ship channel and the adventure team waved goodbye. John and Polecat had to quickly refocus their attention on a plan of attack and what the next move would be.

The wind was picking up quickly and they both knew what that meant. Large white caps and a lot of turbulent bay water was directly ahead of them. John and Polecat were on their own at this point and there was no way to communicate with anyone if they capsized in the large waves and needed to be rescued. Thank the Lord that they had remembered to bring along the emergency flares that were required in the water safari. If the bay crossing suddenly turned into a swimming marathon and they found themselves in bad trouble, the flares would be very important. Hopefully someone would see the flares and come to investigate or at least report it to the authorities.

This was crunch time. John and Polecat stared across the large bay with the Corpus Christi shoreline barely visible in the distance. Polecat did not like the bad situation in front of them and it would of not taken much to convince him to abandon this adventure and call it quits. John is an Army veteran, white water guide, and a very good water safari racer and he was not looking at the situation in negative terms. John was focused on trying to figure out how they could get this racing canoe across a very rough bay with three to five foot waves crashing into them.

The silence between them was deafening and Polecat started praying to the Lord Jesus for help and assistance in formulating a plan to get across this last obstacle safely. The Bible clearly says that the Lord does not pay much attention to man's never ending attempts at recognition and personal achievements, but he does care about a personal relationship with each one of us. Polecat was asking the Lord for a safe ending to this adventure and that could also mean just giving them the ability to safely swim back into the closest shoreline after a bad wipe out.

Polecat's prayer was ending and John started talking out loud about a white water canoe trip he had been on a couple of years earlier. John explained that he and his partner had to both get on their knees in the middle of the boat and paddle on opposite sides in order to successfully get through a very turbulent rapid.

Polecat has a passion for white water canoeing and getting on your knees for stability is a very common procedure in turbulent rapids, but both paddlers moving to the middle of the boat did not make any sense. John went on to explain that when he and his partner got into the middle of the boat one behind the other, the boat stability improved and they were able to avoid plowing straight through the large waves. The body weight of both paddlers was shifted to the center of the boat and they were able to paddle over the top of the waves instead of the bow being driven directly into the wave. That gave them the ability to avoid taking on large amounts of water. John said that the only negative thing from that experience was that after moving to the middle of the boat they did not have the ability to quickly turn the boat when needed. The situation they were in called for out of the box thinking and that is exactly what John was doing. Polecat's response to John's plan was short and sweet. "Let's get in the boat and give it a try because I don't have any better ideas".

There was not much time to waste on debate so they moved the damaged spray skirt out of the way and awkwardly squeezed their bodies into the middle of the USCA C-2. John was in front of Polecat and the back of his head was right in his face. There was a very limited space in between the center thwarts. This was a very unusual and uncomfortable position for Polecat but the situation they were in called for drastic measures.

John and Polecat started paddling out into the open water of Corpus Christi bay and the southerly winds were increasing to over 20 miles per hour and the waves were two to four feet. John was paddling on the right side and Polecat was on the left side as they cautiously paddled over the top of the large waves. It took a while for them to adapt to this weird setup but the boat stability seemed to be good and they were not taking on large amounts of water.

There were no huts being called out because switching sides with their paddles would probably cause them to quickly lose boat stability in the turbulent waves. Polecat was leaning out to the left of the boat while paddling forward and then would quickly put a hard brace out with his paddle when they would clear the whitecap and violently slide down into the valley between the waves. John was doing the same thing on the right side of the boat.

The next hurdle was when they cleared the whitecap and were in the valley between the waves they had just a few seconds to try and turn the boat back into a 45 degree angle before the next wave hit. This procedure seemed to be working but it was very hard on them physically and there was a lot of open bay ahead. John and Polecat were going over the top of the waves instead of through them. There was still some water splashing into the boat when the whitecaps rolled over the gunnels.

The spray skirt was still covering the bow of the boat but the middle and stern section were not covered. The bilge pump was not working anymore and the Polecat had no choice but to stop paddling when he could in between the waves and scoop out water with the emergency hand scoop.

This was shaping up to be one of the hardest things Polecat had ever done in a canoe. The waves were getting bigger and the wind was blowing harder as they tried their best to make some limited progress across the bay. There was very little conversation going on because they were so focused on keeping the boat upright and headed in the right direction.

A large shrimp boat suddenly pulled up close to them and slowed down their engines. The boat captain started to talk to them through a loud speaker, "are you in trouble", "can we help you", "do you need to be rescued"? John and Polecat could not stop paddling because of the constant wave bombardment they were battling through. Polecat hollered back to the captain that they were alright and asked how far it was to Emerald beach in Corpus Christi. The boat captain answered back, "it is going to get a lot worse out here", "you will not make it across in that boat and in these conditions". The captain continued, "we will get closer and try to pick you up", "your boat will have to stay out here". John was quiet at this point so Polecat answered the captain for both of them, " thank you for the offer but we are headed for Emerald beach".

There were a couple of men on the back deck of the shrimp boat and they were waiting to start the rescue operation. John and Polecat waved at them and then had to refocus on the turbulent wave that was crashing into them. The shrimp boat captain was just trying to help and make them realize how bad the conditions were. John and the Polecat were determined to finish this adventure, paddling or swimming.

The sight of a low profile tandem racing canoe with two people crammed into the center of the boat in the middle of a very rough Corpus Christi bay was probably something that the shrimp boat crew had never seen before. The best way to look at that sequence of events is that they gave them something to talk about at the local bar with their friends. The boat captain probably reported them to the Coast Guard. The shrimp boat started pulling away while they struggled to paddle over the top of the three to five foot waves.

John and Polecat could not even take the time to drink some water because of the constant maneuvering and bracing that was required to keep the boat upright. This constant up and down motion over the large waves could eventually cause a person to suffer from motion sickness but they were not experiencing those kind of problems yet.

The harbor bridge was within view and they noticed a very large aircraft carrier that was moored next to the shoreline. John and Polecat did not know that the historic World War 11 aircraft carrier, the U.S.S.

Lexington had just been towed in to Corpus Christi bay the day before. The entire bay was closed down on Wednesday while they towed in the very famous aircraft carrier to its final destination. It would soon be turned into a floating museum with military aircraft from the same time period on the flight deck.

The waves were getting larger but they were still upright and were making some very slow progress towards Emerald beach. The outline of shoreline drive was coming into view and they focused in on the Holiday Inn motel beachfront because that was pretty close to the official finish line in the 1963 water safari. It was a blessing to still be upright and not having to swim in to the nearest shoreline with a submerged canoe in tow. The Holiday Inn hotel was within sight and something very strange was happening in front of them.

There were two good looking ladies at the end of the long rock jetty that extended out about one hundred yards into the bay. These two young ladies were yelling and waving at them but they could not make out who they were. There were still a lot of waves to navigate over before they were safely in calmer water next to the shoreline. One of the good looking ladies was whistling at them very loudly and that unique sound was very familiar. Polecat finally realized who these ladies were.

Darla and Ginsie were at the end of the rock jetty and they were enthusiastically encouraging them to paddle on in to the beach front and finish this adventure. Polecat had tears streaming down his face as they paddled in the last few yards and ran the boat up on to the beach front. There were several hotel guests sitting in lawn chairs along the beach watching the show.

John and Polecat awkwardly tried to crawl out of the boat and stand up. Polecat quickly lost his balance and fell down face first into the sandy beach. The constant up and down motion and being on their knees for the last several hours had taken a physical toll on both of them and it affected Polecat's balance and the ability to stand up.

Darla and Ginsie came running up to them while they both tried to get up and greet them. Darla and Polecat hugged each other tightly and Polecat struggled to stand up on his own while Darla wiped away the tears of joy on his face. Polecat thanked her for all of the loving support and for being there to greet them. Three Dots and Vowery were standing close by and they all celebrated a successful end to this amazing adventure.

Darla logged the unofficial finishing time as 12 noon on Thursday and this added up to exactly 43 hours after they had launched the boat at the water safari finish line in Seadrift on Tuesday afternoon. The actual time they were on the water paddling across those four bays was somewhere around 27 hours. The extra miles ended up taking longer to complete than the 265 mile Texas Water Safari did.

The Corpus Christi adventure turned out to be just as physically and mentally challenging as the Texas Water Safari was. The 80 miles across four large bays was a test of physical endurance and mental toughness that John and Polecat were not expecting. This added on adventure helped make both of them realize how tough that first Texas Water Safari race course was and it gave them a lot of additional respect for those water safari racers who participated in those early races.

There were only two teams that finished the 1963 race that ended in Corpus Christi at Emerald beach. Lynn Maughmer and Jim Jones won that first water safari in an elapsed time of 110 hours and 35 minutes. Fred Hurd Jr. and Sam Hare came in second place with a total elapsed time of 145 hours. The 1963 Texas Water Safari was a twelve day race that was done in several stages and the official finishing time of both teams did not include the required down time from the four legs. Roger's one page description of that race on the water safari website says it best and he concluded his brief description of that race by saying "the 1963 TWS was the most difficult and challenging thing I have ever attempted. And I almost finished it solo without food from Victoria on except for what I could find. I still regret not making that 3 miles into Ingleside".

John and Polecat took the time to retrace that first Texas Water Safari race course and it gave both of them a better understanding of how hard that first race in 1963 must have been. The Corpus Christi adventure made a long lasting impression on Polecat. Texas Water Safari weekend turned into a 342 mile adventure and a six day event for him.

It was time to load the boat up and take their lovely wives to one of the famous seafood restaurants on shoreline drive to celebrate. Three Dots and Vowery came along and joined them for the victory celebration. John and Polecat needed some down time and rest to recover from all of this self inflicted physical abuse. John and Ginsie were their guests at Floodplain ranch for a couple of days before they had to head back home and they really enjoyed the visit.

Polecat reflected back on this adventure and tried to compare that first race and their limited equipment to the way the race has evolved over the years. They were definitely at a disadvantage from San Marcos to the bay because of the heavy aluminum and fiberglass boats they were using at the time. They probably had an advantage over the low profile Kevlar and carbon boats used today while navigating across the four open bays to Corpus Christi. Sailing and rowing through rough and turbulent water in large aluminum boats sure seems like a better way to go than what John and Polecat had just experienced. The 1992 canoe racing season was officially over for Polecat and now it was time to focus on his beautiful family. It was time to load up and take them on the sometimes annual family vacation.

Polecat and John Dunn passing super tankers in the Corpus Christi
ship channel while paddling towards the first finish line at Emerald
beach

CHAPTER 18

1993: Moving into the multi man division

1993 came around very quickly and Polecat just assumed that Lone Wolf would want to team up again and defend the three straight USCA C-2 division wins. The TWS was not mentioned very much around Polecat's house after the race was over because helping Darla with three young boys would take up most of his free time at home. The Running man would soon be a common sight again on the back roads around Thomaston with his river dogs in hot pursuit.

The Houston Marathon was on the tentative schedule for the middle of January and it was something he really wanted to do but it would not be planned out very far in advance. The Running man had to talk Darla into it by framing it as a weekend away from children. This would be a weekend away with reservations at a very nice hotel in downtown Houston and dining out at a popular restaurant in the area. The Running man was looking forward to his fourth straight Houston marathon and the thinking was that he could possibly have the experience and training necessary to be able to run a faster race than he did in 1990.

The early Sunday morning start of the race was uneventful. The Running man had learned the hard way to be sure and line up with the other runners in his projected finishing time group. Lone Wolf and Mary had joined them the night before for dinner and were planning on following the race. The start of the Houston marathon is chaotic because five thousand runners were jockeying for position and were trying to get over the several narrow overpasses at the start without getting knocked down. The race will wind around the downtown Houston area and then head towards Rice University. It was a beautiful Lord's day and the Running man thanked Jesus through prayer for his undeserved blessings and for watching over his beautiful family.

The starting group he was in finally made it up to the official starting line several minutes after the gun went off. The pace started picking up very quickly as the Running man tried to hang with the three hour and thirty minute group. The plan was to follow these runners as long as he could and then hang on and try to break his personal record of three hours and thirty seven minutes.

The first half of the race was uneventful and was moving along without any significant problems. The Running man eventually made it to the twenty mile mark where the belly dancers were in the middle of the street putting on a big show. The Running man felt good and ran a good race up to this point but ended up slowing down a lot over the last six miles and finished the 26.2 miles in an official time of three hours and forty nine minutes.

This was twelve minutes slower than his best finishing time in 1990 but he felt good at the finish and was able to walk through the convention center and collect all of the free stuff that is given away to the finishers. The finishing time was disappointing but the Running man did not dwell on the negative stuff and just focused on the positive things. The Running man had his fourth straight Houston marathon finish in the books. It was time to load up and let Darla drive back home. The Running man stretched out and slept on the passenger side of the vehicle during the three hour ride.

Lone Wolf had briefly talked about the water safari during the dinner the night before and he had mentioned that we should seriously think about moving into the multi man division for this years race. That conversation surprised Polecat because they had done pretty well in the

USCA C-2 division over the last three years. Polecat was not very excited about the idea of switching divisions and did not enthusiastically jump on board.

Lone Wolf had some experience in the multi man division from earlier races and he wanted to get back into that kind of a boat. Polecat's racing experience had been in the solo and tandem divisions. Polecat had steered a tandem unlimited boat down river with a rudder before and that is a lot easier than trying to navigate a USCA C-2 down the race course with single blade paddles.

The brief conversation ended with Polecat saying that they needed to talk about this some more before making any hasty decisions. Lone Wolf had already been talking to John DuPont about the possibility of the three of them teaming up for the 1993 water safari. The idea of moving into the multi man division would have to wait for a few weeks in order to give Polecat some time to think about it before making any future race plans.

Polecat was headed to Lafayette, Louisiana for a week of safety training in February and was looking forward to the trip because of the great Cajun restaurants that dominate that area. The exciting possibility of eating shrimp gumbo, craw fish etouffee and boiled craw fish every night was making him very hungry. Polecat had become addicted to the great Cajun seafood cooking that he enjoyed at work offshore and this trip would give him the opportunity to try out a few more interesting restaurants. Polecat's water safari friend from the Corpus Christi adventure, John Dunn, was now living in the Lafayette area with Ginsie and was attending paramedic school there.

Polecat contacted John and he wanted Polecat to come over to his house for dinner and a visit while he was in the area. The idea of moving into the multi man division was still being debated and it was getting very close to the time of year when those kind of decisions had to be made in order for the planning and training to start. Polecat started thinking that if he did agree to go into the multi man division with Lone Wolf, adding a very good water safari racer like John Dunn to the team would make a lot of sense. That could possibly make them a dark horse contender for the Argosy cup.

The Argosy cup is the traveling trophy that the winner of "The World's Toughest Boat Race" gets to put their name on. Everyone that competes in this race dreams about having their name engraved on this trophy. If your name is engraved on this trophy it will stay there and will be on display for all of the future water safari racers to see and it will never be removed. Polecat would love to have the opportunity to get his name on the Argosy cup but that is not the real reason why he does this race.

The reason Polecat competes in this race is because it pushes him well beyond his self imposed limits and it helps him realize that he needs a strong and personal relationship with the Lord. Polecat desperately needs Jesus to help him navigate through life's turbulent rapids.

John and Ginsie invited him to their home for dinner in Breau Bridge Louisiana. This is a small community on the Achafalaya basin and is located just a couple of miles to the east of Lafayette. They had a great time talking about what they had been doing since the water safari and the Corpus Christi adventure paddle last June.

Polecat mentioned that they were thinking about a multi man run in the water safari and asked John if he would be interested in joining the team. John was surprised to hear that Polecat was leaving the USCA C-2 division after three straight wins. John didn't have to think about the offer for very long before replying, "count me in". Polecat was pleasantly surprised at the quick answer from John and his positive response meant that more details needed to be discussed. It was getting late and Polecat needed to head back to the hotel. The evening ended with an agreement to stay in touch and continue the discussion on all of the details and training plans going forward. It was going to be difficult for John to come to Texas for training runs on a regular basis because of his paramedic training. The plan would be to get together whenever they could and make it work somehow.

Polecat called Lone Wolf and gave him the good news that he had just recruited one of the best water safari paddlers there was out there.

Lone Wolf was excited about the news and confessed that he had been talking to John DuPont about teaming up with them and he was on board with that as well. That all sounded good but they had just put together a very competitive four man water safari team with no plan and no boat.

The first priority would be to reach out to the many water safari veterans that they knew and try to locate a reasonably priced four man racing canoe that was for sale. There were very few four man racing canoes out there and it should not take very long to find out if there was one for sale. If none were available the only other option would be to try and get one made by one of the very few people who did that kind of work.

The new Cowboy four man team should be competitive because of the experience factor but it was a long ways away from becoming a reality. A long hitch at work offshore had just ended when John called Polecat at home with the bad news. The conversation started out good and they were just getting into the water safari plans when John said that he had just gotten off the phone with Joe Mynar. There was a long silence on both ends of the phone because Polecat knew exactly where this conversation was headed.

Joe, Fred, and Brian had won the water safari a couple of times over the past few years and were known as one of the fastest multi man teams in the race. Polecat's response probably surprised John because he was not mad or upset and just started laughing after the few moments of silence ended. "You got the call and now you are going to tell me that you can't team up with us this year". John explained that he was not expecting any offers from other teams and the call from Joe surprised him.

Polecat told John that he did not have to follow through with his commitment to team up with the "Cowboys" after receiving the "call". Polecat understood the difficult situation he found himself in. John apologized for having to back out of his handshake commitment and he was hoping that we could still be friends. Polecat assured him that they were still friends because he really enjoyed the adventure trip to Corpus

Christi with him last year and that this phone call would not change that. Dumping the Cowboys ended up being a great move for John because he teamed up with the Mynars and they went on to win eight Texas Water Safari's together. There was no way the Cowboys could have even come close to matching that.

The Cowboys had just lost the best water safari paddler on our new team to the Mynars. This all happened before a four man racing canoe was purchased and they were back to square one. The funny side of this story is that the Cowboys often talk about this experience among themselves during training runs and joke with each other that they can't make a commitment to the team because they are expecting the call to come at any time. The call has never come and it probably never will.

Lone Wolf and Polecat were in agreement that since he had already recruited John DuPont as a teammate, they needed to keep moving in that direction. The Cowboys found a well used three man racing canoe for sale and were able to make a deal on it for nine hundred dollars. This would only be three hundred dollars each. Polecat was on board with it because that amount would be a lot easier to try and explain to Darla.

The boat needed some major repair work and they needed to get some training time in. The Cowboys came up with a plan to get this new team moving forward. John DuPont seemed to be pretty good at boat repairs and boat rigging. Lone Wolf and Polecat always seemed to struggle with these type of issues in their previous races so this was a big step forward in the right direction.

" The World's Toughest Boat Race" requires a lot of boat rigging and figuring out where to install the necessary equipment. Lone Wolf and Polecat were usually able to get these things done in a very simple and primitive way. This would sometimes come back to bite them in the rear end during the race when bow lights quit working and bilge pumps didn't pump. It was good to finally have someone on the team who seemed to have good ideas on how to rig out the well used racing canoe.

The next step would be to purchase a new double blade paddle because Polecat had been single blading in the USCA C-2 division for the last four years. Tom was able to fix Polecat up with a brand new lendle double blade paddle with fiberglass blades and it was much lighter than his old paddle. These type of paddles are not cheap but they are necessary if you want to be competitive in the multi man division.

The Cowboys started training on the San Marcos river near Luling because John DuPont lived near Austin and this was more of a central location for the three of them. Polecat was starting to warm up to the new multi man team after a couple of training runs. The Cowboys seemed to be moving along at a very good boat speed while using double blade paddles.

The biggest problem was that there were way to many John's in the boat and it was a high priority for the new Cowboy team to come up with a racing nickname for John DuPont. Polecat can't remember exactly why the name Possum Belly was chosen, but it seemed to fit their new racing partner even though he was not very happy with it at first. John had a new canoe racing name and it did not matter if he liked it or not.

The decision was made at the last minute to enter the Buffalo Bayou Regatta in down town Houston and use the twenty mile race as a training run for the water safari. Lone Wolf and Polecat had competed in this race before and were very familiar with the unusual start and the race course.

This is a big event in Houston and it is followed closely by the local television stations and newspapers. Lone Wolf, Possum Belly and Polecat were waiting patiently when the starting gun went off and all of the entered teams started dragging their boats down the very steep bank towards the bayou. Polecat had learned from experience that the fastest way to start this race is to slide down the bank on your rear end and firmly hold on to the boat. It is important to keep your feet in front of you while sliding down the steep bank in order to push off the numerous trees and thorn bushes.

The Cowboys were able to slide down the steep bank and drag the boat behind them without crashing into the many obstacles. Polecat was going to slide straight into the deep bayou and then try to keep the bow of the 27 foot long racing canoe from going completely under as it slide into the water behind him. Polecat went completely under but managed to keep the bow above the waterline as the boat ran over the top of his submerged body. Lone Wolf and Possum Belly were able to turn the boat and get it up next to the bank while Polecat crawled up on higher ground. The Cowboys then jumped into the boat one at a time.

The Cowboys were one of the fastest teams into the water and it was time to pull the double blades out and start paddling. There were several very fast multi man and tandem teams entered in this race and they all had water safari experience.

The crazy start worked to the Cowboys advantage and they were now in the lead followed closely by several fast tandem teams. The stroke rate was very fast and there was a big battle shaping up for first place. This was a sprint race and to have any chance at winning the Cowboys were going to have to increase the stroke rate to a level they were not used to. The competition was very intense and the Cowboys were able to slowly increase their lead. The final turn towards the finish line was just ahead.

There was a band playing and a large crowd watching when the Cowboys crossed the finish line in first place. The crowd was applauding and the television cameras were filming the action while they made their way over to the take out spot. This was a very unexpected and surprising scene that the Cowboys had just paddled into. They were in shock at the reception they were getting.

The size of the crowd and all of the attention they were getting was totally unexpected. The Cowboys were introduced by the announcer as the official winners of the Buffalo Bayou Regatta. Television reporters were crowding around and were asking questions while they jumped out and pulled the boat up onto the bank. Microphones were constantly being shoved in front of their faces and the questions were coming from every direction.

Polecat can't remember exactly what he said in response to the questions. Lone Wolf was stuttering and mumbling and his rambling words did not make any sense. The reporter kept trying to get him to answer his question. There was a television camera aimed directly at him and he could not get any coherent words to come out of his mouth. Lone Wolf completely froze up and stood motionless while he stared at the camera. Possum Belly and Polecat noticed the embarrassing situation their teammate was in and they both walked over and started answering the question for him.

Lone Wolf quickly turned and walked away to try and regain his composure. Several more boats were crossing the finish line and the reporters started to redirect their attention towards them. The take away from this very unusual sequence of events is that the Cowboys were not very well prepared for all of the attention and being suddenly thrust into the spot light. Polecat had no idea at the time that this would be the only canoe race he would ever win. Polecat has competed in many canoe races over the past forty years and has come very close to being the first boat across the finish line several times but he was never able to match that day on the Buffalo Bayou again.

The 1993 Texas Water Safari was coming up very quickly and the training and preparation shifted into high gear. The river levels for that race were shaping up to be in the moderate range. The Cowboys started double blading throughout all of the training runs in anticipation of a very fast and competitive water safari. This was a big change for Polecat because he had not used a double blade in the water safari since the 1988 race with Three Dots. Double blading will put a lot of stress on your hands, wrists and shoulders. The Cowboys were putting in long training runs using their new lendle double blades in order to get ready for the big dance. There was probably no way they could be competitive with the two fastest four man teams that were entered that year but there was a good opportunity to finish in the top four overall. The Cowboys would have to run a fast race with no serious boat damage and wasted time in order to accomplish that.

Race day finally arrived on that first weekend in June with 46 teams lined up in rows of six. Tom led everyone in a beautiful prayer before firing off the starting gun. Possum Belly, Lone Wolf and Polecat started on the first row because of a top five finish in the pre-lim race a month earlier. The race started fast and the field quickly spread out while the

Cowboys made their way down the upper San Marcos river. Lone Wolf was doing a good job maneuvering the 27 foot long three man racing canoe through the many obstacles and rapids. Polecat did not have to straighten the bow up as much through the obstacles and hard turns. The rudder was doing most of the work in the turns and this enabled Polecat to stay focused on keeping up a faster stroke rate. Cotton seed rapid was next in line and the Cowboys were in a back and forth battle for third place overall with Grady's three man team. The Cowboys navigated through the rapid with no problems while a large crowd watched and cheered them on. Polecat's three year old son Jordan was standing on the edge of the river bank at the end of the rapid yelling out, "go Polecat go" while Brandon and Wade were standing behind him.

A filming crew from the Texas parks and wild life magazine was set up there filming the action. A video of Jordan, Brandon and Wade yelling out encouragement was included in their coverage of the "Worlds Toughest Boat Race". Polecat has that video and it is a great reminder that the race has always been a family event.

The race was moving along with just a few minor problems and the Cowboys were now in third place with Grady's team not very far behind. The Cowboys were moving along at a fast stroke rate and only one boat was close enough to put any pressure on them. The top two four man teams were battling each other for first place and the Cowboys and Grady's team were battling for third. The rest of the field was getting further behind and would not be able to catch up unless something bad happened and valuable time was wasted.

The first night and most of the second day were uneventful except for the big back and forth battle with Grady's team. Maintaining a fast stroke rate with double blade paddles was taking a toll on everyone physically but they had to keep it going in order to stay close to the competition. The Cowboys approached the swinging bridge checkpoint at Bloomington right at sunset on Sunday. Grady, Jon and Chris were just a few minutes ahead of them at this point. The stroke rate started picking up even more when they approached the logjam cuts just after dark. The logjam cut was runnable without portaging but it required a lot of maneuvering in order to get through the low hanging tree limbs and brush. The logjam cut was the only way to go in order to get around the two mile long logjam that blocked the Guadalupe river.

Grady's bow light was right in front of them. The Cowboys paddled into the cut and started crashing through the thick tree limbs and brush that infested the area. The Cowboys were able to get through most of the thick vegetation without having to come to a complete stop but it seemed to be getting worse while they carefully navigated through the narrow cut. The cursing and yelling coming from Grady's boat was very loud and clear because they were right behind them. They were experiencing as much trouble and difficulty as the Cowboys were.

Polecat didn't use any bad words but he was constantly yelling back to Lone Wolf and Possum Belly to paddle backwards. Tree limbs covered with thorns were laying on top of Polecat and he was pinned down in a horizontal position in the bow. Lone Wolf and Possum Belly would have to paddle backwards for a few strokes in order to free Polecat from the tree limb and then they would paddle forward and try another angle to get through the hazard. This seemed to go on for a while and it got even worse the further along they ventured into the cut. Blood was oozing out of the many deep scratches and gouges that were all over Polecat's arms and upper body. The expensive resistol Cowboy hat on Polecat's head was taking a terrible beating and was probably beyond repair at this point but it was helping to protect his head and face from being lacerated with deep scratches.

The only thing that could possibly happen that would be far worse would be for a water moccasin to drop into the boat and pay them an uninvited visit. Polecat has come very close to stepping on water moccasin's and copper head snakes during portages over the many years he has participated in the race but thank the Lord that he has never been bitten yet. The end of the brush and tree infested cut was finally within sight and they made their way into Alligator lake. There were several sets of red eyes staring at them from the bank. The Cowboys finally made it back into the river after a pretty fast sprint across the open lake. Grady, Jon and Chris had increased their lead on them through the cut and they were going to have to pick up the pace even more if they had any chance to catch them.

San Antonio bay was choppy but was manageable. The Cowboys snapped on the spray skirt at the mouth of Seadrift cut and headed for the finish line in Seadrift. Possum Belly, Lone Wolf and Polecat ended up coming in fourth place overall with a finishing time of 43 hours and 25 minutes. This ended up being a fast race and it was Polecat's tenth straight finish. Moving into the multi man division was a good move even though Polecat was very reluctant to make that move at first. The future looked bright at this point. The Cowboys just needed to put the right team together in order to become contenders and get their names on the Argosy cup. This was the first time that any of them had managed to finish in the top four. It was time to pry the double blade paddles out of the blister infested hands and celebrate. Three Dots and the party bunch were patiently waiting at the finish line to help kick off the celebration.

John Dunn, Joe, Fred and Brian Mynar won the race with twenty seven teams making it to the finish line.

Polecat talking to his Dad just before the start of the race in 1993

CHAPTER 19

The Freeport Adventure

The finishers banquet ended on Tuesday afternoon and the small crowd that remained was standing around telling water safari stories and were trying to look over the way other boats were rigged out. John Dunn was busy getting his picture taken with the Argosy cup and doing an interview with Tim from the Victoria advocate. Possum Belly and Polecat were watching all of this from a distance and were busy cleaning out the very dirty and bug infested three man racing canoe.

John and Ginsie eventually ventured over towards them after the interview ended and they congratulated John on his first Texas Water Safari win. John had a few interesting stories to tell them about his experiences in the race with the Mynars. The conversation eventually shifted back to the Corpus Christi adventure that John and Polecat did the year before. The stories from that extended trip were getting bigger and bigger. John talked about the extremely rough bay conditions they had to overcome during that adventure and everyone was laughing at the stories. Possum Belly changed the subject and brought up the idea of paddling to Freeport, the finish line for the Texas Water Safari in 1965. Possum Belly had done some research on this and he told them that it would be a 120 mile adventure across several open bays and it would probably end up being more of a challenge than the Corpus Christi trip was.

Lone Wolf was listening to the discussion and responded that he had other plans. "Count me out." was his blunt answer. John Dunn liked the interesting idea but Polecat was a little hesitant at first because he knew that it would be a hard sell to Darla. The Texas Water Safari was over and that usually meant that they would be loading up the boys and heading out on their sometimes annual family camping trip. Darla was not involved in this conversation at the time because she was standing at the sea wall watching Wade and Brandon. They were swimming and playing with several other kids in the shallow water next to the pier.

The real reason why Possum Belly had brought up the idea of paddling to Freeport was because his family owned a house that was located on the bay front just behind the intra coastal canal at Sargent beach. The bay house was used for weekend trips and family vacations and was previously owned by his parents. The motivation behind his Freeport plan finally came out when he explained that he and his family were planning on staying there for a few days after the water safari was over. The conversation shifted and focused on the fact that Sargent beach is a little more than half way to Freeport from Seadrift and it would be a good stopping point for some food and rest. That would be a good place for a long rest stop if everyone decided to move forward with this adventure. The offer of a bed to sleep in along with a home cooked meal was very appealing and definitely added something positive to the on going discussion.

Possum Belly made an offer to Ginsie that she could stay with Veronique and his daughters at the bay house. John liked the tentative plan and was on board with the adventure trip. John said, "let's do it". Everyone started staring at Polecat and were patiently waiting for his response. There was no way Polecat could commit to this before consulting his better half and getting her approval. Darla ventured back over to where they were standing and started listening in to the conversation. It was obvious from the expression on her face that she was not thrilled with the idea. She could tell from the back and forth comments that it was probably going to happen. They were just waiting for Polecat to throw his cowboy hat into the ring and join the party.

Darla and Polecat were planning on heading out for a family vacation in a few days. If Polecat decided to join the party, the adventure paddle to Freeport would have to be finished by Friday or Polecat would be in big trouble with the family. Darla could not get involved because she had three young boys to contend with and her adventure seeking husband would be on his own. Polecat agreed to team up with John and Possum Belly only if this adventure trip could be finished by Thursday.

"Thank you Lord Jesus for putting a woman in my life who will support me unconditionally and who can deal with my adventure seeking personality. A devoted wife who probably knows me better than I know myself. Amen"

The plan started coming together and the first thing they needed to do was to launch the three man racing canoe back into San Antonio bay and start paddling towards Freeport. The plan was to try and make it to Possum Belly's vacation house at Sargent beach by Wednesday afternoon. This also meant that they would have to paddle through most of the night after starting the journey in order to make it into the Port O' Conner area before taking any breaks. The Freeport adventure team would then paddle into western Matagorda bay on Wednesday morning.

Tim, the reporter from the Victoria advocate was still at the sea wall talking to other water safari finishers. Tim noticed that they were putting supplies and paddles back into the canoe instead of unloading it and placing it on top of a vehicle for the ride back home like everyone else was doing. Tim ventured over to check out what they were doing and started listening in to the conversation. Tim became very interested in the Freeport adventure plan and listened very closely to the tentative plans that were being made. Tim told Polecat that he would not be able to follow them like he did last year but he would be very interested in interviewing the team after they finished in order to hear all of the details. Tim wanted to write an article about the trip to Freeport for the newspaper.

It was getting late and they needed to get started. The Freeport adventure team quickly finished up with the boat rigging and loaded up left over water safari food. Several water jugs were filled up and were secured in the boat before launching the three man racing canoe back into San Antonio bay. Polecat hugged Darla and his youngest son Jordan. "Thank you for supporting me and for not being too upset". Wade and Brandon were in the waist deep water and were helping to hold the boat steady while the three adventure seekers started to climb into the seats one at a time. Ginsie and Veronique, along with a small group of water safari veterans and race officials were gathered on the sea wall watching the show. The newly formed adventure team waved at them and started paddling towards Freeport.

John was the Texas Water Safari champion and he was in the bow seat. Polecat was positioned in the middle seat and Possum Belly was in the stern operating the rudder pedals. The official starting time was 5:30 pm on Tuesday afternoon and there was 120 miles of open bay ahead of them before reaching the final destination at the Freeport park and pier near the mouth of the Brazos river.

There was just a light wind blowing out of the south and San Antonio bay was fairly calm while they paddled out of sight. The long range forecast was predicting strong southerly winds on Wednesday and Thursday. The weather forecast meant that they would have to kick it into high gear and get as far down the route as they could before the wind speeds picked up and caused turbulent bay conditions.

Polecat's hands were blistered and his wrists were very sore from all of the double blading down the water safari race course over the last few days. The mutual agreement between everyone was that the double blades would remain stored away and they would only use single blade racing paddles during this adventure trip. That would make sense unless the bay conditions became so rough that they would be forced into using the double blades to help maintain boat stability.

It took a while for the three adventure seekers to get into sync and back up to a good stroke rate because of all the physical abuse that they had just put themselves through. The water safari champion was in the bow and they were able to increase the stroke rate and eventually make their way back to the intra coastal canal. The real reason why

John decided to team up with them was never talked about. Polecat just figured to himself that maybe John felt bad about dumping the Cowboys after getting the call. It didn't really matter what the reason was and it was not important because Possum Belly and Polecat were very happy to have him on board.

The sun started making it's glorious descent on the western horizon with amazing and beautiful colors lighting up the skyline. Sunset was always the best time of day while Polecat was at work on the oil production platforms in the Gulf of Mexico. The magnificent colors that light up the skyline and radiate across the open Gulf waters as the sun goes down are just amazing.

Several large barges pushed by a tugboat were headed towards them while they made their way down the canal. The Freeport adventure team was forced to pull the boat up onto the shoreline when they passed because of the large waves the long line of barges was pushing out.

It was a very dark night and they were still several miles away from Port O' Conner, but they were determined to get in as many miles as they could before the winds picked up on Wednesday. The water safari stories were getting bigger and funnier while they tried to keep each other alert by topping every story told with another one that was even harder to believe. Possum Belly can tell some pretty good stories but he still had a long ways to go before reaching Polecat's level.

Several hours of hard paddling passed by and they were all getting very tired. The decision was finally made to pull over and take a short break before daylight. The boat was pulled up on the canal shoreline and they laid out in the sand for a quick nap. The Adventure team had a long day of paddling in front of them if they had any chance of getting to Sargent beach by Wednesday.

The salt water sand crabs and bugs were having a field day crawling all over them while they unsuccessfully tried to get some rest. John and Possum Belly had sleeping bags to lay on but Polecat had to lay out in the sand with no protection. The sun started making it's glorious appearance on Wednesday morning and they finally had to give up on the attempt to get any rest because of all the bugs and sand critters that were crawling on them. Thankfully, no alligators had shown up to join in on the party during the short break. Port O' Conner was not very far down the canal from them at this point. That would give the Adventure team a great opportunity to stop at the popular boat dock and bait house that is located there for coffee and a breakfast taco.

Polecat worked in the Gulf of Mexico out of Port O' Conner for several years and crew changed out of the PHI heliport that was located there. Polecat also had some great memories from all of the time spent fishing and hunting in the back bays around Port O' Connor with his friend Steve when he was a teenager.

The bait shop would have fresh coffee and taco's and they were motivated to get there as quickly as they could. This would be a good spot for a quick break before heading in to the wide open Matagorda bay. The boat ramp was busy with several boats waiting in line to be launched and the fishermen standing there were staring at them when they beached the canoe next to the pier. The unusual sight of a 27 foot long racing canoe with three people on board was drawing a lot of attention. Two fishermen ventured over towards them and were checking out the boat. Polecat asked them if there was fresh coffee and taco's for sale inside the bait house and the answer was yes, "this is the only place on the canal down here where you will find that kind of stuff for sale".

Polecat quickly jumped out and headed for the bait house to get a cup of that fresh coffee while it was still available. There wasn't much time to waste so they quickly downed a couple of taco's and several cups of hot coffee while watching all of the expensive fishing boats being launched into the intra coastal canal. The wind was starting to pick up a little as the Adventure team got back into the boat and started paddling towards the western part of Matagorda bay. The canal is not protected in this area. It winds its way across the western end of Matagorda bay towards the mouth of the Colorado river.

Thank the Lord that they were much better prepared for this adventure compared to last year's Corpus Christi trip. The bilge pumps were functional and the brand new spray skirt that Paula had made for this boat was snapped on and was in good condition. The ultimate test of how well they were prepared to navigate through some very turbulent bay conditions was about to begin.

The south winds soon picked up to over 20 knots. The adventure team was able to keep up a good stroke rate and paddle over the waves with just a few minor problems. The winds were steadily increasing and the bilge pump had to be left on continuously because the waves were crashing over the bow and salt water was slowly soaking through the spray skirt into the boat. The waves were starting to hit John about chest high in the bow, but they were still making progress and managed to stay upright with the single blade paddles. The Adventure team eventually made it across the open part of the bay and were able to get back into a section of the canal that was protected by a barrier island. The most interesting section of this trip was within view in front of them. The TWS champion and his two helpers were quickly approaching the mouth of the Colorado river.

There is a man made lock system that controls the water levels in that section of the intra coastal canal and the mouth of the river. The lock chamber is a stationary box constructed in the intra coastal canal with two matching gates at each end that close. The lock chambers are 1,200 feet long and 75 feet wide, with a lock situated on both the east and west sides of the Colorado river on the intra coastal canal. The gates open or close to allow water levels to correspond with either the intra coastal canal or the Colorado river. One set will open to let the boat enter and then closes to allow the water level in the chamber to be raised or lowered, depending on the direction the boat is going.

The opposite set of gates then will open to let the boat leave. The filling and emptying of the lock chamber is done by gravity flow that controls the flow of water into and exiting the lock. The boat traffic that is coming through that area will make contact by radio with the lock operator and coordinate their passage through the lock.

John, Possum Belly and Polecat did not have the luxury of a radio or phone on board to call in ahead of our expected arrival time. They had to try and make visual contact with the operator before the lock could be lowered and they could enter the chamber area. The lock operator had probably seen a lot of interesting vessels pass through the lock many times before. The unusual sight of a 27 foot long racing canoe that was covered with a spray skirt and had three people wearing big cowboy hats on board probably was something he had never seen. The operator finally noticed them and talked loudly through a speaker to give the strange looking boat some important instructions.

The chamber gate located directly in front of them started to lower so they could enter into the chamber. The operator told them to paddle into the mouth of the Colorado river and the chamber gate would close behind them. This was a very weird sequence of events and they were now trapped in between two chamber walls while they patiently waited for the water level to equalize. The down stream chamber wall finally started to lower and the lock operator started giving them more instructions to follow. "I hope you make it safely to wherever you are going", "proceed and have a nice day". Polecat glanced back to wave at him and noticed that he was standing outside of the small control room with a camera in his hand and was taking pictures of the Adventure team. That was probably something that the lock operator talked about with his co-workers and friends for a long time and he even had a picture to prove it.

Time was starting to become a factor and the Adventure team still had another large open section of Matagorda bay to cross before reaching Sargent beach and Possum Belly's bay house. The south wind had picked up to 25 knots with occasional gusts up to 30 knots. The TWS champion and his helpers picked up the stroke rate and paddled out of the protected canal back into the open eastern section of Matagorda bay.

The Adventure team was only able to make very slow progress forward because of the large waves breaking over the bow. The bow would occasionally disappear as the boat plowed through them. The bilge pump was still working and had to be left on because of the constant wave bombardment. Possum Belly had done a pretty good job of rigging up the bilge pumps and they were now getting the ultimate test. The battery would hopefully hold up long enough to help them get across this large section of open turbulent water.

Polecat was not used to being in the middle seat of a multi man racing canoe. The primary job of this position in this kind of turbulent situation was to help keep the boat stable and maintain a 45 degree angle heading into the next large wave. This was done by constantly increasing and decreasing the stroke rate and occasionally putting out a hard brace. This roller coaster ride through the three to five foot waves seemed to drag on for an extended period of time. The Adventure team was still upright and headed in the right direction.

It was getting late on Wednesday afternoon when they finally made it in to a more protected section of the intra coastal canal. The waves were getting smaller and a little more manageable. This was a much needed break from the constant pounding and they took advantage of that by eating some of the left over water safari food that was secured in mesh bags under the seats. The Adventure team was hoping that this would be the last time they had to resort to eating this terrible tasting left over food because Sargent beach was next in line and a home cooked meal was waiting on them.

The sun made its glorious disappearance on the western horizon and they were now located several miles into a section of the canal that was semi-protected from the strong southerly winds. It had been a very long day of paddling through some rough sections of open bay and everyone was physically and mentally drained. Sargent beach was still about ten miles in front of them when they had to pull over and drag the boat up on the sandy shoreline to avoid a long caravan of large barges that was approached from the opposite direction.

The barges started to slowly pass by and everyone agreed that they needed to take a short break before continuing on to Sargent beach. The plan was to pull the boat farther up onto the sandy bank and turn it side ways. They could lay out in the sand behind the boat and use it as a wind block. The Adventure team had not slept since Monday night and it was starting to catch up with everyone in a hurry. John and Possum Belly pulled out their sleeping bags and Polecat dug a small hole behind the boat in the soft sand to lay in. It didn't take very long for the limited conversations to end and for the snoring to begin.

The next thing anyone remembers is when Polecat heard John getting up out of his sleeping bag. The sun was starting to light up the sky and make its glorious appearance on Thursday morning. Polecat's sand bed was not very comfortable and the only padding was a life jacket which was being using as a pillow. Polecat was laying on his side in the sand facing the boat. That is when one of the scariest sequence of events he has ever experienced before started to unfold.

John was walking around the boat when he quietly said "Polecat, don't move". The comment did not alarm Polecat at first because he was in a delirious state and was still half asleep. All of a sudden, Polecat heard the distinct sound of a rattle taking place right behind him. John then repeated himself, "Polecat, don't move". "There is a large rattlesnake coiled up right behind you".

Polecat was having a hard time understanding exactly what John had just said. The bad situation he was in became very obvious because every time he started to move one of his arms, the loud and distinct sound of a rattle would take place right behind him. A large rattlesnake had ventured out of the sand dunes during the night and had become an uninvited bed partner. Polecat's new friend was comfortably coiled up next to his back.

Polecat's new bed partner was attracted to the warmth of his foul smelling body and was coiled up next to him taking a nap. Every time Polecat flinched a muscle or tried to talk, his new friend would give out a distinct warning with a loud rattle. This was a situation that Polecat had never been in before so he had to lay there quietly. John and Possum Belly were trying to come up with an idea between themselves on how to scare away his new bed partner without getting bit. There were no good ideas coming out of their team conference. Polecat finally had to come up with his own plan because of impatience and frustration.

Polecat slowly started the process of getting himself out of the sand bed by digging his free hand into the sand and then pulling his body out of harms way one inch at a time. This was a very slow process. Polecat's new bed partner would rattle his tail with a warning to immediately stop or suffer the consequences every time he inched forward. Polecat would heed the warning and lay motionless for a while and try to remain calm and not panic. The getting out of bed one inch at a time strategy was slowly working and he didn't have any fang marks in his back yet.

"Lord Jesus, thank you for your many undeserved blessings. I humbly bow my head in prayer and ask for your help and guidance to get through this very unusual situation because I know you are in charge of everything and even the reptiles on this earth obey your instructions. Amen".

John and Possum Belly were constantly giving Polecat encouragement and updates on exactly where his bed friend was located and what he was doing. John and Possum Belly were keeping their distance. One inch at a time is probably the best way to describe what was happening while Polecat slowly pulled himself towards safety. The warning rattle was getting louder every time Polecat managed to move a little farther away from his new friend.

The rattlesnake incident finally came to an end when Polecat's teammates informed him that his lower legs were the only parts of his body that were still within striking distance. The one inch at a time move to safety finally came to an end when Polecat quickly jumped up and moved out of harm's way. The five foot long rattlesnake seemed to be very annoyed with Polecat when he looked around and realized that he had just lost his heat source. The Adventure team quietly watched him slowly slither back into the sand dunes and disappear.

It took a few minutes for Polecat to calm down and get over this unique experience. Polecat stood there in a state of shock while trying to understand what had just happened. There was not much time to waste talking about this crazy event because they had to start loading up and paddle on down the canal towards Possum Belly's bay house.

Veronique's home cooked meal was waiting on the stove for them. The Adventure team picked up the stroke rate down the protected canal and reached Possum Belly's bay house around mid morning on Thursday. Veronique was expecting them to show up sometime the night before and had been up most of the night patiently waiting. The food was cold because it had been put in the refrigerator, but it didn't take long to warm it up and get down to business. The original plan was to get there on Wednesday night and get a few hours sleep but that did not happen. The Adventure team only had a couple of hours to waste before needing to get started again on the journey. The Freeport adventure had to end sometime on Thursday because Polecat had a family vacation planned and that was supposed to start on Saturday. Everyone was enjoying the reheated home made meal and side dishes while Polecat enthusiastically retold the rattlesnake story to Veronique and the girls.

The Adventure team still had almost fifty miles to go before reaching the old finish line in Freeport. It was time to get back in the boat. There was enough time allowed for Possum Belly to make a pot of fresh coffee and to hug his family before he had to say goodbye and head back down the canal towards the mouth of the Brazos river. The good news was that the majority of the intra coastal canal in front of them was protected by a barrier island and that would help eliminate the potential hazard of having to cross open bays during high wind conditions.

The stroke rate picked up some while they made their way towards the Brazos river. The Adventure team would have to slow down occasionally and position the boat at the proper angle before plowing through the large waves after a long line of barges passed by. The physical abuse their bodies had endured through since the start of the Texas Water Safari five days earlier was starting to catch up to all three of them and they were ready for this Freeport adventure to end.

The Brazos river lock on the intra coastal canal was wide open and they didn't even have to slow down. The official Texas Water Safari finish line in 1965 at the Freeport park and pier was just a few miles ahead. The Adventure team was in a big hurry to end this thing and they crossed the 1965 finish line at 8:19 pm on Thursday afternoon as the sun was starting to make it's glorious disappearance on the western horizon.

There was no cheering and no crowd gathered there to greet them when they crossed the old finish line and pulled up to the boat launch just past the highway bridge. The only greeting they received was from a large group of irritated seagulls because the Adventure team had disturbed them at the takeout point. The plan was to hide the boat up on the bank somewhere and hike over to the nearest seafood restaurant for a celebration meal. Possum Belly would then be able to call Veronique on the public phone and ask her to please come pick them up.

The final time was a total of 50 hours and 49 minutes to make it from Seadrift to Freeport. There was approximately 37 hours of that time actually spent in the boat. The total time was longer than it took any of them to finish the 265 mile Texas Water Safari just a few days earlier. The newly crowned Texas Water Safari champion and his two helpers were very excited to finally be able to store away the paddles after 385 miles of paddling.

This adventure helped give all three of them a better understanding and appreciation of what the racers who competed in those early years of the Texas Water Safari had to endure through. The "Worlds Toughest Boat Race" has always been very hard on the competitors but those early races back then were even more demanding and challenging. The finish line was moved to Freeport from Corpus Christi in 1965. This added 120 miles to the race course from Seadrift and there were only 34 teams entered. Ten teams were able to go the distance and finish that year. Al Widing and his younger brother Pat Widing finished just minutes ahead of the 2nd place team. Gib McEachern from Canada and Ed Adams from Michigan finished second in a total time of 77 hours and 16 minutes.

1966 proved out to be the toughest Texas Water Safari on record. After eight days of racing, the first place prize of two thousand dollars was awarded to J.L. Bludworth and his brother Harold. There were fifteen boats entered that year and the Bludworth brothers were the only team that crossed the finish line. Three teams were disqualified during the race because they were caught traveling across land. The temptation of winning a lot of Prize money will sometimes cause people to make bad decisions.

Polecat had previously promised to buy his teammates a seafood dinner at a nice restaurant in Freeport when they got there and it was time to pay up. Veronique drove down to the restaurant to pick them up a little while later. The Adventure team loaded the boat on her vehicle and started heading back towards a previously scheduled meeting spot. Darla and Ginsie were patiently waiting there to take over custody of John and Polecat. John and Ginsie spent the night with them and then headed back home to San Marcos. Polecat's beautiful family had been waiting for him to get back home so they could finally get started on the family vacation.

Tim from the Victoria advocate called the next day and wanted to hear all of the details about the extended trip to Freeport. Polecat enthusiastically told him about all of the rough and turbulent bay crossings and the rattlesnake incident. Tim wrote a nice article about the adventure and it was published in the Victoria advocate a few days later. The article started with the headline, "Extra miles tough for Thomaston man, teammates". Thomaston man suddenly became one of Polecat's new nicknames and it seemed to catch on with his water safari friends.

CHAPTER 20

1998: A life changing year

The older Polecat gets, the more he realizes just how fast time can fly by because the next several years of water safari racing just seemed to all run together into one story. The "Thomaston Running Man" refocused on marathon running again and was able to go on and finish ten Houston marathons before knee problems and offshore work schedules finally got in the way and ended his running career. The running man was never able to beat his finishing time from that first marathon in 1990. The last nail in the coffin happened when the clown finally beat him to the finish line in his last Houston marathon and that was the wake up call that was needed to give up marathon running and throw the well used new balance running shoes into the nearest trash can. After fifteen years, six months and seven days of "running for no reason", the Thomaston Running Man's marathon days were now over.

The next eleven Texas Water Safari races that Polecat participated in were all in the multi man division with many different partners and boat configurations. Two more three man races were followed by seven four man and two six man races with many different characters on board as teammates. The only thing that stayed the same during this time period was that Lone Wolf and Possum Belly were usually in the boat with Polecat. Three Dots was always part of the team and was either in the boat or on the bank as the team captain. There are many great stories to talk about from these races but there are only a few of them that can be written about in order to spare the innocent from embarrassment. The Cowboys would run fast and competitive races during this time and would consistently finish in the top seven but were never able to put together a team that could get their names on the Argosy cup. In hindsight, the three Cowboys with the critter nicknames were probably the main stumbling block for never being able to put a team together that won the TWS.

The top teams did not usually look at them as a strong threat to beat them to the finish line so the Cowboys eventually became the training team that the young and talented and inexperienced racers would try to team up with. They would agree to join the team in order to gain experience and then hopefully get the "call" to move up into the next level. There was a large group of home schooled young men from the Houston area that would go through the Peter and Cathy Derrick school of canoeing as part of their home school program. That would usually spur their interest in "The World's Toughest Boat Race". Peter and Cathy Derrick were very successful water safari racers for many years and they would pass on these canoeing skills to the home schooled group that enrolled in their program. This group of young and talented teenagers was usually a good place to start when you were looking for teammates to fill up your multi man boat. Possum Belly and Lone Wolf would take the lead on recruiting these young teenagers because Polecat was always skeptical about teaming up with young men that had very little or no water safari experience.

Marathon canoe racing is mentally and physically challenging and you never really know how someone is going to hold up to two days of non stop paddling until they have finished a race and have some experience behind them. Tommy was the first of several racing prospects that the Cowboys recruited from the Derrick school of canoeing. Tommy had just started college and his Christian parents were not very thrilled with the idea of him teaming up with the Cowboys. Tom was also a close friend of theirs and he agreed to intervene and he assured them that the Cowboys were very harmless and only looked like a bunch of shady characters with weird critter nicknames. Tommy started training with the Cowboys in the spring and Polecat was very impressed with his paddling technique and his strong stroke rate. It became obvious during their training runs that Peter had taught him well and Polecat could probably learn a better paddling technique from him instead of the other way around. The Cowboys started calling Tommy by his new nickname, Needle Nose, in honor of the famous needle nose gar fish that dominates the lower Guadalupe river. The nickname seemed to fit and it became his new racing nickname. It did not matter if he liked it or not.

The 1998 Texas Water Safari was a fast race with moderate river levels and Needle Nose was a good addition to the team. The race evolved into a big back and forth battle with the Prochaska and Horsefly four man teams for third place through the lower sections of the race course. The Cowboys were finally able to establish a lead on Horsefly's team and finish strong in fourth place overall. Several canoeing friends told the Cowboys that their picture appeared on the front page of the San Antonio Express newspaper sports section a few days later. The picture was taken as the Cowboys paddled through cotton seed rapid on the upper San Marcos river. The headline said "Go With The Flow", for the most challenging action afloat, nothing matches the annual "Texas Water Safari." Polecat dominated the photograph because he was reaching out with his double blade paddle to straighten the bow after clearing the rock lined rapid and he blocked Possum Belly out of the picture. An article on Michael Jordan's pending retirement decision was right next to the picture. That was an unbelievable honor to have a picture of the Cowboys paddling through cotton seed rapid right next to a picture of Michael Jordan on the front page of a major newspaper's sports section.

Tommy would team up with the Cowboys one more time a few years later before getting the "call" and stepping up to the next level. Tommy would go on to win the Texas Water Safari several times with different teams.

The most interesting race Polecat ever participated in happened a few months later when Lone Wolf and Mary talked Darla and Polecat into going with them to Ireland in September of 1998. Mary's family is from Bally Mote, Ireland and the plan was to stay with her extended family and look over the area for several days. Mary's brother and sister in law offered to let Darla and Polecat stay at their place during the visit and they would also be the guides around the area. This was shaping up to be a great adventure to a part of the world Darla and Polecat had never been to before. The main focus of the trip was to enter the Jameson Liffey Descent canoe race in Dublin, Ireland.

Lone Wolf had been telling Polecat all about this whitewater canoe race on the Liffey river near Dublin. The river was intentionally flooded during irrigation season when they opened the flood gates of an upstream dam for a few days in early September. The whitewater canoe race would be scheduled at the same time in order to take advantage of the high water conditions. The Jameson Liffey Descent is a 30 kilometer race that goes over 10 weirs and has one long mandatory portage before reaching the finish line in Dublin. Lone Wolf, Mary and their young daughter Molly, along with Darla and Polecat arrived in Dublin and then rented a car. The group loaded up and drove all the way across the country in order to get to Bally Mote, which was located on the western side of the country next to the Atlantic ocean. Mary's family was very nice to Darla and Polecat and everyone enjoyed the visit and the guided tour of the area.

It was time for the racing team to head back to Dublin in order to get ready for the race. Lone Wolf was comfortable doing all of the driving because for some unknown reason they like to drive on the wrong side of the road over there. The only racing equipment that was brought across the pond with the team was single blade racing paddles due to the limited space on the airplane. Polecat's brand new resistol cowboy hat was getting a lot of attention out in public and the locals would just stare and smile at the very unusual sight of a bearded character wearing a cowboy hat. Lone Wolf had been in contact with one of the race officials several weeks earlier and was able to get a racing canoe loaned out to them. It was good publicity for the race to have two guys from Texas entered and they tried very hard to help the Texans any way they could.

Lone Wolf, Darla and Polecat arrived at the check in on the afternoon before the race and were escorted over to the racing canoe by one of the officials. It was basically just a standard plastic canoe, sixteen foot long with two built in plastic seats. This boat was something that would normally be used in a river or lake for recreational paddling. The only positive things Polecat could see was that it was in good condition and it was lightweight. This boat would fit into the standard division of the TWS but it would probably have a hard time making it to the finish line because of the very thin and flimsy plastic bottom. There was no spray skirt offered on this borrowed boat and they had to fill the interior of it with large, lightweight air bags. This strategy should help the Texans be able to keep most of the large waves they would be paddling through from filling the boat up with water. The bags were inflated and stuffed into the boat and there was just enough room left to squeeze their bodies into it. This would also require the Texans to position themselves on their knees for stability.

Whitewater paddling is a passion and Polecat was really looking forward to the race even though the Texans were not familiar with the race course and the many hazards. Lone Wolf, Darla and Polecat finished up the boat rigging and headed for the hotel in order to get some rest before the big event started early on Saturday morning.

This is a big annual event that is sponsored by Jameson Irish Whiskey and there were racers from all over Europe entered. Lone Wolf and Polecat were the only one's there from the great state of Texas. They were expecting somewhere around four hundred boats to start the race and it was a staggered start with multiple divisions. The fastest teams were in the K-1 and K-2 divisions and they would start first and that would soon be followed by the open kayak division. The canoe division would start last. Starting in the last group worried Polecat a little because he figured that the Texans would be a lot faster than most of the whitewater kayak's starting just ahead of them. That would force the Texans to do a lot of passing on a narrow and flooded race course.

The three Texans arrived back at the starting point early the next morning and Lone Wolf quickly handed the car keys over to Darla. She looked at him in disbelief because there was no way she felt comfortable following them down the race course while having to drive on the wrong side of the road. This was a situation that the Texans had not talked about before and there was no time for debate because it was time to get into the boat and get lined up.

Darla and Polecat hugged each other tightly and Polecat told her that the only options she had was to stay there and wait for the Texans to return or to try and find a ride with someone back into town. A race volunteer was standing close by and was listening in to the emotional discussion. She walked over and told Darla that she could ride with her down to the finish line after the race started. This was the answer to Polecat's urgent prayer request and that took a lot of pressure off and eliminated some of the tension. It allowed the Texans to refocus on the challenge ahead. Lone Wolf and Polecat thanked the race volunteer and quickly headed for the starting line.

The K-I and K-2 divisions had already started and the open kayak class was next in line while the Texans watched from the bank. There was probably somewhere around two hundred whitewater kayak's crammed together into a large group at the starting line when the starting gun fired off. The canoe division teams started launching their boats into the river to warm up and then crowd in as close as they could get to the starting line. Several of the boats around the Texans started making funny comments about Polecat's beautiful cowboy hat and were making fun of the Texas Cowboys.

There were a couple of boats lined up close to the Texans with the nice hats that were friendly and were very interested in where they were from. The rude remarks from the other boats close by were starting to get on Polecat's nerves. The Texas Cowboys inched up as close as they could to the starting line. The gun fired off and the Texans with the nice hats were able to sprint out into the lead pretty quickly. There were a couple of other canoe's right behind them as they approached the first obstacle.

The first flooded weir was just a little ways in front of the Texans with the nice hats and the intense stroke rate was over 60 strokes per minute. The weir was basically just a cement dam that had a large volume of water flowing over the top of it. Lone Wolf and Polecat didn't have much time to figure out the best route to take over the weir because they were the first boat in the canoe division to get there. The Texans stayed in the main current and paddled over the top of the submerged weir. The Texans made it cleanly over the top and were sliding down into the main current on the backside of the weir when all of a sudden they slammed into a very large six foot standing wave at the very bottom of the drop.

The Texans made it over this large standing wave upright but there was more to come. The next wave was a little smaller but the boat had already taken on a lot of water from the first wave crash and the Texans violently flipped over into the turbulent water. They were able to slowly crawl out from under the air bags and then quickly swim back up to the top of the water to catch their breath. Polecat's beautiful resistol cowboy hat was ripped off his head during the wipe out and was nowhere to be found. The hat was strapped down with a chin strap but the turbulent water managed to yank it off his head and give it a burial at the bottom of the river. There was no time for a prolonged search or for a memorial service because the Texans were busy swimming the submerged canoe over to the bank. The boat was not damaged and they still had their racing paddles in a tight grip.

The Texans quickly dumped water and started getting back into the boat as fast as they could. Some of the same teams that were making fun of them before the start of the race were paddling by and were laughing and yelling out rude comments. "Look, the Cowboys from Texas lost their hats", "Ha", "Ha", "Ha". The comments were making Polecat very angry because he was mourning the loss of his beautiful Cowboy hat and he felt half naked. The stroke rate suddenly went into over drive as Polecat tried to vent his anger through the racing paddle.

The Texans with no hats quickly got back into the race after the unscheduled pit stop. The area over to the right side of the weir revealed the route that they should have taken in order to avoid most of the large waves. The teams that were making fun of them just a few minutes earlier were very quiet when the Texans with no hats quickly sprinted by them. There were nine more weirs to go over. Since the Texans with no hats didn't do very well at the first one they were hoping that a hard lesson had been learned and that they would do much better the next time.

The Texans sprinted by most of the boats that had passed them at the first weir wipe out. The next obstacle was going to be trying to maneuver through all of the whitewater kayak's that started in the large group ahead of them. It did not take long before the Texans were right behind a large group of them and they were blocking the entire river at this narrow spot. Lone Wolf tried to politely ask them to move out of the way and give the Texans a passing lane but they were not listening and did not respond.

The anger Polecat was feeling from the first weir wipe out incident was still dominating his thinking and he was not slowing down. Polecat's stroke rate increased as they started to plow into several of the slower kayak's that were at the back of the large group. The Texans were a lot heavier and moving much faster than they were. Every time the bow slammed into one of the kayak's they would be forcibly pushed into the brush lined bank. The Texas Water Safari mentality of not slowing down for anything that you can paddle through or around was kicking in. The Texans with no hats were running over these kayak's at a frantic pace because they refused to make room for them to pass.

The yelling and cursing that several of them were directing at the Texans was very loud and should not be repeated. The Texans continued to crash into their boats and force them into the bank. The kayak's in front of this group could hear all of the cursing behind them and looked back just in time to see the Texans making a path way through the large group of kayak's directly behind them. They were finally catching on that the Texans were not going to slow down and if they did not want to get run over they needed to open a passing lane in a hurry. A narrow passing lane started to quickly open up as they got out of the Texans way and let them pass.

The loud cursing continued as the Texans finally made their way through the large group and the river opened back up again. The interesting take away from that incident was that Polecat had never been cursed out like that before. Polecat worked in a rough environment in the offshore Gulf of Mexico oil fields but had never been cursed at like that before. Irish men yelling out profanity and insults at him in their very different and unique accent as the Texans plowed over their boats is something Polecat will never forget.

The next weir came up on the motivated Texans pretty quickly and they were now paddling with the faster boats and were able to follow several of them. The Texans needed to let the experienced racers show them the best route over the weir and at the best angle. The best route would help them avoid most of the large standing waves at the bottom of the drop. It didn't take long for the Texans to adapt to the commonly used technique of slowly sliding over the weir at a 45 degree angle. That would allow the boat to float over the top of the large standing waves at the bottom of the weir at an angle instead of plowing straight into them at racing speed and taking on large amounts of water. The borrowed standard canoe they were in turned out to be an advantage because of the stability it had while riding over the top of the large standing waves.

There were big crowds gathered all along the race course waiting to be entertained with the next violent wipe out. The racers were making their way down the flooded river towards the finish line in Dublin. Rescue teams with scuba divers were stationed at strategic locations along the race course and were very busy plucking people out of the river. The Texans with no hats were moving along at a sixty stroke per minute pace and were passing a lot of teams. The more important factor was that they were getting much better at successfully navigating over the flooded weirs and staying upright.

There was a long mandatory portage around a weir that was not runnable next in line. The Texans passed several teams as they sprinted around the roped off area with the canoe up on their shoulders. Lone Wolf and Polecat were very motivated at this point and were determined to win the canoe division. A race official at the portage yelled out to them that they were currently in third place in the canoe division and the other two boats were just a couple of minutes ahead. This was good news and energized the Texans to pick up the pace even more. The Texans were trying to overcome the bad wipe out at the start of the race and finish strong.

The finish line was within sight and the two teams in front of the Texans were just a few yards ahead as everyone sprinted into Dublin. There was a large crowd gathered along the banks cheering and applauding as several K-1 and K-2 teams crossed the finish line. The borrowed standard canoe the Texans were in was gliding on top of the water as they put the pedal to the metal and paddled as hard as they possibly could.

A race announcer with an Irish accent was on a loud speaker and was describing the battle for first place in the canoe division to the spectators. The three leading boats were next to each other as they sprinted in to the finish line. In an exciting finish to a very unusual race, the Texans with no hats came in third place overall. The Texans crossed the finish line with the bow of the boat banging into the stern of the second place team. The wipe out incident at the first weir ended up costing them the victory but it did help create an interesting story to tell. It definitely helped to keep them motivated for the rest of the race.

Polecat scanned around the large crowd that was gathered at the finish line and was searching for his lovely wife. Darla was standing on the bank with her new friend. The race volunteer they had met at the start had become her new friend and had given her a ride to the finish line in Dublin. Lone Wolf and Polecat shook hands and were a little disappointed in the third place finish but were comforted with the fact that they did the best they could with no experience on this race course. The first two teams walked over and congratulated the Texans on a good race and the conversation was very friendly. They asked the Texans several questions about their canoe racing experiences back home. This gave Lone Wolf and Polecat the great opportunity to tell them about "The World's Toughest Boat Race" and invite them to come try it out next June.

Lone Wolf wanted to wait around for the awards presentation that was going to start in a couple of hours but Polecat quickly reminded him that their kayaking friends that they ran over early in the race would be finishing pretty soon. It would probably not be very wise for the Texans to be there and provoke another heated discussion with them. The thought of being confronted by an angry mob of kayakers did not make any sense to Polecat. They needed to just load up into the transport van that was being provided to the racers and head on back to the rented vehicle at the start. Lone Wolf finally agreed and they turned their borrowed racing canoe back in to the race officials at the finish line. The Texans headed over to the awards table to tell them they would not be able to hang around for the awards ceremony because they needed to go back to Bally Mote as soon as possible.

The race official thanked the Texans for participating in the Jameson Liffey Descent and then handed over the reward for the third place finish in the canoe division. A very nice Irish green colored pull over collared shirt along with the third place medal was awarded to them along with two bottles of Jameson Irish Whiskey. The Polecat couldn't help but stare at the bottle of Irish Whiskey and was very tempted to open the bottle right then and there and start downing it as fast as he could. Polecat then remembered that he had given up drinking alcohol a few years earlier. Polecat would end up giving it away to Mary's brother back in Bally Mote. The Texans with no hats loaded into the van with their racing paddles and bottles of Irish whiskey and the driver drove them back to the starting line where the rental car was parked.

It was time to get to the hotel and get cleaned up before taking Darla out to one of the local restaurants in Dublin to enjoy an Irish meal before having to head back to Bally Mote the next day. The plan was for Lone Wolf and Polecat to spend at least one day playing a round of golf on one of the famous golf courses that was located along the Atlantic Ocean coastline. Lone Wolf and Polecat had a great time playing on a very hilly course that was right next to the ocean. Walking eighteen holes over some very steep and severely inclined fairways with your golf bag in tow was very hard but it was well worth the effort. The view of the Atlantic Ocean and the very steep Ireland coastline from several of the greens was breathtaking. Polecat's score card for eighteen holes on such a hard course was not very important and was conveniently lost into the trash bin.

The Ireland trip was a lot of fun and the drive across the country revealed a lot of beautiful and unique scenery but it finally came to an end. Darla and Polecat had to get back to the boys and the summertime heat in South Texas. Polecat never had the opportunity to go back to Ireland and enter the Jameson Liffey Descent for a second time and that ended up being his only opportunity to compete in an overseas canoe race.

1998 took a big turn in the wrong direction in October when a life changing weather event happened. The remnants of a tropical cyclone that came across Mexico from the Pacific Ocean made its way into Texas and stalled out in the central part of the state. The storm dumped enormous amounts of rain throughout central and south Texas for several days in the middle of October. The historic once in a lifetime 500 year Guadalupe river flood was about to take place and it soon became a life changing experience for Polecat. After several days of torrential downpours and a lot of local flooding the warning was issued that a flood of historic proportions was heading their way from the hill country of central Texas. Polecat had a lot of previous experience with flooding on the Guadalupe river and had a tentative plan in place for what needed to be done in order to prepare for this massive flood that was coming right at them. Moving furniture upstairs to the highest point available in the house was the first step. That was followed by loading out several trailers with what was left and hauling them up the road to a neighbors house for storage.

Evacuating his beautiful family to his in-laws house in town was a top priority and that had to be done before the county road in front of the place went under water. The river dogs would not leave without

Polecat so they stayed behind to help with the last minute preparations. The last step in the evacuation plan would be to load them up in the truck and evacuate. A law enforcement vehicle drove up to the house with the sheriff of Dewitt county driving and he began to explain to Polecat that he was making the rounds through the area to warn people of the massive flood coming their way. The conversation was serious and it was obvious that he was very concerned about what was going to happen throughout the county. Polecat respectfully replied that he was getting ready to leave but there was still a few more last minute preparations to finish. The sheriff stared at him and said, "Evidently, you don't understand what I am trying to tell you," "this is the worst flood anyone has ever seen in this area and we have been rescuing people off their roof tops all morning long in the northern end of the county." "You need to leave right now."

The sheriff was very clear with his warning and Polecat completely understood the evacuation orders. Polecat thanked him for driving out there to check on the people in harms way. Polecat assured him that he would be right behind him on the way out. The river dogs were loaded up and the last thing on the to do list was to turn his Mom's Emu birds loose. Polecat smiled and watched the comedy scene while they enthusiastically ran down the fence line enjoying their new freedom.

That is when a drastic change in the evacuation plans happened because his neighbors from down the road were still there and were trying to pull a travel trailer out at the last minute. They were stuck down to the axles in the muddy pasture. There was no way Polecat could leave the area with his neighbors still there. Polecat drove over as close as he could get to them and looked over the situation. There was no safe way to pull them out of the mud pit because Polecat could not get close enough with his truck to even make an attempt. Steve and Walter were about to give up and were depressed at the thought of their truck and travel trailer going under water. That was the reality they faced and Polecat convinced them to load up what they could on the back of his truck. "Let's all get the heck out of here before it is to late".

They loaded what they could on the farm truck and started heading down the county road. Polecat drove up on a low section in the road and could not go any further because the floodwaters were rising very fast and the road was already several feet under water at this spot. The reality was that they were stranded and there was no possible way to get out of the flooded area without having to swim. Polecat made the decision to go back home and load up one of his canoes. Steve and Walter had no choice at this point except to follow his instructions.

Steve, Walter and Polecat were eventually forced to drive over to another neighbor's house that was close by. Shane's house was located on higher ground. The flood waters were rising dramatically all around them. The great river flood of 1998 was in full swing and they reluctantly found themselves right in the middle of it. The flood waters kept rising around them at a very intense rate and they were eventually forced to climb up on to the roof of their neighbor's house to avoid going under.

Polecat had brought along his whitewater canoe as the emergency escape vessel and it was securely tied up to the roof and was on standby if they had to make a quick getaway. The sun was starting to make it's glorious disappearance on the western horizon. The loud and continuous sound of turbulent rising water all around them was kind of like being camped out right next to a very loud whitewater rapid.

Walter noticed a vehicle light about a half mile away and it looked like it was parked on the county road. There was no electricity on at the house and Polecat did not have a flashlight so it was very hard to make out exactly what they were staring at. Polecat could not help but think that it could possibly be someone stranded in their vehicle on the road and they might need help. Polecat's three river dogs, Precious, Spooky and Buddy were on the roof with them and Walter was given the job to please try and keep them there.

Polecat was going to get in the canoe and paddle over to check out the vehicle on the road. This did not work out very well because all three of them jumped in to the swift flood water as Polecat paddled towards the stranded vehicle. Precious was the strongest of the three and was able to keep up but Spooky and Buddy were swept away by the strong currents and disappeared from his sight. There was nothing Polecat could do about it because he was having a hard time keeping the boat straight in the strong currents and he did not have a good light to attempt a rescue. It still bothers Polecat to talk about this because he did not have the opportunity to say goodbye to his canine friends and he never saw them again.

Precious was swimming as hard as she could and was close enough to where Polecat finally was able to grab her and pull her into the boat. The boat was barely moving forward even though Polecat was paddling as hard as he could into the strong rising current. It was a slow process but Precious and Polecat were finally able to reach the stranded truck. Polecat finally able to get close enough and recognized Ben and Denise sitting in the front seat. The quickly rising flood waters were up to the top of the dash in the truck and they were sitting in chest deep water.

Denise recognized Polecat and called out his name when the bow of the canoe bumped into the flooded truck. There was a lot of emotion and panic in her voice when she asked if she could get in the canoe. "That is why I paddled over here", Polecat answered. Denise quickly climbed out the open window on the passenger door and crawled into the bow of the canoe. The boat almost capsized when she fell head first into the bottom of the boat but Polecat was able to keep it upright.

Ben was nervously sitting in the chest deep water on the drivers side. Polecat yelled out to him to crawl over to the same window and follow Denise into the canoe. Ben responded that they had several pets in cages stored away in the bed of the truck. "What should I do with them". Ben asked in desperation. A very large heavy pig and a large dog barely had their heads above the water line because of being trapped in their transport cages. It didn't take long for Polecat to yell out an answer. "Turn the pig loose because we don't have room in the boat". "He should be able to swim well enough to have a chance at surviving". "Bring the dog with you".

Ben slowly crawled into the bed of the truck and let the pet pig out of his flooded cage and they watched in horror as he grunted and tried to swim. The pet pig was keeping his head barely above the water line before quickly being swept away into the dark night. The flood current was very strong and Polecat was having a hard time keeping the boat close to the truck. Ben pulled his dog out of the cage and threw him into the canoe. Ben was then able to slowly climb into the bow and Denise was able to move into the middle of the boat with Precious and their dog. Turning the canoe back towards the direction they needed to go was a long process because of having to slowly turn the bow into the current at an angle to try and avoid an abrupt turn and rollover. Thank the Lord Jesus that we were finally able to make it back to the neighbors house safely.

Ben and Denise were able to climb up onto the roof with their dog and were closely followed by Precious and Polecat. There were now five people stranded on the roof along with two dogs and no supplies. It was going to be a long stressful night watching the flood waters rise. Polecat's immediate concern was if they were high enough to avoid being swept away and his job was going to be to make sure everyone stayed calm and didn't do anything that could cause an injury or worse. The last resort would be for all of them to pile into the canoe and try to paddle across the very intense and turbulent water to safety. This would be very difficult because five people in a seventeen foot long whitewater canoe trying to navigate across swift cross currents could be a recipe for disaster.

Polecat bowed his head in prayer. "Lord Jesus", "Thank you for helping all of us survive this dangerous situation we are in. I know you have put me here for a reason and I pray that you use me to carry out your will". Amen.

Believers can be sure that whatever the Lord calls us to face, we can move forward without fear knowing that even the most overwhelming and impossible tasks are in God's capable hands.

Precious and Polecat stood watch on the roof while the four neighbors tried to get some rest on the hard and severely angled roof top. The sight of the ranch truck eventually going completely under water in the driveway next to the house just added some more emotional stress to the situation. The constant sound of wild life screams and cows bellowing in the distance were very loud and disturbing because there was nothing Polecat could do to help these animals. It was a very dark night and the stars were shining brightly. Polecat just sat there in a trance, quietly trying to make sense of it all.

Sometime around four in the morning it started to get eerily quiet and it took Polecat a while to realize what was happening. The rising flood waters were slowing down and the river level was about to crest. The most disturbing thing was that all of the animal sounds Polecat had been listening to for the last several hours came to an abrupt end. They had all been swept away down river.

The sun started making its glorious appearance and Polecat was finally able to see the unbelievable sight around him. The open cow pastures around the immediate area were now completely under water and it looked like he was sitting in the middle of a large lake. All of the livestock fences around the area were under water and the only thing showing above the water line was the tops of large trees and floating debris.

Polecat's father had purchased property in this area thirty years earlier. Darla and Polecat had lived here for almost nineteen years at the time and Polecat had never seen anything like this before. Sitting on a rooftop in the middle of a flooded lake was kind of like finding your-self trapped in a terrible dream or water safari hallucination. Ben kept asking Polecat if they could try and paddle over to his house to check on the animals that he and Denise had left behind. The river had crested and the wild and turbulent cross currents that were there the night before had significantly slowed down. Polecat reluctantly agreed to load up and make an attempt to paddle over to his house and check things out. The motivation behind this decision was that he wanted to go see if his house was still standing. Polecat could not help but think the worst and that it had been knocked down and swept away down river.

Precious was not going to be left behind and she jumped into the canoe with Ben and Polecat. They started carefully paddling across the flooded lake towards Ben's house. The cross currents were still very strong and with Ben's help in the bow we were able to slowly paddle across the flooded lake and keep the boat upright. Ben's house was more than a mile away and it took a lot of effort to carefully maneuver across the open water at the right angle in order to avoid dipping a gunnel and sinking the boat. Ben and Polecat paddled close to something that was bobbing up and down in the turbulent water. Polecat suddenly realized that it was his son's four wheeler and it was hung up in the neighbors barbed wire fence. It was upside down and bobbing up and down like a cork in the water. This caused Polecat to just shake his head in disbelief because this was probably only going to be the first of many bad things they would see on this journey.

Ben and Polecat finally made their way over to Ben's house safely and noticed only about two feet of the roof still above the water line. It was still there and in one piece as far as they could tell. Ben started calling out the names of the barn cat's they had left behind and one of them answered him from the top of a large pecan tree nearby. Ben and Polecat paddled over to the tree and found the large orange cat clinging to a branch above the water line and he appeared to be OK. Ben kept trying to get him to climb down to us but there was no way he was going to let go of that tree limb. There was no easy way to safely reach him so we had no choice but to leave him behind and pray that the flooded river would soon start dropping.

Ben and Polecat started paddling towards Polecat's house which was located over a mile further upstream. Polecat had already convinced himself that it was not going to be a pleasant sight. The area around them was not recognizable because it looked much different under water. The branches of large trees extended out above the water line and they had to carefully be avoided along with the many cross currents. The partially submerged trees had to be paddled around but there were no fences to worry about because they were all several feet under water.

Several critters were clinging to tree limbs barely above the water line and they were staring at us while we slowly paddled by. Ben and Polecat were finally able to paddle their way into Floodplain ranch but Polecat did not recognize the surrounding area. The roof top of his mother's house came into view and then he knew where they were because several Peacock's were perched on top of the roof and were squawking at them. Polecat's primary focus at this point was to try and find what was left of his house and he didn't even slow down to check on the the Peacock's.

The very odd sight of his second story bedroom barely clearing the top of the water line caught his attention. Ben and Polecat paddled over the top of his submerged car port and storage building. Thank the Lord that the house was still there and had not been swept away down river. The main sections of the house were completely under water. The only thing showing was the second story bedroom and it was barely above the water line.

There were no tears of sorrow in his eyes at this time because he was expecting to find a much worse situation. Ben and Polecat were having a hard time keeping the boat close to the house because of the strong currents. That is all Polecat needed to see, so they turned back towards his neighbor's house. Steve, Walter and Denise were nervously waiting for them to return.

Ben and Polecat were finally able to paddle back over to the roof top sanctuary at my neighbor's house and join the other three. A rescue plan was being discussed on the roof top sanctuary. That is when we noticed a large boat with an outboard motor in the distance. It appeared to be heading in our general direction. The boat turned out to be a volunteer rescue boat that was patrolling the area and they were looking for people that needed help. Denise was frantically waving at them trying to get their attention. The rescue boat finally noticed her and they started heading over towards us.

Polecat probably could have safely paddled everyone to freedom and dry land two at a time but that would have been a risky adventure and would have been attempted as the last resort. It was a welcome sight to have a rescue team find us and then give everyone a ride back to a safe location on higher ground. Precious and Polecat stayed behind and waited for the second trip because of limited space on the boat. This gave Polecat another opportunity to gaze out over the unbelievable scene that surrounded him one more time. The sight of this entire area being under water was something Polecat will never forget and it is firmly etched into his mind.

Darla was patiently waiting for Polecat and Precious at the rescue operation staging area with a smile and a big hug. There were no words needed at this time, just tears of joy.

"Thank you Jesus for helping me and my neighbors safely make it out of this once in a lifetime event and I pray for everyone who is still in harm's way and in need of help. Amen".

This unbelievable once in a lifetime event changed Polecat's limited understanding of God's complete control of events and it brought him even closer in his personal relationship with the Lord.

The final tally of our personal losses ended up being a house that had to be gutted and completely remodeled along with many personal items and furniture that could not be salvaged. The 1978 ford one ton farm truck that went completely under water. Twenty five cows along with several chickens, ducks, Peacocks and two Emus. Five Texas Water Safari plaque's that floated out of a damaged window and were never found. Fences around the property that ended up taking several years to replace and rebuild.

The most important loss by far were my beautiful canine friends, Spooky and Buddy. They were part of the family and Polecat missed them dearly. The situation we found ourselves in forced my family to adapt to some new living conditions. Polecat purchased a used travel trailer to live in and his friends at work loaned him a portable offshore living quarters that the boys lived in for the next six months. Three Dots and Vowery came down for a visit and offered to help any way they could. Tears started streaming down Vowery's face after she saw most of our personal belongings in the front yard piled up in a pile, waiting to be hauled off to the nearest landfill. Thank the Lord that Polecat does look at the loss of personal belongings that way because it was just stuff that could be eventually replaced. It took us several years to fully recover from the historic 500 year flood in 1998. Polecat will always remember that experience as a life changing event.

The next several months would be spent trying to remodel our flooded home after it was completely gutted. Some of the rebuilding would have to be contracted out because Polecat had to spend a lot of time in Houston on a new offshore deep water project that he was assigned to.

One of the few bright spots from that busy rebuilding time was when our oldest son Wade played in the class AAA state championship football game. The fighting Cuero Gobblers advanced to the state final against Aledo in the Astrodome in early December. The entire town of Cuero was pumped up about this game and it would be a great opportunity for the community to take a break from all of the damage repairs that the great flood had inflicted on the surrounding area. Darla and Polecat loaded up the family and headed to Houston on that beautiful Saturday afternoon in December. The Astrodome was packed on both sides of the field. The game was very exciting and well played by both teams with Aledo eventually pulling out the win at the end, 14-7. That was disappointing but was not nearly as important as getting the opportunity to watch our son play in a state championship football game. This helped make the on going flood recovery a little more tolerable. Thank you Jesus

Paddling over one of the flooded weirs during the Liffey Descent

Polecat standing on his porch in chest deep water a few days after
the great flood of 1998

CHAPTER 21

The Rest of the Story

The rest of the story almost seems anticlimactic compared to the great flood story, but there were some very interesting canoe races with different characters that Polecat was involved with after 1998.

In 2000 the Cowboys teamed up with another home schooled young man from the Houston area who had also graduated from the Derrick school of canoeing.

David was a young man who had a passion for music and he was also a very strong paddler. David didn't have any water safari experience at the time so he eagerly accepted the "call" from the Cowboys. David had a very good paddling technique that he had learned from the Derrick's and he ended up being a very good addition to the four man team that year.

The story that Polecat remembers most from that year happened early in the race on the upper San Marcos river. The Cowboys were moving along at a good stoke rate and were in the top seven overall when they paddled under some very low hanging branches in a swift section of the river. All of a sudden the boat came to an abrupt stop even though they were double blading at a fast pace.

The scream Polecat heard from behind alerted him to a very bad situation that was taking place in the stern of the boat. Lone Wolf was barely still in the boat and was desperately trying to hang on to one of the low hanging tree branches that Polecat had just leaned under with no problems. Possum Belly was talking to him while everyone else tried to figure out what was going on back there.

"Paddle backwards" is all they could hear coming from the back of the boat. They were now at a complete stop. The three of them started paddling backwards because it was pretty obvious that something serious was going on back there. Possum Belly checked the water depth level they were in with his paddle and it was only about three foot deep and he quickly jumped in to go see what the problem was with Lone Wolf.

Possum Belly then yelled out to Polecat to get the pocket knife out of the secured bag under his seat and come back here as fast as he could. David and Polecat both jumped out on opposite sides of the boat and Polecat was able to find the knife before making his way through the very swift water back towards the stern. The sight of Lone Wolf hanging onto the large tree branch with both hands and his feet locked in under a cross thwart in the boat was very strange.

The bad situation became much clearer when Polecat got closer and noticed a drop line hanging from the tree branch. The large barbed hook that was located at the end of the line was deeply embedded into Lone Wolf's right ear lobe. There was a lot of blood on his shirt and it was obvious that he was suffering from severe pain. Polecat was able to quickly cut the drop line just below the limb and they cautiously pulled the boat over to the left bank with Lone Wolf sitting in the stern seat.

Lone Wolf got out of the boat with the hook and drop line dangling from his ear. Lone Wolf laid down on the sandy bank as Possum Belly and Polecat tried to figure out what to do next. Valuable time was wasting and this was a race. Polecat's suggestion was to leave the hook in his ear and get moving down river before another boat passes by. The sarcastic comments continued and he jokingly said that the hook made it look like Lone Wolf had an ear ring in his ear and it gave him the appearance of a Pirate wearing a cowboy hat. Lone Wolf did not see the humor in that.

Possum Belly was in agreement with Polecat's assessment of the situation but Lone Wolf did not like the plan. He said that they were going to have to get that hook out of his ear before anyone headed down river. The barb at the end of the hook was all the way through his ear lobe. The only option available would be to cut the end of the hook off and then push it back through his ear in the opposite direction.

The drop line incident was starting to get serious now because another multi man team paddled by while they debated what to do next. The Cowboys watched from the bank while the other team quickly paddled by. The leather man tool they were using had a pair of pliers attached to it and that would have to be used to try and cut off the barbed end of the hook. If that was successful they could then push the hook on through the swollen ear lobe and get this comedy show back on the river.

Lone Wolf was wiggling in pain and shouting out bad words at them while Polecat tried very hard to hold him down. Possum Belly was in charge of the surgery and was cutting the barbed end of the hook off. David was sitting under a large tree a few feet away and was being entertained with the drama while he gobbled down a pre packaged meal. The shouting and name calling got much worse as the ear surgery continued and another boat passed by.

The pressure was getting more intense to quickly finish the ear surgery and get back to racing. Possum Belly was finally able to cut off the barbed end of the hook and push it back through Lone Wolf's lacerated ear lobe. An antibiotic cream that was in the first aid kit was then applied to the pierced ear. They were finally able to get back into the boat and start racing again. The pierced ear incident was finally over and it was time to refocus their attention on catching the two boats that had just passed by during the unscheduled surgery stop.

Lone Wolf's damaged ear eventually swelled up so much that he temporarily lost his hearing in that ear. Thankfully it did not effect his paddling ability and the Cowboys were back to racing again. Lone Wolf's loss of hearing forced everyone else to loudly yell out instructions to him when he needed to quickly turn the boat in one direction or the other to avoid the many obstacles in the river. The hearing problem lasted for the rest of the race.

The 2001 and 2002 water safari races were the last of the four man teams the Cowboys put together. Possum Belly and Lone Wolf were able to recruit a young man from Seattle, Washington for both of these races. Liam had some water safari experience after previously finishing second in the USCA C-1 division. Liam has a good sense of humor and Polecat enjoyed listening to him talk about what it was like living in the Seattle area. Liam would always be enthusiastically involved with the constant and never ending battle of who could tell the funniest and most interesting water safari story during the long training runs. Liam reluctantly had to accept the nickname Hellgrammite, in honor of the famous water bug that lives under rocks and is sometimes used for catfish bait. They are usually found under submerged rocks next to gravel bars that line the banks of the lower Guadalupe river. The odd nickname seemed to fit him perfectly.

The 2003 Texas Water Safari ended up being a year of big change for the Cowboys. Lone Wolf and Possum Belly were successful in getting Polecat to go in with them and purchase a six man racing canoe. The selling point that was used was that they could finally move up into the next level and hopefully be able to put some pressure on the top teams. Maybe even be able to put a good enough team together that could compete for the Argosy cup.

The search for young and talented teammates always seemed to eventually go back to the growing pool of home schooled young men that had graduated from the Derrick school of canoeing. Tommy was once again at the top of the list and he was showing some interest in teaming up with the Cowboys for the second time. Tommy suggested that we should also try to recruit a good friend of his. Tim was also from that small group of young men from the Houston area that had gone through the Derrick school of canoeing.

These were two very talented canoe racers who had some experience and they would be very solid teammates. This six man team was slowly coming together but they needed one more young and talented teammate in order to have any chance of getting their names on the Argosy cup.

Wade is from the College Station area and he was another young man who had a good track record in the water safari. Wade was showing some interest in joining the six man team because of Tommy and Tim. The Texas Water Safari has always been a big family event and Wade had grown up watching his father race before getting involved himself. Pete and the Polecat had raced against each other many times over the years and their families were always involved in the race somehow. Wade was more interested in teaming up with Tommy and Tim than he was with the Cowboys. There was an open seat available and this was his opportunity to team up with them.

The "All Star Team" finally came together but there were only three all stars on the team and that did not include the three who had weird critter names. It did not matter who the real "All Stars" were at this point because this team had the potential to be a factor in the race and maybe even be able to put some pressure on the big boys. The new Cowboy team came together towards the end of the training season and things seemed to be working out after the few limited training runs they were able to get in before race day.

The 2003 Texas Water Safari started with river levels on the low side in early June. The Cowboys and the three all stars were able to sprint ahead of the pack and put themselves all alone in second place. The Cowboys were able to stay pretty close to the Mynar six man team on the first day down the San Marcos river. The sun made it's glorious appearance on Sunday morning and they were still in second place with a substantial lead over the boats behind them.

Tim was in seminary college at the time and he gave the team an inspiring devotional that perked everyone up after a long night of non stop canoe racing. The devotion ended with Tim leading everyone in prayer. Polecat started singing one of his favorite gospel songs and several of his teammates joined in. The loud singing was echoing down river on that beautiful Lord's day. The early morning hours are a great time to try and pick up the stroke rate in order to take advantage of the slightly cooler temperatures before the day quickly turns into an over heated oven.

Tim's devotion and prayer was a great way to start the new day and honor our Lord. The isolation they were all feeling because of being close to the front and having a big lead on the boats behind them would last for the rest of the race. Polecat was in the bow for most of the second day and was feeling the physical effects of a very fast stroke rate and a change needed to be made. Wade volunteered to take over the bow position for the remainder of the race.

Three Dots was patiently waiting for them at the Tivoli checkpoint for the water hand off and tried to motivate everyone with the fabricated story that they were still within striking distance of the lead boat. Three Dots told them that all they had to do was pick up the stroke rate a little more and they had a chance to catch the Mynar team.

The Cowboys paddled into a choppy San Antonio bay and were paddling as hard as they could when Polecat suddenly yelled out to everyone, "let's give it everything we have left because this could end up being the best finish some of us will ever have". Nobody responded to Polecat's challenge. He was just trying to motivate himself because he had never been in this situation before.

The Cowboys and the three all stars finished strong in an official finishing time of 40 hours and four minutes and in second place over-all. This finishing time was well over two hours behind the winning six man team and it also ended up being exactly what Polecat had predicted during the bay crossing. It was the best finish Polecat ever had in the Texas Water Safari. The three young and talented "All Stars" who teamed up with them eventually got the "call" and all three of them moved up to the next level and won the Texas Water Safari several times with different teams.

The 2004 Texas Water Safari was a completely different story after a mandatory delay of two weeks because of a flooded race course. The Cowboys once again ended up consisting of three talented home schooled young men along with the Polecat, Lone Wolf and Horsefly.

Possum Belly had to drop out of the race after the delay due to a planned family vacation trip to France.

The new Cowboys came together very late in the game and they had little opportunity to train together. There was really no good way to judge how this team would stack up against the competition. This was definitely going to be an interesting challenge for the three older Cowboys to quickly bring this team together and try to be competitive in the multi man division. The young men had no water safari experience but they had all graduated from the Derrick school of canoeing. Two of the young men were named Jonathan and the youngest of the two was only fifteen years old at the time of the race. Jeremiah was the third young man and he was the oldest of the three at seventeen.

This race ended up being a very fast and exciting race as the Cowboys navigated through the many turbulent rapids and obstacles that were created due to the very high river levels. Polecat stayed in the bow with Lone Wolf and Horsefly occasionally switching out with each other in the drivers seat. The three young teenagers were able to keep up a very good stroke rate and they were definitely a positive factor in helping the team stay in the top three overall down the flooded race course.

The self appointed coaches that were located in the back two seats were constantly barking out orders and instructions to the young teenagers. They were focused on trying to keep them motivated and alert. Polecat was in a world by himself. He set the pace for the rest of the team and was constantly yelling out warnings to the driver about obstacles just ahead of them. The lack of training time together did not seem to be a problem. The Cowboys were moving down river with very few problems and were able to maintain their third place position.

The Cowboys successfully cleared the lower river logjams and alligator lake on late Sunday afternoon. The intense heat and stress of paddling at a very fast stroke rate for well over 30 hours was catching up with the younger Jonathan and Jeremiah. The older Jonathan started to take over as their new coach and kept trying to talk them through this mental and physical down time they were both experiencing. It was great for the old racing veterans to watch one of the young guns step up and become their leader.

This took a lot of pressure off the old guys and they could now concentrate on getting this long six man racing canoe successfully through the many obstacles ahead of them. Jonathan would eventually enlist in the military and become an officer a few years later. After his service to our country ended he got the "call" and moved up to the next level of canoe racing and won the Texas Water Safari with his brother Tommy.

The Cowboys finished strong in third place overall with an official time of 37 hours and two minutes. This ended up being the fastest finishing time Polecat ever had in "The World's Toughest Boat Race". Three Dots and Polecat were smoking their traditional victory cigars after the finishers banquet ended and the conversation shifted to what their future water safari plans were.

Three Dots had been a team mate in the boat with Polecat five times and had been his team captain for 15 years. Three Dots emotionally admitted to Polecat that he had endured through enough after twenty years of participating in the TWS and this would be his last year. The race was becoming a big burden for him and it was time to turn in his official retirement notice.

This did not surprise Polecat because he had been thinking the same thing. Polecat had accomplished just about everything he was going to be able to do in this race and he needed to move on and re focus his attention on his beautiful family and international oil field career.

Darla and Polecat had two sons in college and the youngest son was getting ready to start high school. This was putting a big burden on them financially. Polecat's priorities were drastically changing and he needed to take a break from this great race and take a step back. Twenty one straight finishes in "The World's Toughest Boat Race" had taken a big toll on him physically, but the more important factor was that the TWS had taken away a lot of quality time that he probably should have spent with his wife and sons.

Three Dots and Polecat came to an agreement between themselves that this was their last race and that it was time to move on to other priorities. Three Dots lived up to his part of the agreement and he never came back again, not even as a spectator. Polecat has asked him many times since then to come back and join the fun and watch the pain and suffering from the river bank, but he never has. Three Dots is a great friend and he made a big impression on everyone that new him in this race for twenty years. It is very hard for Polecat to put into words how much he appreciated the friendship and all of the time and effort that Three Dots put into being his team captain and racing partner.

The Cowboys were never really the same after that when both of the original Cowboys retired. Polecat did not live up to his part of the agreement and he came out of canoe racing retirement four years later when Brandon started showing some interest in doing the race. Brandon was playing college football at Angelo State University and he had followed the TWS since he was a young boy. The Texas Water Safari was always a family event.

Brandon and Polecat had talked about teaming up together someday for the race but playing football and going to college had dominated most of his time for the last several years. Brandon asked Polecat to come out of his self imposed retirement and team up with him for the 2008 water safari. This caught Polecat completely by surprise and it got the competitive juices flowing again but he didn't have a racing canoe that could make it to the finish line anymore. Polecat called Lone Wolf and he was more than happy to let them join the Cowboys six man team that year.

The Cowboys were able to recruit two more old racing friends and Polecat was looking forward to being on the same team with them. Preacher Jim was a church pastor and he lived in the College Station area. Preacher Jim had a good track record of strong finishes with several different teams.

Horsefly accepted the offer from Lone Wolf to fill the last open seat on the six man team. This was shaping up to be a team with many interesting characters on board and it would turn out to be a very hard and long race in low water conditions. Brandon and Polecat were able to get some much needed training time in with the team even though his college schedule and Polecat's offshore work schedule in Angola, Africa did not match up very well. The 28 days on and 28 days off schedule with no vacation time could be a big problem. The only way Polecat could manage this was if his scheduled days off lined up with the scheduled start of the race. Thankfully, the scheduled days off lined up with the start of the water safari that year and he was able to throw his expensive cowboy hat into the boat and have the great honor of racing on a team with his son Brandon.

The Cowboys started out strong and were basically paddling by themselves in fourth place overall for most of the first day on the San Marcos river. Horsefly's wife Kristen was their new team captain and she was doing a great job keeping them supplied with cold water while they tried to navigate down the San Marcos "creek" towards Gonzales. Kristen does not have the crazy and funny personality that Three Dots has but she is very organized and she was self motivated to do the best job she could do while carrying out her team captain responsibilities for a six man team by herself.

Brandon seemed to be holding up pretty well in the extreme heat and low water conditions. That all changed in a hurry when the Cowboys paddled into the logjam area on the lower Guadalupe river. Stephan and Jonathan were a very strong tandem team and they were right behind the Cowboys while they carefully made their way through the narrow and brush lined logjam cut.

Brandon was starting to say crazy things and would abruptly stop paddling while talking to himself in an unknown language that no one could understand. Polecat was in the bow and could not see what was going on behind him. Everyone was talking to Brandon and they were desperately trying to bring him out of the mental fog he was going through.

Brandon would start paddling again for a while and then would just stop and start mumbling to himself. Brandon would start pointing his paddle at objects along the bank and then talk to himself in a strange language. The Cowboys were in a heated battle for fourth place at this time and could not afford to have one of their team mates stop paddling for no reason.

Everyone behind Polecat was trying very hard to talk Brandon through the mental lapse he was experiencing. Jonathan and Stephan eventually passed them and they were not able to catch back up. This was the same Jonathan that Polecat had paddled with in his last race in 2004. Jonathan was on an extended leave from the military.

Brandon was struggling to get out of this mental fog he was in when the Cowboys paddled into Seadrift cut and headed for San Antonio bay. Preacher Jim had taken over the bow spot at the last checkpoint and was setting a good stroke rate when the 40 foot long racing canoe suddenly came to an abrupt stop. The water hyacinth plants that are normally very thick and line the banks throughout Seadrift cut had grown across it and were now completely blocking it off.

These plants grow on top of the water and they had taken over the cut. The plants were so thick that they stopped the Cowboys forward movement cold and they were now stuck in the middle of a big patch of it. The Cowboys tried to pick up the stroke rate and plow through it but that did not seem to make any difference. The boat was at a stand-still and was not moving forward.

Preacher Jim suddenly jumped into the deep water and tried to swim forward through the thick plants while the rest of the team carefully and slowly paddled the boat behind him. Preacher Jim would grab and pull the plants loose with his hands and then try to make a narrow pathway through the middle of this water hyacinth garden. There was not much the rest of the team could do to help him so they just kept paddling forward. Preacher Jim would have to occasionally grab the bow of the boat in order to catch his breath before continuing on with the plant removal operation.

Preacher Jim was kind of like a dredge and was slowly able to clear a path forward. The hyacinth garden started thinning out some and they were finally able to paddle over the thick vegetation. Preacher Jim was extremely exhausted when he slowly attempted to crawl back into the bow of the boat so the Cowboys could get back up to racing speed again.

The water hyacinth incident was something Polecat had never experienced before and it just ended up adding another hard obstacle to overcome in this very difficult race. That is why they call it "The World's Toughest Boat Race".

Preacher Jim then asked Polecat to hand him one of his five hour energy bottles that were secured under the seat. Polecat then had to give him the bad news that they were not there. Someone had apparently stolen and drank them and there were only a couple of empty bottles laying on the floor of the boat under the seat. This made Preacher Jim very mad and he would not talk to anyone or answer any questions for the rest of the race. The five hour energy drink thief never came forward to admit what he had done and this cold case is still a mystery that was never solved.

The Cowboys paddled into the finish line in fifth place overall with a finishing time of 49 hours and 59 minutes. Brandon finished his first Texas Water Safari and this race was the catalyst that motivated him to get better and come back next year. Polecat once again announced that he was done with the water safari after 22 finishes and he handed his favorite racing paddle over to Brandon in an emotional event after the finishers banquet was over.

The 50th anniversary of "The World's Toughest Boat Race" came around in 2012 and Polecat had officially retired from his offshore job with BP in February of 2011. The plan was to eventually go back to work as a contract consultant somewhere over seas after retirement but the phone remained silent and no one called with a job offer.

Polecat's first attempt at finishing the Texas Water Safari was on the twenty year anniversary in 1982 and the temptation was overwhelming him to come back one more time and enter this milestone race. This ended up being a last minute decision and the Cowboys already had their team put together and it included Brandon. Brandon was now recognized as a very talented water safari racer after four straight finishes and he was getting some attention from the top teams.

Andrew is a long time friend from his high school days in Cuero and they had teamed up together for the last three water safari's. They had finished every race in the top fifteen and were patiently waiting for the "call" in order to get the rare opportunity to step up to the next level and get their names on the Argosy cup.

Andrew is a very interesting character who did not have any canoeing experience when he started going with Polecat and Brandon on the sometimes annual trips down the lower canyons of the Rio Grande river below Big Bend national park. Andrew seemed to enjoy the water safari stories that Polecat would ramble on about while they all were gathered around the campfire. Andrew told Polecat later that these stories had a big influence on him when he decided to enter the water safari with Brandon for the first time. That was a great compliment but the only thing Polecat can take credit for is that he just flamed the fire that was already burning in him. In some small way it helped to spark his interest in "The World's Toughest Boat Race".

Polecat entered the USCA C-1 division and Darla was not very happy with this decision. She kind of warmed up to the idea after Polecat was able to recruit their oldest son Wade as the team captain. This made it more of a family event and she was happy with that because of the rare opportunity to hang out with Wade and Julia.

Darla and Polecat were very excited when Wade and Julia were married in Cuero six months earlier in December. Wade is a graduate of Texas A&M university and Julia has a degree from St. Thomas university in Houston. Their wedding day was an answer to their prayers and Julia has been a great addition to the family. Darla was looking forward to the opportunity to being able to hang out with her new daughter in law.

Wade would usually just shake his head in disbelief at Polecat when he told him and his brothers that good things always happen at canoe races. Wade met Julia at the Colorado 100 canoe race when he was a team captain for Polecat and his brother Jordan. That meeting eventually turned into a marriage proposal. Good things happen at canoe races and they are proof of that.

Polecat did not end up putting the required time in and doing the necessary training for the 2012 TWS. It became pretty obvious that he was going to have a hard time in this race and would probably finish way back in the pack. Polecat is not very fast in a USCA C-1 and he was going to finally get his opportunity to do an Owen race.

Owen is the well known cigar smoking water safari veteran who had several strong finishes in the water safari when he was younger but eventually he acquired the reputation of consistently being the last boat to cross the finish line later in his racing career. This was going to be Polecat's first good opportunity to personally experience an Owen race.

Polecat was lined up on the last row because of the last minute entry. The stern of his USCA C-1 was bumping the cement barrier that marked where Aquarena Spring lake started. This was the first time Polecat had started the race on the last row and it was going to be an uphill battle from this point forward.

Tom led everyone in prayer and shot off the starting gun as 135 teams made their way to the first island portage. Polecat was eventually able to move up into the middle of the pack. Everyone was struggling to find the deeper channels because of the low water levels on the upper San Marcos river. That is when things started changing in a hurry.

Martindale dam was next in line and Polecat quickly jumped out of the boat and carried it around the dam portage. Polecat was able to paddle through the low water bridge rapid that is located just below the dam and his boat ran aground on the gravel bar just below the bridge and came to a complete stop. That is when a three man multi man team slammed into the stern of his USCA C-1 racing canoe and the bow of their boat had completely penetrated through the Kevlar exterior.

This crash opened a large gaping hole in the stern of his boat just above the water line. Polecat was caught of guard and was surprised because they came out of nowhere. Polecat just could not stop staring at the large gaping hole in his boat as they backed up and started paddling down river. One of the boat crashers casually looked over at Polecat and apologized for the damage while they quickly paddled down river and out of sight.

Polecat had to pull over at the nearest available accessible river bank and let the exterior of the boat dry. Polecat pulled out his only roll of gorilla tape and started applying it in layers over the large hole until the roll of tape was completely used up. Racing canoes were constantly paddling by during the boat patching repair job. This was a make or break moment when Polecat was finally able to launch the boat back into the river and get back to racing.

Thank the Lord that the patch job appeared to be holding and Polecat was back into the race. The sad reality started to set in that he was now dead last. Polecat was going to have to pick up the stroke rate in order to make up for the lost time. Passing boats is a lot more exciting than being passed and the first day turned out to be a long day of passing boats as Polecat tried to make his way back up into the middle of the pack.

This was going to be a long and hard race because of the low river levels and it was going to get even harder after the boat crashing incident.

There was a record number of boats entered in this race because of the 50 year anniversary and there was nowhere to go at this point except up. The most interesting pass that Polecat made on that first day was when he caught up with the first paddle boarder to ever enter the race. Polecat can't remember his name but a friendly conversation was started with him and Polecat respectfully started calling him the Cajun Man. The Cajun Man reminded Polecat of his friends from south Louisiana who would stand up and paddle their pirogue dugout canoes around the bayous of south Louisiana.

The paddle boarder was from a northern state and he was very depressed by the reception he had received before the start. Several water safari race veterans and officials had told him that he had no chance of finishing this race on a paddle board. This story resonated with Polecat because that is exactly the way he was treated 30 years earlier in his first race. Polecat tried to motivate the Cajun Man with encouraging comments.

Polecat was trying to make up for lost time so he had to leave his new friend behind and keep moving as fast as he could down river. The Cajun Man paddle boarder eventually was able to cross the finish line in Seadrift just before the cut off time and he became the first paddle boarder to ever finish the Texas Water Safari.

This was an endurance event instead of a sprint race because of the low water conditions and that should have worked to Polecat's advantage. The lack of training and Polecat's advancing age was becoming a huge factor and he was starting to struggle on the lower sections of the race course just like everyone else was.

The inexperienced teams around Polecat were paddling hard and were moving along at a good water safari pace but the biggest mistake many of them were making was wasting time at the checkpoints. They would also waste time by pulling over and jumping in the water for a few minutes to try to cool down some because of the scorching south Texas heat. Polecat's water safari mentality would not allow him to do that.

The hardest portage Polecat had ever experienced before was next in line at the famous logjam that was located below the swinging bridge checkpoint. The cuts around the logjam were blocked with logs and were impassable due to the extremely low water levels. Polecat ended up having to drag his USCA C-1 for almost two miles around the massive logjam before reaching open water again. There was a friendly aluminum tandem team making the portage at the same time and they kept each other alert with conversation.

Polecat was able to finally make it through the last checkpoint somewhere around the 80 hour mark with no unscheduled rest stops or wasted time at the check points. The only wasted time in this race so far was for the repair job after the boat crashing incident. The boat repair had held up and Polecat was somewhere in the middle of the pack again with only a bay crossing left in front of him.

Polecat was getting very close to Seadrift cut when he unexpectedly caught back up to his boat crashing friends in the three man unlimited boat. They were the one's that had caused all of the damage and wasted time after plowing into his boat at the rapid below the Martindale dam low water bridge. They all stared at Polecat in amazement and could not believe that he was still in the race.

This was one of the few highlight's during this difficult race and now it was time to put everything he had left into passing them. Thank the Lord that Polecat does not hold grudges and he does not seek revenge because the Lord Jesus Christ has given him an ability to forgive and forget.

The conversation was awkward at first and they eventually understood that the only thing Polecat was focused on at the time was getting to the finish line as fast as he could. Polecat wanted to get out of this boat because he had been sitting in it for over 80 hours without a break. The awkward conversation soon became friendly and the boat crashing incident was not talked about in a negative way. Polecat told them that this is "The World's Toughest Boat Race" for a reason and things like that happen. The key to success is to figure out a way to adjust and overcome every time an obstacle is placed in front of you.

Polecat's boat crashing friends paddled with him for a while before they eventually pulled out the double blades and slowly started pulling away. A very choppy San Antonio bay was next in line and Polecat was focused on the finish line in Seadrift. There was still enough time left to make it in to the finish line before sunset.

Polecat paddled over the two to three foot waves and angled towards the barge canal point. Everything was starting to look dramatically different around him and his mind was gradually shifting into neutral after almost three and a half days of non stop paddling. It is very hard to explain this to someone who has never experienced this before. Things can change in a hurry after pushing yourself for this long with no sleep. This was shaping up to be the longest time it had ever taken Polecat to reach the finish line in Seadrift. This was an unfamiliar situation that he found himself in.

Polecat vaguely remembers paddling across the barge canal point and there were only two miles left across the open water to the sea wall and the finish line. Polecat paddled over to some shallow water close to the shoreline and got out of the boat for no apparent reason. The next thing he remembered was when someone started yelling and waving at him from about a hundred yards away on a sandy beach front.

The yelling and waving caught his attention and Polecat slowly loaded himself back into the boat and paddled over to see what this person wanted. The fisherman was rod and reel fishing with his young son on the beach front and he was trying to wave Polecat over closer to them. The severely damaged USCA C-1 ran up onto a shallow shell reef and suddenly stopped.

The fisherman walked over to Polecat with a concerned look on his face. "I have been watching you for over an hour and you have just stood there holding on to your canoe," "Is everything OK or do you need help?" Polecat does not remember how he responded to that question.

The fisherman then invited Polecat to walk over with him to their primitive fishing camp. That is when Polecat suddenly stumbled and fell face first into the sand. The fisherman hesitated and did not try to help him get up. "Are you involved with that canoe race that finishes at the sea wall"? Polecat cannot remember how he answered that question.

The fisherman yelled at his wife who was sitting in their car several yards away and asked her to come over and join us. The fisherman's wife walked over and joined in on the conversation. They were talking back and forth between themselves while Polecat just stared off into San Antonio bay with a blank look on his face. The fisherman's wife got into their car and drove off as the fisherman and Polecat continued with their very awkward conversation. "My wife is going to drive over to the finish line and report to them that there is a canoe racer over here that needs help". Polecat must have been answering his questions but cannot remember what was said.

Two cars drove back up to the sandy beach where they were sitting and all of a sudden a woman that Polecat recognized ran up to him. "What are you doing"? Darla loudly yelled out as she got closer. "We have been waiting for you at the finish line for the last several hours". She was very upset and the chewing out intensified, "Get back in that boat and get your butt to the finish line so we can end this race and go home".

Polecat's lovely wife's voice was starting to bring him back to earth and reality. Polecat vaguely remembers saying, "where are we"? Darla quickly responded, "The finish line is right over there and you need to get back into your boat and go that way". She was pointing at the finish line off in the distance and was patiently waiting for Polecat to follow her instructions.

Polecat staggered back up onto his feet and crawled back into his damaged USCA C-1. The sun was making it's glorious disappearance on the western horizon as he paddled in the direction she had pointed towards. The yellow blinking light at the finish line caught his attention. The mental melt down Polecat was going through was starting to ease up a little while he tried to pick up the stroke rate and head straight for the yellow blinking light.

A very large crowd was gathered at the sea wall because the finishers banquet had been moved to Wednesday in coordination with the 50th anniversary. There were several hundred people gathered along the sea-wall partying and waiting for the next boat to come in.

Polecat was next in line and after 23 finishes in "The Worlds Toughest Boat Race" he had never seen a crowd that large before at the finish line. The yelling and applauding was overwhelming as Polecat bumped the bow of his severely damaged USCA C-1 into the steps at the pier and his official finishing time was logged in at 85 hours and 34 minutes. This was the longest time it had ever taken Polecat to get there.

Darla was standing on the seawall with a big smile on her face while several race volunteers helped Polecat climb the steps and get up onto the sea wall. The warm welcome was very appreciated and it brought a big smile to his face. Polecat likes to reflect back on that unique moment sometimes because twenty eight years earlier he was standing at the very same spot after finishing the water safari for the first time in ninth place overall. There were only four people standing there to greet him and three of them were part of his bank crew. This race is getting bigger and more popular and it has been an honor and privilege for Polecat to have witnessed that change.

Polecat did not know until later that a young man had tragically lost his life during the race while paddling through the Gonzales area. This terrible sequence of events is what everyone was talking about at the finishers banquet. This had never happened before in the fifty year history of the TWS and it would drastically change the race rules going forward. Polecat was in shock after hearing about the young man's passing and he felt very sad for the parents and extended family.

Everyone joined together in prayer at the finishers banquet to remember the young man and pray for his extended family. "Lord Jesus", "Please help this family during this difficult time of sadness and grief and we pray that you will help comfort them". "Amen".

Polecat, Possum Belly, Hellgrammite and Lone Wolf paddle over Rio
Vista dam

The Cowboys and the "Three All Stars" clear the Luling dam

CHAPTER 22

"I had a Good Run"

Brandon and Heather were married on the river bank at Floodplain ranch in November of 2014. This was the answer to many prayers and Darla and Polecat were excited for them. The wedding ceremony took place on top of the bank overlooking the Guadalupe river and it was well attended by many friends and the extended family.

A young lady was playing blue grass music on her fiddle and the unique sound of a fiddle being played was echoing down river on that beautiful Saturday afternoon. Pastor Mike was leading the ceremony and the young couple was just about to say "I do" when everything drastically changed.

A neighbor from upstream started shooting his semi automatic rifle and everyone was startled by the loud sound of a high powered rifle. Pastor Mike jumped about a foot in the air in reaction to the loud gunfire but he never lost grip of the Bible he was holding. The ceremony went into a pause mode while Pastor Mike tried to regain his composure.

Everyone sitting there was looking around trying to figure out where the gunshots were coming from. Darla started violently jabbing Polecat in the ribs with her elbow. "You need to go over there and tell our neighbor to stop the shooting because we are in the middle of a wedding". Polecat did not want to disrupt the ceremony any more than what had already happened and he was hesitant to follow her orders. The gunfire finally ended and everyone started to calm down.

Pastor Mike restarted the ceremony where it had abruptly ended and the young couple were finally able to say "I do". Everyone started cheering and applauding as the young couple kissed each other and the gunfire started again. This was a dramatic end to a very unusual wedding ceremony. Polecat apologized to Pastor Mike for the unscheduled disruption after the wedding was over. Pastor Mike replied with a big smile on his face, "Now I know what a shotgun wedding is like".

A self imposed retirement from canoe racing started after the 2012 Texas Water Safari and Polecat watched from the bank while Brandon (Pavos) got a lot better in this race over the next few years. Several of Brandon's high school friends from Cuero had given him a new nickname. Pavos means turkey in Spanish and that seemed to fit him perfectly because he had been a standout player on the fighting Gobblers high school football team a few years earlier.

There is really no good way to explain it but 2015 rolled around and Polecat started getting the Texas Water Safari fever again. It had been four years since starting early retirement from the offshore oil fields and three years since his last canoe race and he needed to get physically active again.

A bad case of shoulder arthritis had set in and Polecat missed the personal challenge and the competition. The competitive drive that once dominated his thinking was trying to make a comeback. The next step would be to contact his good friend Possum Belly and get up to speed on the latest water safari news.

Possum Belly and Lone Wolf are very close friends after all of the time they spent together in a racing canoe during training runs and races over the last 25 years. The call was made and the conversation jumped all over the place until Polecat finally got to the point. Could he recommend a young and talented canoe racer that had some water safari experience and that might still looking for a teammate? The Cowboys already had their boat filled up with young talent for the race and that took the pressure off and made it a lot easier for Polecat to ask him for a name.

Possum Belly told him about Matt, a young man from the Houston area with water safari experience who had done a training run with them a few weeks earlier. Polecat called Matt and he seemed to be interested with the offer to team up with an old water safari veteran who was way past his prime and was getting very close to senior citizen status.

The new team came together and they decided to enter the USCA C-2 division. It had been 23 years since the last time Lone Wolf and Polecat had raced in the USCA C-2 division and Polecat really wanted to get back into that kind of boat again.

The training was going along pretty well when a big flood event happened two weeks before the scheduled start of the water safari. The historic Memorial Day flood of 2015 on the Blanco and upper San Marcos rivers wiped out everything in its path downstream, including a young family that ended up being trapped inside a house during the flash flood near Wimberley.

This was a terrible event and the water safari had to be delayed several weeks because of the flooded race course. The historic Memorial Day flood did not end up affecting the lower Guadalupe where Polecat lives as much as the Blanco and San Marcos rivers were.

Matt and Polecat had to hold off on doing any more training runs on the San Marcos river until the river levels started receding. The levels returned back to a more manageable level a few weeks later and they decided to meet up and do a training run in the Martindale area. The destruction and flood damage throughout the area was much worse than what Polecat was expecting to see while they paddled down river just below Martindale.

A large volunteer group was searching through a very dense section of flood debris that was piled up along the river bank near Martindale when they paddled by. It finally dawned on them that they were training for the Texas Water Safari while these volunteers were searching for the missing bodies from the Wimberley area. The fact that they were training for a canoe race while an intense search for bodies was going on right next to them really depressed Polecat and he asked the Lord Jesus to please forgive him in a short prayer.

Matt and Polecat did not talk about it very much but watching these volunteers search for bodies while they paddled by affected both of them in a negative way. The training run finally ended and they drove back up to the put in spot at the Martindale bridge. This is where the shuttle vehicle was parked and they were going to move the racing canoe back over to Polecat's truck.

All of a sudden a starving kitten came out of a large pile of downed tree limbs and flood debris that was piled up next to the bridge and started rubbing his head on Matt's leg. Matt was very surprised to see a cat rubbing on his leg. The kitten looked harmless so he reached down and started petting the flea infested flood cat. The kitten eventually headed back over to the debris pile while they continued with the boat transfer. A few minutes later Polecat looked down and noticed the kitten rubbing up against his leg, The starving kitten was staring at him with some very sad looking eyes. Polecat is not a cat person but the sight of this orange flood kitten staring at him with a very sad look was getting his undivided attention.

The boat transfer was completed. Matt and Polecat shook hands before heading out in different directions. A strange feeling that Polecat can't explain suddenly came over him that he should not leave that flood cat there. The truck was in gear and Polecat was about to drive off when he looked over at the flood kitten one more time and noticed that he was still staring at him. Polecat had no choice but to grab him and gently place him on the back seat of the truck for the long ride home.

The Lord must have a sense of humor because he laid on Polecat's heart that this orange flood cat was the only reward he was going to get after 33 years of canoe racing. Marcos the flood cat is staring at Polecat right now and is patiently waiting to be fed while this unique story is being written about him eight years later.

The 2015 Texas Water Safari started after a month long delay with higher than normal river levels. Matt and Polecat had a pretty good first day while they cautiously paddled through all the rapids and obstacles on the upper San Marcos river with just a few minor problems. This was the first water safari Polecat had participated in after a major rule change was implemented that allowed the team captain to give you any type of food or drink you wanted.

Polecat did not like the new rule change at first because this was a big change from the way he had always done the race in the past. The planning and storing of enough lightweight food in the boat to last you for the entire race was a big part of the pre-race preparations in previous years and now that was all changing. The balance of having enough food and supplies checked in and stored away on board at the start and the canoe not being to heavy was always a major factor in the pre race planning.

This rule change really altered the way everyone prepared for the race in a dramatic way and Polecat was experiencing it for the first time. This put a lot more pressure on the team captains because they had to basically become a traveling waiter/waitress. The young water safari competitors that enter the race now expect food and water to be handed to them at the designated hand off spots. This did not affect Polecat as much as it probably would have in the past because he had primarily become a liquid only canoe racer. High energy meal replacement drink mixes were what he relied on.

The technology had changed for the better over the years and several drink mixes were now available that provided all the ingredients you needed in order to keep your energy level at the right balance. The old days of peanut butter and honey sandwiches, energy bars and left overs out of the refrigerator securely stored away under your seat were now long gone.

Matt and Polecat were currently in second place in the USCA C-2 division when they paddled in to the Gonzales gravel bar checkpoint and their team captain was there for the food and water hand off. Polecat watched Bill hand Matt a large pizza that had just been purchased at the local pizza place and it was still hot. Matt was very excited when he started downing the large pizza.

Polecat slowly sipped on the meal replacement drink mix out of a sports bottle when he could in between strokes. The sight of Matt stuffing large slices of hot pizza into his mouth made Polecat jealous and hungry but there was no way his gut would have been able to handle that after 18 hours of hard paddling down the San Marcos river. Matt paid a huge price for this a little while later when he started having stomach cramps and was experiencing some nausea problems. Polecat was not showing any sympathy and said that he was just going to have to suck it up and keep paddling because they were in a heated battle trying to catch up to the first place USCA C-2 team.

Matt and Polecat were finally able to catch up with Ken and John just before daylight on Sunday. Polecat told Matt that they needed to increase the stroke rate even more in order to sprint by them as fast as they could. This is an old water safari technique where you try to give your competition the impression that they can not keep up with your stroke rate and boat speed and the race is basically over at that point.

Experienced water safari veterans know that this is a long marathon race and things can change in a hurry on the lower sections of the race course. The serious racing usually does not start until below Victoria and they were not even close to that point yet. Matt and Polecat were able to pick up the stroke rate and pass Ken and John after a very brief and friendly conversation with them.

The Hochheim checkpoint was next in line and they were now in first place in the C-2 division. This was something that Polecat had not experienced since the 1992 race 23 years earlier. Bill handed Polecat a cup of hot coffee in a travel mug and he immediately became the best team captain that Polecat ever had. Polecat was gradually starting to warm up to the new rule change because this was the first time his team captain had ever handed him a hot cup of coffee during the race.

Matt and Polecat were able to gradually increase the lead throughout a very long and scorching hot Sunday afternoon. Bill handed Polecat an ice cold coke at the handoff spot just below Victoria. Polecat was downing it as fast as he could when Matt suddenly and without any warning jumped out of the bow seat and into the river in order to get himself wet after a long day of canoe racing in 100 degree temperatures. Polecat lost his balance and the canoe rolled over. The ice cold coke he had just opened was now floating in front of him and was full of river water. Polecat stared at Matt in disbelief and gritted his teeth in anger. Bad words were exchanged between them and they did not talk to each other for the next several hours. The stroke rate increased and Polecat vented his anger through his racing paddle. The coke spilling incident was not talked about any more.

They paddled through the swinging bridge checkpoint around 2 am on Monday morning and then successfully made their way in to the open cut that was located just above the mile long logjam. That is when they suddenly noticed three sets of bow lights paddling towards them going in the wrong direction. Hellgrammite and Edoh were in the first boat and they were very excited when they recognized Polecat. Matt and Polecat were cautiously paddling towards them when Hellgrammite yelled out, "Polecat, there is no good way to get through this cut because it is blocked off with tree limbs and brush". "We are headed back to the main river channel to try and find a better route".

There was a long pause before Polecat finally responded to his old friend and former partner. "Follow us because we know how to get through this area". Matt was very surprised that Polecat was offering to help them.

Taking the time to do several training runs through this area before the race starts will sometimes give you a big advantage over the competition. Polecat probably should have stayed quiet and given them the impression that they were all lost but Hellgrammite was a good friend and a former racing partner. Polecat felt obligated to help him get through the area.

There was a lot of boat maneuvering required to get through all of the low hanging tree limbs and thick brush due to the high water levels. All three of the lost teams were able to follow Matt and Polecat into Alligator lake. That is when the stroke rate picked back up again and they found themselves in a heated battle with the same lost teams that they had just helped.

The close friendships that Polecat has made while competing in this race over the years have been very special to him but the friendly discussions and the exchanging of funny stories usually have to wait until the finish line.

Matt and Polecat paddled into a very choppy San Antonio bay and were still in the lead of the USCA C-2 division on Monday morning. There was a slim chance of breaking into the top fifteen if they could just pick up the pace a little more and have a clean bay crossing. Matt and Polecat made it to the barge canal point upright but had to quickly pull over and dump water because of continuous bilge pump problems.

Everything started going downhill in a hurry at that point and they struggled to stay upright over the last couple of miles into the finish line. They ended up having to walk the boat in to the finish line over the last half mile because of the choppy bay conditions. Matt and Polecat managed to maintain their lead in the USCA C-2 division and finished in the official time of 49 hours and 33 minutes and in nineteenth place overall.

Pavos finished three hours ahead of them in eleventh place overall and was the second solo unlimited boat to cross the finish line. Darla and Polecat were very excited to see Pavos doing so well and he was quickly becoming one of the top racers in "The World's Toughest Boat Race". Pavos finished way in front of Polecat and now he had the family bragging rights.

Matt awkwardly laid down under under one of the tents they had set up at the finish line after the brief team celebration at the flagpole and he was still laying in the same spot the next day when Polecat returned for the finishers banquet.

The race officials asked Polecat to lead the prayer before the banquet started and that was one of the greatest honors and privileges that Polecat has ever had. A very large crowd was gathered there and Polecat appreciated the opportunity to honor our Lord and Savior through prayer.

Matt and Polecat accepted the USCA C-2 traveling trophy and Polecat was able to get his name back on it after a twenty three year absence.

This race ended up giving him the motivation he needed to try and stay in good physical shape and maybe even attempt to come back next year.

The Cowboys called in March of 2016 and offered Polecat a seat on their six man team. Polecat was a little reluctant to go back into the multi man division because it had been eight years since the last time he had teamed up with his cowboy brothers. They were in the process of putting a strong team together and there was a good possibility of maybe getting back into the top four. The main reason Polecat ended up accepting the offer was because the phone was silent and the "call" never came in from anyone wanting to team up with him for a USCA C-2 race.

The training runs were filled with the funny back and forth contests of who could tell the best water safari stories and then were followed with competitive golf matches after a hard day of training. The training runs brought back a lot of good memories from years past.

The Cowboys started on the front row and were able to stay in the top five for the first day of the race while they navigated down the San Marcos river in above average water conditions. Pavos was racing in the solo unlimited division and he was having a very fast first day and was not very far behind the Cowboys while they paddled their way down the upper San Marcos river.

The Cowboys paddled into a hard turn that was partially blocked by a large tree that had fallen into the river. The large tree was blocking about two thirds of the narrow turn. Lone Wolf did not have enough time to react and try to turn the 40 foot long canoe. The bow of the boat ran up on top the downed tree trunk and the boat came to a sudden stop.

Panic was starting to set in because it was very swift in this section of river and the boat was very unstable because of the bow being elevated and wedged on top of the tree trunk. Lone Wolf and Possum Belly were both yelling out instructions to the rest of the team but they were not on the same page and the situation they found themselves in was quickly getting much worse. The yelling and barking out of instructions was intense but it was not helping much because everyone was frantically trying to maintain their balance and keep the boat upright. Everyone started paddling backwards to try and pull the bow free but no progress was being made. Chris had to finally jump out of the bow seat on top of the large tree trunk and then try to push the boat back.

When Chris jumped out of the bow the loss of his body weight caused the stern to suddenly go under water and start moving sideways into the current. This caused the 40 foot long racing canoe to violently flip over and all of a sudden everyone was swimming. The boat was upside down when the strong current pushed it into the downed tree and pinned it there.

Polecat has experienced this kind of situation before and it can end very quickly with the boat breaking in half over the tree. Thankfully that did not happen because the current had it wedged firmly into the tree and the boat was floating just above the water line. It took a while but after a lot of team effort they were finally able to carefully pull the boat back into some calm back water that was next to the left bank. Some of the competition paddled by at this point and they had to stop and walk their boat through the tight turn because the Cowboys were blocking most of the river.

They probably should have thanked the Cowboys for that but there was no conversation between the boats. The boat pinning incident could have ended very badly for the Cowboys but they were able to overcome the near tragedy and get back to racing. .

This was turning into a very competitive race and the Cowboys found themselves in a big back and forth battle with two more multi man teams and one very fast tandem team. Pavos was still back there but they were not paying much attention to him because of the multi man teams close by.

Jason handed Polecat a fresh cup of hot coffee in a travel mug at the Hochheim checkpoint and he immediately became the best team captain Polecat ever had.

Polecat was asked to get into the bow seat at Cuero and he stayed there all the way down to the swinging bridge area near Bloomington. This pretty much completely wiped Polecat out physically. The intense stroke rate he tried to maintain combined with the scorching south Texas one hundred degree Sunday afternoon temperature was taking a heavy toll on him.

Polecat had to eventually move back to seat number five to try and regroup. JT jumped into the bow seat and took over setting the stroke rate for the team when they entered the last section of the race course. Willie was sitting in seat number four and was trying to talk Polecat through the down period he was experiencing. The Cowboys tried to increase the stroke rate while watching the sun make it's glorious descent on the western horizon.

Willie is Possum Belly's nephew and he had a lot in common with Polecat because he was starting his career in the overseas international oil business and Polecat was working in Angola, Africa.

JT was doing a great job yelling out instructions to Lone Wolf while they navigated through Seadrift cut with a bow light that was not working very well. JT has very good night vision and that was a big advantage for them due to the bow light problems. The Cowboys successfully paddled through the numerous low hanging tree limbs and finally made it to the mouth of Seadrift cut.

The decision was made to stop and quickly snap on the spray skirt because of the choppy bay conditions that they were getting ready to paddle into. That is when Possum Belly noticed a bright bow light that had all of a sudden appeared right next to them. This immediately caught everyone's attention and Polecat yelled out "where did that light come from".

Possum Belly answered that it was Pavos and he was right next to them. The team was focused on getting the 40 foot long spray skirt snapped on and this completely caught everyone by surprise. Jason did not mention Pavos being close to them when he was giving updates at the last checkpoint.

Someone shined a light on Pavos and he had a big smile on his face. He quickly jumped out of his canoe and started snapping on his spray skirt. This unexpected surprise motivated the Cowboys to shift into a higher gear and get this show back on the road. Polecat was very proud of Pavos doing so well in this race but there was no way he was going to allow him to beat them to the finish line. The thought of Pavos in a solo boat beating the Cowboys was just way more than Polecat could handle.

The Cowboys still had a chance at third place overall. The stroke rate increased and they gave it all they had left while they tried to pull away from Pavos. The irony of this situation was that Polecat had humbly prayed many times over the years to the Lord Jesus asking for support and guidance while he helped Darla raise their three boys. Polecat specifically prayed and asked the Lord for all of them to eventually grow up and become better men than he was in everything they attempted to do. That prayer was being answered right before his eyes.

The third and fourth place teams were just barely in front of them and the Cowboys gave it all they had left while they paddled the last few miles across San Antonio bay towards the seawall in Seadrift. Most of Polecat's attention was focused on the boat behind them because he was more worried about being passed from behind than he was about passing anyone in front of them.

The stroke rate was intense and they were doing the best they could while they watched the third and fourth place teams finish just eight and nine minutes ahead of them. The Cowboys finished in an official time of 39 hours and 11 minutes and in fifth place overall. Pavos ended up finishing just eleven minutes behind them.

The third through sixth place teams were only twenty minutes apart at the finish line. Polecat was standing in the waist deep water at the finish line and was the first person to greet Pavos with a big smile and hug while tears were streaming down his face. Pavos told him later that he had been paddling with Virginia, a very fast female solo paddler through several sections of the lower race coarse and that he had to pick up the stroke rate and paddle as hard as he could in order to stay in front of her.

Pavos smiled when he told Polecat that catching up with the Cowboys at the mouth of Seadrift cut was the biggest highlight of the race for him. Pavos said that when he paddled up next to them and everyone recognized him that the rest of the race did not seem very important. The Cowboys finished about as well as they could in this race even after wasting valuable time during the boat pinning incident. The most important thing that happened was when they barely were able to hang on and beat Pavos to the finish line.

The 2017 water safari training season came around very quickly and the phone was silent. Advancing age was gradually becoming a factor and the young and talented water safari racers did not have much interest in teaming up with an old Polecat. The previous two races had gone pretty well and Polecat was keeping himself in decent physical shape. The motivation was there to come back and try again.

Pavos and Heather were expecting their second child to be born into this world in May and he was very limited on what he could commit to that year. Pavos had finished nine straight water safari's and he really wanted to enter his tenth straight race but family obligations were holding him back from committing to one of the top teams. The old Polecat was definitely not his first or second choice for a teammate but he was still available and time was running out. Pavos asked Polecat to be his partner in the water safari and he was shocked and at a loss of words. Pavos is one of those young and talented water safari racers that the top teams are looking for. Polecat is one of those water safari veterans that can tell funny stories but is way past his prime.

The team came together late in the game and then they had to try and figure out what division they were going to enter. After some intense discussion the standard division was agreed upon. There was a big problem with that decision because they didn't have a standard racing canoe that could make it to the finish line in one piece. Pavos contacted John to find out if he still had a standard racing canoe available to rent out.

John is a water safari veteran that has won the race several times over the years with different teams. John builds some very durable carbon racing canoes that have a good reputation and track record in the water safari. Pavos and Polecat drove out to his place and looked over the standard racing canoe that he still had available. A quick test run down a short section of the San Marcos river was all that was needed to come to an agreement that this was the boat they should use in the race. John told us that the difference in his model compared to other racing canoe's was that you can paddle this boat over anything. "Don't portage around anything that can be paddled over because this boat can handle it" .

Landry was born into this world on May 17th and he is a blessing from the Lord. Heather came through the birth with no complications and Pavos celebrated the arrival of a new son. Darla and Polecat had the opportunity to proudly welcome a new grandson into the family.

Pavos and Polecat were able to get a few more training runs in and their picture appeared in the Victoria advocate sports section one week before the race. A reporter for the paper contacted Pavos and wanted to write an article and get a picture of them during a training run. The headline below the picture said "Family Affair", "father-son duo one of many competitors preparing for the grueling 265 mile canoe race".

This kind of unmerited publicity is an honor and is appreciated but it ends up putting a lot more self inflicted pressure on you before race day arrives. Pavos and the Polecat started the 55th Texas Water Safari on the second to last row and almost dead last. There were 141 teams entered and they had to start at the back of the field because of not running the pre-lim race together.

Tom led everyone in prayer and blew the starting horn before the mass chaos started. Starting almost dead last and then trying to make your way through all of the slower boats can be very challenging. This can sometimes end up with your team having to swim across Aquarena spring lake with your submerged canoe in tow.

Pavos and Polecat were able to fall in behind a very fast multi man team that started in the back of the pack with them. They were opening up a clear path towards the first island portage. The slower teams were reluctantly giving the six man team an opening to get through so they would not run over them. Pavos and Polecat were able to make it to the first portage upright and in good shape.

Pavos was constantly yelling out instructions to Polecat when they quickly carried their racing canoe over the island. This section of the race course was crammed full of racing canoes and they found them-selves in the middle of a large group. Rio Vista dam was next in line. Pavos and Polecat quickly portaged around the first drop and then jumped back in and successfully paddled over the next two drops with several submerged canoes floating upside down next to them.

They maneuvered over the last drop and ended up right next to a very fast five woman team. Pavos and Polecat could only paddle on the left side because their boat was right next to them. Pavos was barking out loud instructions when Polecat suddenly lost his composure and started yelling back. The constant criticism and orders that Pavos yelled at Polecat was something he was not used to and it was starting to get under his skin.

Polecat raised his paddle and yelled back, "You might as well be talking to this paddle because I'm not listening to you". Several of the young women in the long racing canoe next to them started laughing because they thought Polecat's response was funny. Pavos did not think his comments were very funny but he started to finally calm down a little and focus on what was ahead of them instead of what Polecat was doing.

Pavos was setting a good stroke rate and he refocused his attention on the next obstacle ahead of them instead of constantly critiquing everything Polecat was doing. This team was shaping up to be kind of like a horse and a donkey being on the same team with the horse con-stantly pushing the donkey to go faster. The old grey bearded Polecat was doing a good job keeping up with the intense stroke rate and was successfully helping maneuver the boat through the numerous obstacles on the upper San Marcos river.

Pavos and Polecat were following John's advice and were paddling over everything without having to portage. They were constantly pad-dling over the top pof partially submerged rocks and tree limbs. These were potential hazards that they would normally try very hard to avoid. This was helping them catch up with some of the competition and move into the top 20 overall while the sun started making it's glorious disappearance on the first day.

The stressful first day of the race was now behind them and they were the first standard canoe through the Gonzales checkpoint. Pavos and Polecat were both holding up pretty well at this point but it was going to be a long night of paddling while they made their way towards Hochheim. They tried to sing along with each other in order to stay alert and to maintain the good boat speed.

Joseph and Wade handed Polecat a hot cup of coffee at the Hochheim checkpoint and they suddenly became the best team captains Polecat ever had. Joseph went to Cuero High School with Pavos and he is the brother of Wade's wife, Julia.

Joseph and Wade were doing a great job and Pavos and Polecat deeply appreciated everything they were doing. Taking on the responsibility of being a team captain in "The World's Toughest Boat Race" is usually a thankless job that requires you to stay awake for hours on end while patiently waiting for your team to show up at some very isolated locations along the race coarse. The team captain's job is to perform a quick hand off of food and water before loading up and moving on down to the next spot to repeat the process.

The sun was making it's glorious appearance on Sunday morning and they celebrated the beautiful Lord's day by singing their favorite gospel songs and then bowing their heads in prayer.

Lord Jesus, thank you for your many undeserved blessings. We pray for the safety of everyone involved in this race and especially for those who are struggling today. We pray that you will help them and that they will accept you into their hearts and give you all the credit and honor you deserve. Amen.

"Pavos" is a believer and his adult life has reflected that faith. It was an honor and privilege for Polecat to be in the same boat with him on that beautiful Lord's day..

The second day turned out to be another scorching one hundred degree afternoon when they paddled into Floodplain ranch with the extended family cheering and yelling out encouragement. Polecat's beautiful grand kids, Aiden and Josie were standing there and that brought a big smile to his face. They briefly talked to each other while Joseph and Wade quickly changed out water containers.

This was the confidence boost they needed and the stroke rate started increasing. Pavos and Polecat would occasionally splash water on each other with their paddles and this would help their over heated bodies cool down a little. Polecat's expensive resistol cowboy hat would always come in handy during these extremely hot Sunday afternoon's. Polecat would occasionally take the time to dip it into the river and then put it back on top of his head full of water.

Pavos and Polecat were maintaining a pretty good stroke rate when they paddled through mile 200 at the Victoria riverside park check point. Friends and family were gathered at the checkpoint to encourage them while the sun was making its glorious disappearance on the western horizon.

Most of the water safari veteran racers Polecat knows do not like the lower sections of the race course below Victoria because this section is called hallucination alley for a reason. The mile long logjams below the swinging bridge checkpoint can be very difficult to get around and they move and change every year. Pavos and Polecat had an advantage over a lot of the competition because they lived close to this area and they would usually spend a lot of time training there.

Polecat was holding up to the intense stroke rate and extreme heat after 40 hours of racing but the hardest part of the race course was still in front of them. Pavos and Polecat paddled in to the swinging bridge checkpoint around two am on Monday morning. Pavos had stopped trying to be Polecat's personal coach earlier in the race but that mentality was starting to make a comeback when they paddled through the logjam cut and into Alligator lake. Polecat was not paying much attention to the constant critiquing and was focused more on all of the red eyes that were staring at them.

Pavos and Polecat paddled into the Tivoli checkpoint at the salt water dam just as the sun was starting to make it's glorious appearance on Monday morning. The bay crossing was reported to be rough but they didn't even stop and snap on the spray skirt. The standard racing canoe they were in has taller gunnels and it sits a lot higher above the water line. John's advice was to not waste time snapping on the spray skirt because the boat could handle a rough bay.

The funny part of that story is that Polecat mentioned to Pavos that maybe they should consider pulling over and snapping on the spray skirt before they entered into the turbulent San Antonio bay. Pavos did not respond to Polecat's comments. Several minutes of silence passed by before he finally gave him the bad news, "I forgot to put the spray skirt into the boat at the check in and it is still stored away in the back of the truck", was his surprising answer. That self inflicted oversight could have eventually forced them to swim across the bay and walk in to the finish line but they did not end up needing the spray skirt that was left in the back of the truck.

Pavos and Polecat were the first standard canoe to cross the finish line with an official finishing time of 47 hours and 8 minutes and in seventeenth place overall. Family and Friends were cheering and applauding while they watched them painfully crawl out of the boat they had been sitting in for two days. The crowd watched them awkwardly try to stand up and hug each other while tears were streaming down Polecat's face. Competing in "The World's Toughest Boat Race" with a close family member can be very challenging and filled with controversy but this race turned out to be a great experience and it was one of the most rewarding water safari's Polecat had ever done.

2017 went downhill in a hurry when Hurricane Harvey made it's unwelcome appearance in August. The eye of the category three hurricane came right by Floodplain ranch before stalling and then turning around and back tracking over the area for a second time. One hundred and ten mile per hour sustained winds and twenty inches of rain pounded the area and created a lot of damage.

The barn was completely leveled and damaged canoes were scattered all over the open pasture. Thank the Lord Jesus that the river flood that came knocking at the door after twenty inches of rain over a three day period did not get high enough to threaten the house. Darla and Polecat were stranded at home with no electricity and were cut off from the outside world for five days due to the county road being several feet under water.

The Guadalupe river had a lot of erosion and large sections of the river bank collapsed because of the local flooding causing the landscape around the river to dramatically change. Hurricane Harvey inflicted severe roof damage to a large percentage of the buildings throughout the area and the list of people that needed help included many friends and extended family.

The next several months were spent volunteering to help with tree removal and replacing damaged roof shingles on homes that needed repair. The take away and lessons learned from all those long days working on top of a very hot roof replacing shingles was that Polecat would never attempt to try and make a living doing that kind of work. Polecat did not want to climb up on another roof anytime soon. It took a lot of families in the area several years to fully recover from Hurricane Harvey. It was a blessing from the Lord to see volunteers from all over the country show up and offer to help with the recovery effort.

The Cowboys called in 2018 and wanted the old Polecat to team up with them and fill one of the seats in their six man boat. This caught Polecat by surprise because the old grey bearded Polecat was slowing down a lot and was just about at the end of his canoe racing career.

The thought of hanging his favorite racing paddle on the wall as a display at home and calling it quits had seriously entered his mind after the great experience with Pavos from the year before. The call from his cowboy brothers changed his thinking and gave him some motivation to come back and race with them one more time. Polecat accepted the offer because the six man team they were putting together also included his old friend, Hellgrammite.

This team was shaping up to be sort of like a reunion of the four man team they were both a part of back in 2001. Mike and Max rounded out the six man team and it looked like they had a good chance of possibly getting into the top five over all after a strong performance in the pre-lim race. The pre-lim ended up being a very fast sprint race that required them to double blade all the way down the 34 mile race course in order to finish in the top six. Double blading in a fast sprint race for that distance was something Polecat had not experienced in several years. That brought on a lot of joint stiffness and soreness that took the old grey bearded Polecat a few days to get over.

A very interesting event happened just a couple of days before the start of the TWS when Darla and the old Polecat were in Seadrift setting up their travel trailer in preparation for the race. They were walking out of a local restaurant towards their vehicle when Polecat looked down to see a flea infested and hungry puppy rubbing up against his leg. This starving puppy had the saddest look on his face that Polecat had ever seen and that caught his attention. He cautiously reached down to pet him. The large mixed breed puppy was soaking up the attention Polecat was giving him and he was very friendly. Darla was patiently waiting in the truck. Polecat reluctantly told his new friend goodbye and got into the truck for the long trip back home.

The parking lot was very busy and the puppy was in danger of getting run over. Polecat glanced over at him one last time. The starving puppy was staring straight at him and they were about to drive away when Polecat suddenly stepped on the brake and looked over at Darla. She knew exactly what he was thinking and before he could say anything she loudly said, "No, we don't need any more river dogs". Polecat had to get out and go pet him one more time. He brought him over to the truck in order for Darla to get a better look at the flea infested mutt.

It did not take long for Darla to change her mind after petting on him and he was soon loaded up into the back seat and was headed home with them. Jake is now part of the family and is a valuable member of the Floodplain ranch river dog security team. There is really no good way to explain this other than the Lord had once again laid on Polecat's heart that Jake was going to be the final reward for thirty six years of canoe racing. The only rewards that had any long term meaning for competing in "The Worlds Toughest Boat Race" were now completed with a flood cat from Martindale and a rescued dog from Seadrift.

The 2018 Texas Water Safari started with Mike, Max, Hellgrammite, Possum Belly, Lone Wolf and Polecat starting on the second row with

134 teams lined up in rows of six in Aquarena Spring lake. The first day was very fast and uneventful while the Cowboys paddled their way down the upper San Marcos river towards Gonzales. The first night was interesting. Lone Wolf and Polecat tried to keep everyone alert by competing against each other on who could tell the most unbelievable water safari stories from previous years. Polecat moved into the bow position at Hochheim. Joseph handed him a hot cup of coffee and he once again became the best team captain Polecat ever had.

It was turning into a very hot Sunday. They paddled their way down towards Floodplain ranch where they would be enthusiastically greeted by family and friends and the ranch river dogs.

Polecat was setting the stroke rate for the rest of the team from the bow position on Sunday and was feeling the effects of the fast pace and the one hundred degree temperatures. Mike took over at mile 200 in Victoria and Polecat was put back in seat number four in order to try and recover after a long hot day. The second night was very intense while the Cowboys carefully maneuvered their way through the low hanging tree limbs and brush at the logjam cut area.

The sun was making its glorious appearance on Monday morning when the Cowboys approached the salt water barrier checkpoint. Joseph gave them the bad news that there was a very rough San Antonio bay waiting ahead and everyone in front of them was having a very hard time getting across. The spray skirt was snapped on at the mouth of Seadrift cut and the decision was made to go straight across and follow the island barriers instead of angling across the wide open bay.

The primary bilge pump was not working and this was adding more stress to the situation because they had to pull up on the shoreline a couple of times in order to dump water. The Cowboys made their way over to the barge canal point and caught up with a multi man and tandem team that were desperately trying to figure out how to get through the very turbulent six foot waves.

The tandem team shoved off and decided to swim across the point with their boat in tow behind them. The Cowboys watched the amazing show from the bank. Chris and Shannon did not look like they were having much fun when they occasionally disappeared into the six foot waves. Polecat suggested to the rest of the team that maybe they should try and do the same thing. That was voted down very quickly. That would have been a bad idea for a six man team with a forty foot long racing canoe and would have surely ended in disaster or a boat rescue and disqualification.

The Cowboys slowly crawled back into the boat and started heading across the barge canal point while the large waves were crashing over the bow. The primary pump was not working and the forty foot long racing canoe was slowly filling up with water and was becoming very unstable. The Cowboys were able to successfully maneuver across the deep canal and make it into shallow water before the boat violently capsized.

Six people trying to wiggle out of a tight fitting spray skirt before they drown is something the old Polecat would not recommend for anyone to attempt. Teammates were scattered all over the place when they slowly pulled themselves out of the upside down racing canoe and were frantically gasping for air. Thank the Lord that everyone survived and was accounted for.

The Cowboys pulled the submerged racing canoe into shallow water and started bailing water out as fast as they could because the finish line was within sight. There was another multi man boat having similar problems right behind them. Several team mates were having a hard time standing up after almost 52 hours of continuous paddling and they could not help very much at this point.

The six staggering Cowboys managed to crawl back into the boat two more times but this quickly ended with two more bad wipe outs. The decision had to be made to help push Hellgrammite on top of the seawall because he could not stand up in the very turbulent water any longer. Lone Wolf and Polecat were trying to help each other stand up while they carefully walked through the chest deep water. Large waves were continuously crashing into them.

Mary was watching the chaotic finish unfold from the seawall and was overcome with emotion while she watched Lone Wolf struggle to stand up in the turbulent bay water. Darla was giving Hellgrammite some verbal encouragement while he stumbled and crawled along the top of the seawall. The other three Cowboys were slowly pulling the upside down and submerged forty foot long racing canoe towards the finish line.

The Cowboys finished in an official time of 53 hours and 42 minutes and in eleventh place overall. This was the first time Polecat had ever finished "The Worlds Toughest Boat Race" with the racing canoe upside down and completely submerged and teammates scattered all over the place. This was a very sad ending to an otherwise fast race and it was the last time that Polecat, Lone Wolf and Possum Belly teamed up together in the Texas Water Safari.

Eighteen TWS finishes with Lone Wolf and fourteen with Possum Belly came to an abrupt and sad ending on that windy Monday afternoon in Seadrift. Thank the lord that they have all remained close friends. Polecat still likes to call Lone Wolf and Possum Belly his cowboy brothers.

The 2019 water safari training season came around very quickly and Polecat was thinking about sitting out a year when Preacher Jim called and wanted to team up with him in the USCA C-2 division. Preacher Jim and Polecat are good friends and were teammates on the 2008 Cowboy six man team. This was turning into a family event again because Polecat was able to talk his youngest son Jordan into being the team captain.

Jordan and Polecat teamed up together for a couple of short canoe races in 2011 and then Jordan spent the next five years serving our country in the Marines. Jordan did the one hundred mile Colorado river race with Polecat and then was seriously considering being his water safari partner in 2012 but joined the Marines instead and headed out for boot camp in San Diego. The only communication Darla and Polecat had with him during his twelve weeks of boot camp was through hand written letters.

Jordan wrote them a letter not long after boot camp started and it brought tears to Polecat's eyes when he read it. Jordan said in his letter that the drill instructor told them to stand on the yellow foot prints at the entrance to the training base and then he told the recruits that they were now standing on the same foot prints where thousands of former Marines have stood before. Jordan then realized that he was standing in the same place where his grandfather had stood 63 years earlier. Darla and Polecat would spend a lot of time in prayer over the next five years humbly praying to the Lord Jesus to please watch over Jordan and his fellow Marines while they spent a lot of time rotating in and out of the war zone in Afghanistan.

Preacher Jim and Polecat were able to get a lot of training miles in together because he was working in Rockport with a flooring company. A funny event happened on their last training run on the upper San Marcos river just two weeks before the start of the water safari. The biggest mistake they made was to put in at the city park in San Marcos on a busy Saturday morning. Tom had told Polecat many stories over the last few years about how the tubers had taken over the upper sections of the San Marcos river and it would be very chaotic and crammed full of tubers on the weekend's.

Preacher Jim and Polecat got to see this up close and personal when they paddled around a tight turn on the upper river and were staring in amazement at the sight of approximately 500 tubers all bunched up together. This extremely large mass of tubers had the entire river blocked off from bank to bank and they had no choice except to completely stop and politely ask the tubers in the back of the pack to please open up a path way so they could safely pass.

This was just a training run and was not a race so wasting valuable time having a discussion with tubers was not an issue. The bad thoughts of just plowing through them like Lone Wolf and Polecat did to the kayakers in the Ireland race were dominating his thought process but Polecat was able to reject that temptation. Some of the tubers seemed to be a little irritated by the request when they slowly tried to paddle around them. The tubers were quick to reply with angry comments but they were able to stay calm and eventually work their way through the chaos. That was something Polecat had never experienced before and it was in stark contrast to what the San Marcos river was like when he first started paddling on it 40 years earlier. Polecat was praying this would not be a problem on race day because most of the water safari racers he knew would not slow down for tubers that were blocking the river.

Race week was quickly approaching and Preacher Jim had to withdraw from the race due to a family emergency. Polecat had to make a tough decision at this point. Sit this one out or go solo. Darla was not very happy with the decision to go solo at the last minute. Polecat was able to keep the starting position and remain in the USCA C-2 division even though he was technically doing the race solo in a USCA C-1. The legal specifications for these boats are the same and the only difference in the two divisions is if there is going to be one or two paddlers in the boat.

The water safari board had to have an emergency meeting because of his unique situation and they agreed that Polecat could remain in the USCA C-2 division even though he was going solo. The field was wide open in this division and there was a slim chance of doing well if he could just paddle a fast and error free race.

Polecat started on the seventh row with 176 teams lined up for the start of the 57th Texas Water Safari. The first day went pretty well with only a few close calls and a couple of minor wipe outs on the upper race course. This was Polecat's second race in a USCA C-1 and he was much faster and doing better this time around compared to seven years earlier. The average river levels were helping to make this a very competitive race in the USCA C-2 division and Polecat was able to stay within striking distance of the lead boat at the end of day one .

Being in a competitive race was helping to keep him motivated. Polecat made it through the first night without any major problems and Jordan became the best team captain he ever had when he handed Polecat a hot cup of coffee at the Hochheim checkpoint on early Sunday morning.

Sunday turned out to be a long and very hot and humid day. Polecat paddled down river towards Floodplain ranch where Darla, Jordan and the river dogs were waiting to greet him while the sun was making it's glorious disappearance on the western horizon. Jordan gave Polecat the good news that he was hanging in there and was still only about an hour behind the leading USCA C-2 team. Polecat had been chasing them since the start of the race 36 hours earlier.

The second night became a lot more difficult after 40 hours of continuous paddling by himself and with no one to talk to. Hallucination alley started to make it's ugly appearance. The very strange sight of a large cement dam blocking the entire river in front of him suddenly appeared out of nowhere while he paddled towards mile 200 in Victoria. There are no dams located in this area and after the initial shock of this weird sight finally wore off, he just smiled and paddled right through the imaginary dam.

The sun made it's glorious appearance on Monday morning. Polecat was closing in on the swinging bridge checkpoint and the mile long logjam. A couple of tandem teams were following him and he was enjoying the limited conversation. Polecat volunteered to show them where the log jam cut entrance was and how to portage over the downed tree that was completely blocking the entrance. This was over 55 hours into the race and he really needed someone to talk to so he did not mind showing them the best way to get around the logjam.

Polecat was still able to maintain a good stroke rate at this point but the mental and physical fatigue that slowly appears after sitting in a racing canoe and paddling as hard as you can for this long was starting to catch up with him in a dramatic way.

The last section of the race course across San Antonio bay was going to be a few miles longer this year because Seadrift cut was completely blocked off with hyacinth and weeds. This would force everyone to take trailer cut and go through the back end of Mission bay before reaching San Antonio bay and the finish line in Seadrift.

The sun was setting on the western horizon when he paddled by the abandoned fishing camp where he and Three Dots had wasted several hours putting metal art together around the campfire in the 1989 Texas Water Safari thirty years earlier. This was now about 61 hours into the race and Polecat's mental alertness was fading out very quickly. The bay was mostly calm and Polecat did not have to deal with a rough bay crossing like the Cowboys experienced the year before.

Darkness was setting in when he paddled up to the barge canal point and nothing around him looked familiar. Polecat was very confused on where he was. The next sequence of events that happened is very hard to remember in detail. Polecat paddled across the canal point and made it into some shallow water when he noticed that there were several travel trailers parked along the shoreline.

The finish line was only two miles away but he did not have any idea where he was or why he was there. The mental fog he was experiencing was getting much worse in a hurry. The boat drifted up to the shoreline and Polecat slowly stepped out into the knee deep water while staring at all of the bright lights that were lighting up the skyline around Seadrift.

A depressing thought slowly came over him and he convinced himself that the bright lights in the distance were actually cars and trucks driving over the causeway bridge in Port Lavaca. The terrible thought that he had somehow paddled past the finish line in Seadrift and ended up in Port Lavaca was making him very mad and emotionally depressed.

Polecat stood motionless in the shallow water while he stared at the imaginary and very busy causeway bridge. The mental breakdown was getting a lot worse while he tried to figure out what direction he needed to go in order to get back to Seadrift. Polecat started yelling out at the travel trailer that was parked close to him on the shoreline, "Hello, can you tell me where Seadrift is"?

There was no response from the trailer and he kept repeating himself over and over again. If there was someone inside the trailer listening to him ask for directions they were not responding because they were probably on the phone with the sheriff's office. They were probably very busy reporting the strange sight of a very loud and suspicious looking character that was standing in the knee deep water next to their trailer.

All of a sudden Polecat heard a very familiar sounding voice yell back at him, "Dad, what are you doing"? Jordan was standing on the bank close by and was trying very hard to get his attention. "Get back in the boat right now and head that way", was the next thing Polecat heard him say. Polecat suddenly recognized the voice that was yelling at him and started apologizing for taking the wrong turn and paddling to Port Lavaca. "I'm not going to quit, so please just tell me how to get back to the finish line in Seadrift", was the next comment while he tried to regain his composure.

Jordan sounded like a Marine MP that was yelling at a young boot camp recruit when he said, "You are not in Port Lavaca, the finish line is right over there". Another familiar voice then started yelling at him, "Get your rear end in the boat and get this thing over with because we are tired and we want to go home". Polecat's lovely wife Darla has a tendency to be very blunt and usually does not beat around the bush when expressing her feelings. Polecat thanks the Lord Jesus every day for putting her into his life and for their 43 years of marriage together.

The mentally challenged Polecat had a Marine MP and an angry wife yelling at him and it became very obvious to him that he needed to just get back into the boat and head straight to the finish line without saying another word.

Polecat paddled in to the finish line with a large crowd cheering and applauding. The official finishing time was 62 hours and 41 minutes. This was way back in the middle of the field but it was good enough for second place in the USCA C-2 division. Jordan told Polecat later that they were tracking his progress with the GPS coordinates from his spot tracker device and they noticed that he had stopped just two miles from the finish line. They followed the GPS coordinates to investigate.

The new water safari rules requiring every team to have a spot tracker device attached to their boat always seemed like an unnecessary and expensive burden to Polecat until this incident happened and he is completely on board with the new rule now. Darla informed the old Polecat a few weeks later that the 2019 Texas Water Safari would be his last solo race and that was the final word on that.

The 2020 Texas Water Safari was postponed and then was canceled because of the pandemic and nation wide lock downs. This was very disappointing but the old grey bearded Polecat used that down time from canoe racing to catch up on home projects and spending more quality time with his beautiful grand children. Darla and Polecat are blessed to have five healthy grand kids and they thank the Lord for them and that prayer will usually end with a "hallelujah" when their parents take them home after a long play day.

The 2021 training season came around very quickly and once again there was serious thought being considered to hang the racing paddle up on the display wall and retire from canoe racing one more time. Pavos called and wanted to team up with the old Polecat once again because he was very busy with his work schedule and helping Heather raise their three young boys.

Polecat remembered telling him when he was a young man that his day would soon come and the tide would turn and he would have to deal with the same kind of stressful situations that he often would put his parents through. The old grey bearded Polecat was not his first, second or third choice, but the call came late in the game and time was running out if Pavos wanted to enter the Texas Water Safari for the thirteenth time.

The 2021 Texas Water Safari could possibly end up being the old Polecat's 29th finish. The well used USCA C-2 they were planning on using needed a lot of attention and their good friend Horsefly was able to patch it up and put a new coat of resin over the bottom before race day arrived.

Pavos and Polecat were lined up on the last row because of not being able to do the pre-lim race together. There were 138 teams patiently waiting for Tom to lead the prayer and activate the starting horn. Polecat humbly lowered his head in prayer and emotionally thanked the Lord Jesus for giving him the strength and ability to be able to compete in this great race and for all of the many undeserved blessings. Polecat ended the short personal prayer by asking the Lord to please help everyone involved in this race to make it to the finish line in Seadrift safely. "Amen".

There were several strong teams entered in the USCA C-2 division that year and it was going to be hard for them to pull out a victory in Polecat's favorite division. Polecat's name is on the USCA C-2 trophy four times over a twenty five year time period and that was going to be very hard to add to in this race because of the strong competition.

The starting horn went off and Polecat quickly glanced over to the floating platform where his old friend Ralph the swimming pig would grunt in excitement and watch over the start of the race.

This might be the last time Polecat would be lined up to start "The Worlds Toughest Boat Race" and the funny memories were dominating his thinking while they sprinted towards the first island portage. Pavos is thirty years younger and a lot stronger than the old Polecat and they were once again shaping up to be kind of like a horse and a donkey on the same race team.

The old Polecat had learned from experience during their last race together to keep Pavos in the bow position so he would not constantly be motivated to be Polecat's personal coach. The race course was at a high level due to all the rain over the last couple of months and this was going to be a very fast race.

Shannon and Nathan were obviously the fastest team in the USCA C-2 division and everyone in the C-2 division would spend the first day just trying to stay close to them. Pavos and the old Polecat were able to paddle down the San Marcos river with just a few minor problems and were not that far behind Shannon and Nathan at the Gonzales checkpoint. The first night was very fast and problem free while they paddled towards Hochheim. Pavos and the old Polecat kept each other alert by singing their favorite country and western songs.

The great memories of Three Dots bellowing out Willie Nelson songs to Sandy and Janet along this section of the race course thirty three years earlier was putting a big smile on Polecat's face. Sandy and Janet were their racing friends from North Carolina and they always seemed to end up in a back and forth battle with the original Cowboys on the first night of the race.

Wade and Joseph were waiting at the Hochheim checkpoint and Wade handed the old Polecat a hot cup of coffee in a travel mug and Wade immediately became the best team captain he ever had.

The sun was making it's glorious appearance on Sunday morning. Pavos and the old Polecat sang their favorite gospel songs and praised the Lord Jesus through prayer. The second day was extremely hot and uneventful. They paddled into Floodplain ranch with several friends, family, grand kids and river dogs cheering them on. Woody and Jake could not be held back and they jumped into the river behind the boat after the water hand off was completed. The extremely excited river dogs swam as hard as they could and tried to keep up with them but eventually faded out of sight.

The river levels had dropped significantly over the past week and were now in the moderate range when they cleared mile 200 in Victoria and paddled towards the swinging bridge checkpoint. Pavos and the old Polecat were able to maintain a very fast stroke rate but were still well over an hour behind Shannon and Nathan. The reality was that they were probably way to far behind them at this point. Pavos and the old Polecat needed to stay focused and keep pushing themselves towards a strong finish somewhere in the top fifteen. There was a mixed tandem team very close to them below Victoria and that was helping to keep everyone motivated.

Matt and Libby were right behind them when they paddled into the swinging bridge checkpoint just after midnight on Sunday night. Matt was Polecat's teammate back in 2015 and they were keeping each other alert by exchanging funny stories from that race. There were three major logjams ahead of them and this section of the race course would once again become the great equalizer.

Pavos and the old Polecat reached the logjam first and were quickly trying to climb up the steep bank when Matt and Libby suddenly paddled up behind them. Pavos was able to pull himself up onto the muddy and steep bank and was trying very hard to pull the boat up behind him. The old Polecat was struggling to pull himself up the very muddy bank while Matt and Abby watched.

After 40 hours of sitting in a racing canoe the old Polecat was having a difficult time with his balance and mobility. Libby is in her early twenties and was feeling sorry for him. She started telling the old Polecat where to place his foot so he could climb the steep bank and get out of their way. The old Polecat was finally able to pull himself up the steep bank and was trying to regain his balance when he suddenly fell face first into a deep mud hole.

The Guadalupe river had dropped several feet over the past week and all of the banks on the lower section of the race course were nothing more than quicksand and mud holes. The old Polecat fell face first and was completely submerged in the deep mud hole that was blocking the path going forward. Pavos was busy trying to drag the racing canoe around the obstacle and was not very happy with the sight of the old Polecat being completely submerged in a mud pit.

Pavos walked back towards the old Polecat and yelled out in frustration, "get up and stop messing around. I need you to help me drag this boat through the portage." There was no offer of help. The old Polecat slowly crawled out of the deep pit and found himself completely covered in thick mud. The only thing he could do at this point was to try and quickly scrape the slime out of his eyes and mouth with his mud covered hands so he could see again.

There was no time available for a rinse off in the river because they had a fast team right behind them and the logjam cut was next in line. Pavos and the old Polecat had previously discussed the possibility of taking Cowboy cut around the next two logjams and a quick decision had to be made.

There is no good reason why this dense tree limb infested and brush lined cut is named after the Cowboys but the name seemed appropriate because no one ever goes that way any more.

The last portage did not go very well for them. Pavos was convinced that they needed to take Cowboy cut in order to avoid the last two log jam portages. The old Polecat eventually came around to his thinking and agreed that they needed to avoid any more mud pit portages if possible.

Pavos spotted the entrance to Cowboy cut and they quickly paddled into the hard to find opening. This ended up not being a good way to go because they spent the next hour laying on their backs and paddling themselves through low hanging tree limbs and thick brush. This was the hardest logjam cut adventure that the old Polecat had ever experienced.

Trying to paddle at a fast stroke rate while laying in a horizontal position on your back can be very difficult and painful. There was blood flowing out of the deep gouges and scratches that were located all over the old Polecat's face and arms. There were several painful incidents through the cut when the old Polecat would come face to face with a large tree limb that was hanging barely above the water line and it would pin him down into the bottom of the boat.

The old Polecat would then yell out to Pavos that they needed to go into reverse and back up and try another angle. The Cowboy cut adventure seemed to drag on forever before they finally made it into a section that was wider and more open. There was no time to celebrate because they paddled into the Alligator lake entrance and noticed a bow light at the far end of the lake. Pavos and the old Polecat both had the terrible feeling that they had lost a lot of time in Cowboy cut and that they had probably dropped back a few positions.

That was not the case because the boat directly in front of them was Matt and Libby. Pavos was a little confused on the correct route to take across Alligator lake because it looked a lot different after the drastic drop in river levels the past week. The old Polecat knew this area very well and had to correct him on the proper angle to take across the lake and exactly where the exit point was located. This was one of the few times in this race that the old Polecat had the opportunity to correct Pavos and he tried to not make a big deal out of it.

The sun was making it's glorious appearance on Monday morning when they paddled into the last checkpoint at the salt water barrier. Joseph and Wade were busy changing out the water containers when Pavos suddenly noticed that Shannon and Nathan's team captain was standing close by. Chris is a well known canoe racer but he had decided to sit this one out and be their team captain.

Pavos looked over at Chris with a confused look on his face because Shannon and Nathan had been almost two hours ahead of them. That last report had pretty much shut the door on any hope of being able to catch them.

Chris had a depressed look on his face when he started talking to Pavos. Shannon and Nathan were way behind schedule and were somewhere in Alligator lake. The old Polecat was not paying much attention to this conversation because he was busy talking to Wade and Joseph. Chris continued, "You guys passed them somewhere in the lake and it looks like they are just wandering around in circles according to their spot tracker coordinates."

The hand off was over pretty quickly. They started paddling over the submerged salt water barrier dam when Pavos gave the old Polecat the good news. "That was Chris back there and he told me that Shannon and Nathan are lost in Alligator lake." The old Polecat was stunned by this news and it took a few seconds before it finally sunk in that we were now in first place in the USCA C-2 division.

This was very unexpected and his first reaction to the news was to ask Pavos if they were OK or if they were in trouble. Pavos answered, "Chris told me that they are still somewhere in the lake and the spot tracker shows them just paddling around in circles." That was all that needed to be said. Pavos and the old Polecat quickly kicked it into a higher gear because they were now in the lead of their division and they were motivated to stay there.

Seadrift cut was next in line and there was just a light wind blowing out of the south. They were determined to try and get across San Antonio bay before the wind picked up. The stroke rate was back up close to sixty strokes per minute when they entered Seadrift cut and noticed a racing canoe upside down in front of them.

Matt and Libby were swimming towards the shoreline when they paddled up next to their submerged canoe. Pavos asked them, "what happened? are you alright?" Matt angrily replied, "a large needle nose gar knocked me out of the boat and turned us over". The old Polecat looked over at Libby while she swam towards the shoreline and said, "I didn't pay that gar to do that".

Libby didn't think that comment was very funny. Pavos and the old Polecat quickly paddled by and headed for San Antonio bay. It is not uncommon in this section of the race course to sometimes paddle over the top of a partially submerged gar and then they will suddenly jump out of the water and land in your boat. That is what evidently had just happened to Matt and his sudden reaction caused their canoe to turn over.

It was kind of ironic that Pavos and the old Polecat had just passed their main competition because they were taking a long extended tour of Alligator lake and now they had just passed a mixed team that had been knocked out of their boat by a large gar.

It is just amazing how everything can change in a hurry on the lower sections of the race course and that is why water safari veterans call this area the great equalizer. Pavos and the old Polecat had to keep the fast stroke rate going and give it all they had left because there were several fast teams right behind them.

Pavos made the comment that maybe they should consider pulling over and snapping on the spray skirt but the old Polecat told him there was no time for that before heading into the open bay. The old Polecat's thinking at the time was that this was shaping up as an all or nothing event and there was no way they were going to waste time snapping on a spray skirt with a very fast tandem unlimited boat right behind them.

The waves in San Antonio bay were manageable and they paddled straight across the open section of the bay towards the barge canal point and made the last turn towards Seadrift.

Several of the rolling waves were splashing into the boat but they just left the bilge pump running and were able to keep the boat mostly dry and stable. Pavos quickly glanced back and told the old Polecat that Matt and Libby were right behind them and that they were going to have to pick the stroke rate up even more in order to hold them off.

The new finish line at Swan Point added a few more miles to the bay crossing and that just meant that they were going to have to keep the intense stroke rate going for a little longer.

Pavos and the old Polecat crossed the finish line in an official time of 48 hours and 43 minutes with Matt and Libby just two minutes behind them. This was good enough for sixteenth place overall and they were the first USCA C-2 to cross the finish line. Pavos and the old Polecat were enthusiastically greeted by a cheering group of family and friends. They awkwardly tried to crawl out of the boat and congratulate each other.

The old Polecat was crying when he tightly hugged Pavos and thanked him for the great race and for being his teammate. Several of his beautiful grandchildren were standing on the bank waiting to greet them. The old Polecat stumbled and fell backwards into the waist deep water. He could not stand up after 48 hours of paddling and sitting in a canoe.

With some help from his grandson Aiden, the old grey bearded Polecat was finally able to climb up onto the bank where his lovely wife was waiting. They tightly embraced each other. This was a very emotional time for the old Polecat and he thanked all of the cheering and applauding people that were standing there. Darla was trying very hard to help the old Polecat stand up so he could hug and shake hands with everyone watching the show.

This race turned out to be a large family event and there were just a few missing names that would have made the list complete. It would have been great if his parents could have been there. Polecat really missed his Dad because he was his biggest fan and supporter before he went to be with the Lord eight years earlier. Jordan was going to college and working in Kansas. Three Dots was keeping up with the race by following their progress through the spot tracker online. It was time to clean up and get some much needed rest before any celebration could start.

They asked the old Polecat to lead the prayer before the awards banquet started on Tuesday and he was once again very honored and privileged to do that.

"Lord Jesus, we come to you today with humble hearts of gratitude. We thank you for getting everyone here safely. Please watch over everyone that is still on the race course and struggling to get here. I pray that they will seek you out for help and guidance. Thank you for all the race volunteers and for all of the time and effort that they put in to this great race. Thank you for the team captains and the work they do to make sure their team has all the necessary supplies they need in order to make it to the finish line. I pray that your name is honored and glorified by this race and by everyone standing here today. In the sweet and powerful name of Jesus we pray, Amen".

This prayer was once again the highlight of the race for the old Polecat and the Texas Water Safari board needs to be congratulated for continuing this long tradition at the awards banquet.

Pavos and the old Polecat were eventually called up on stage to accept the USCA C-2 traveling trophy and the large crowd seemed to enjoy the mud pit and cowboy cut adventure stories. There were hundreds of people gathered under several large tents at the awards banquet and the sight of such a large crowd was just amazing. The memories from the finishers banquet during the 1980's when there would be less than a hundred people gathered at the local restaurant in Seadrift was the direct opposite of what the old Polecat was seeing in front of him today.

The "Worlds Toughest Boat Race" has exploded in popularity and it has been exciting for the old Polecat to have witnessed the change. His prayer is that it will continue to grow and it will eventually become one of the biggest canoe races in the country.

When the awards banquet concluded the old Polecat took the opportunity to walk around and exchange stories with water safari friends and meet several new racers. This is a very competitive event but after it is over everyone is usually very friendly and they enjoy talking about their experiences on the race course.

Darla had to come hunt the old Polecat down in the large crowd and politely tell him that it was time to load up and head for home. Darla finally told him the bad news about Woody and Jake following them down river and they never came back home. Two of his beautiful river dogs had jumped in behind them when they paddled away from Floodplain ranch two days ago and they were now both missing. This disturbing news put an abrupt end to the old Polecat's race celebration and forced him to focus on a rescue operation.

Most of the next day was spent driving through the area's downstream of Floodplain ranch where there was public access. The old Polecat would occasionally stop to call out the missing dogs names.

Darla called and gave him the good news that someone she knew had posted on social media that a lost dog had been found on the side of the highway close to their place. Darla contacted her and it turned out that Woody had been found walking along the side of a busy highway. The old Polecat was thanking the Lord for that great news when a pickup stopped next to him. The driver rolled down his window asked if he was looking for a lost dog. The friendly man showed him a picture of Jake and explained that Jake was at his fishing camp seven miles down river. The old Polecat enthusiastically followed him to the fishing camp and immediately noticed Jake laying next to the fence. Jake ran up to him and they had an emotional reunion.

That was a great ending to a long race week and Jesus deserves all the credit. It took several weeks of rest and a lot of down time before the old grey bearded Polecat made the hard decision that the 2021 Texas Water Safari would probably be his last race. Big Willy was eventually hung up on the wall for the last time and these words were carefully inscribed on the blade, "I had a good run".

Matt and Polecat race down the San Marcos river in the 2015 TWS

Polecat jumping out of the boat during a portage in the 2016 TWS

The Cowboys in 2016 on the lower Guadalupe river with Polecat in
the bow

Pavos and Polecat race down the upper San Marcos river in 2017

Darla is telling Polecat that there will be no more solo races at the
finish line in 2019

Darla and Jordan with a smiling Polecat at the finishers banquet in
2019

Pavos and Polecat navigating down the upper San Marcos river in
2021

CHAPTER 23

The 30th Finish

2022 came around very quickly and the old Polecat was spending most of his time doing volunteer work and taking care of animals and chickens. The chicken flock had expanded to over 100 birds and that was turning into an expensive and time consuming part time job. Darla and the old Polecat would give away most of the fresh chicken eggs to family and friends or anyone who needed some help with grocery expenses. There were regular costumers that would pay for the delivered eggs but the old Polecat learned over time that you will never become a millionaire selling chicken eggs.

The cattle herd had expanded because there had been plenty of rain in 2021 and there was no shortage of grass. Boudreaux the wild Cajun donkey and his entourage of three female donkeys will usually keep everyone entertained with their very loud braying. Jake, Gus, Chili and Woodrow are the river dogs that lead the ranch security team. Marcos and Harley are the two rescued flood cats that faithfully guard the house and they round out the numbers at Floodplain ranch.

The water safari was not talked about very much because the old Polecat was retired from canoe racing and "Big Willy" was hanging on the wall collecting dust. Another big freeze event hit again in February 2022 and that ended up causing a lot of plumbing problems because south Texas is not prepared very well for those kind of events.

The weather was changing and it started turning very dry in late 2021 through the first half of 2022. The long range for cast was calling for more of the same with no relief in sight. The river levels were drastically dropping because of the lack of rainfall and the old Polecat eventually had to make the hard decision to downsize the cattle herd because of the dry weather conditions and lack of grass.

Pavos was very busy with his job and helping Heather raise their three sons. The Texas Water Safari discussion did not come up during family gatherings because everyone was focused on entertaining the grandchildren. That all changed in March when Pavos asked the old Polecat what his plans were for the 2022 race.

The conversation was a big surprise because the old Polecat had told everyone at the finish line in 2021 that his water safari racing career had ended. There was no way he could top what happened to him in that race. Pavos and the old Polecat had come from behind and passed a much faster team in their division and then they out sprinted a very good unlimited mixed team to the finish line.

The unexpected honor of placing his name on the USCA C-2 trophy for the fifth time was a great way to end his water safari career. There was no way to top any of that and the old Polecat was not in good paddling shape any more. Pavos told him that they were going to team up together because he was determined to help the old Polecat get that 30th finish.

The old Polecat figured that Pavos would get the "call" and end up joining a very fast multi man team that could compete for the Argosy cup. Pavos is a very strong canoe racer and he is well known throughout the racing community. Teaming up with the old grey bearded Polecat would be several steps down the competition ladder and would prevent him from getting on a top team.

Pavos would have to carry a lot of dead weight with the old Polecat sitting in the boat and that is why he was surprised that they were even talking about this. Pavos was determined to put this team together and the old Polecat suddenly found himself in an intense discussion about entering "The World's Toughest Boat Race" for the 31st time.

The one sided debate ended and then shifted to what division and boat they were going to use. The logical choice would be to enter the USCA C-2 division and use the same boat that they used in 2021. It is well used and abused and would require some extensive repairs to fix all of the damage before it would be ready for the water safari again.

The old Polecat said that he would call John to see if there were any boats still available to rent. They rented a standard racing canoe from him in 2017 and won that division. The boat held up very well in that above average water level race.

It became obvious to the old Polecat that his son was very serious about this and he was ready to start the planning and training. Pavos keeps himself in very good physical condition year round so the most pressing issue was if the old grey bearded Polecat could shift into high gear and get himself into canoe racing shape. The old Polecat used to stay in good overall physical shape in the offseason with marathon running and a lot of weight lifting when he was younger, but those days were long gone.

Getting into good enough shape to be able to paddle non stop for 265 miles at a fast stroke rate was going to be a big challenge for a senior citizen that had physically abused his body in this race for 30 years. It was time for the old grey bearded Polecat to get off his rear end and start working out.

The shift work schedule that Pavos had to deal with would limit them on getting training miles in together as a team. The old Polecat would have to start putting some paddling miles in by himself. The well used and abused USCA C-1 solo racing canoe would have to be pulled down off the retirement rack. The spiders, bugs and wasp nests would have to be swept off of it before it could be put into the river again.

Big Willy was pulled down off the wall and the several layers of dust that had accumulated were removed. The old Polecat couldn't hold back the tears when he stared at the words that were written on the blade. "I had a good run" reminded him of all the mental and physical abuse along with all the crazy experiences that he had gone through while competing in "The World's Toughest Boat Race". The irony of that moment was that he was now stepping right back into it after telling everyone that he was done after last years race. Please forgive me for not living up to that promise Lord Jesus.

Darla was not on board with this decision at first but started to warm up to the idea after the old Polecat explained to her that it would be a big family event with several family members involved. She would have the opportunity to spend a lot of time with their daughter in laws and grandchildren.

They would be entertained while watching all of the pain and suffering that usually takes place down the race course. "I knew there was no way you were going to retire from this race", were her sarcastic comments. "The only way you are going to stop doing this stupid race is when you can't physically do it anymore". She was on her soap box and the angry comments continued. "Don't expect me to follow you all the way down to the finish line because I will probably end up being the designated baby sitter". She was right on target with her comments. The old Polecat was very quiet during the soap box lecture and did not try to argue with her. The old Polecat reluctantly nodded his head in agreement that his last water safari would probably be when he could not physically do it anymore. That time was almost here.

It seemed like everything was slowly lining up and falling into place for this new team when all of a sudden everything changed. The Cowboy's had been in contact with Pavos about the possibility of teaming up with them for the water safari. One of the young and talented members on their six man team had abruptly quit and they now had two open seats available.

This offer caught the old Polecat totally by surprise and he was not ready to make a commitment to this. Pavos seemed to be very excited about the offer because he looked at it as as a much faster way to get to the finish line and there would also be four more teammates in the boat to help him get the old grey bearded Polecat to the finish line.

Something just didn't seem right about it. The old Polecat couldn't make a commitment because something was telling him that this was not the way to go. This was going to be a very hard decision and he needed more time to think about it. The five times he had paddled with the Cowboy's on a six man team in the water safari all ended up being very fast races and that was definitely a positive thing.

The 2018 race was the lone exception to that. That race ended very badly with the entire team scattered out and walking into the finish line with a submerged 40 foot long racing canoe in tow because of the very rough bay conditions. That experience at the end of the race was definitely a negative. There are a lot of positives and negatives when you are a member of a six man racing team.

It can be very difficult for six individuals with different talents and interests to mesh together and get along as a team. In the end it usually always works out because everyone has the same drive and motivation and that is to get to Seadrift as fast as you can. The main reason to not accept this offer was that the old Polecat wanted his last race to be more of a family event and it did not really matter to him what place they ended up in.

The old Polecat knew they could be competitive in the USCA C-2 division and the idea of paddling his last race with his son and with the extended family cheering them on down the race course was the overriding influence. The old Polecat called Pavos and told him that he would rather the two of them go C-2 and keep it a family race.

Pavos tried very hard to change his mind because he was worried about the lower water levels and the limited training time they would be able to put in before race day. The discussion went back and forth and finally ended when Pavos reluctantly agreed. The old Polecat told him that he would call Lone Wolf and thank him for the offer but they were going to stick with the original plans. That was going to be a hard phone call to make but it had to be done.

Lone Wolf and the old Polecat have done 18 water safari's together and it was going to be very difficult for him to say thanks, but no thanks. The old Polecat made the call to his racing friend and they talked at great length about what their children were doing. The old Polecat enthusiastically included his five grandchildren into the discussion. The conversation was very pleasant and funny because Lone Wolf has a good sense of humor and can tell water safari stories almost as well as the old Polecat can. The main subject eventually came up when he painfully explained to his friend that they appreciated the offer but they were going to decline. He explained that they were going to stick with the original plan of entering the USCA C-2 division.

The conversation stayed very positive and friendly. The good news was that the Cowboys still had two young and talented canoe racers on standby. That news made the old Polecat feel much better and made it a lot easier to turn down the offer. The phone call ended on a positive note.

Lower body workouts with light weights along with long solo training runs down the Guadalupe river would dominate the old Polecat's time for the next several weeks. He could still paddle pretty hard at a fast stroke rate but he was very limited on flexibility and being able to quickly jump in and out of a racing canoe. The lower body workouts were focused on stretching with weights and it was helping to improve his lower body flexibility.

The first day of the water safari on the San Marcos river is dominated with portages and obstacles and you are forced to jump in and out of your racing canoe very quickly in order to successfully get around all of the difficult hazards. This used to not be a big problem for a young Polecat but time and advancing age was catching up with him in a hurry.

The old Polecat called John to see if he had a racing canoe that was available to rent. John told him that he had damaged his knee while doing some outside work at home and he was told by his doctor that he needed surgery to repair the damage. The old Polecat was very sorry to hear about this because he had endured through two major knee surgeries himself. It was a very painful experience that required a lot of rehabilitation time.

John said that he was hopeful that he would be able to recover in time to start the water safari. John has a lot better overall record than the old Polecat does and they have raced against each other in different divisions several times over the years. They are both very competitive during the race but are always friendly to each other after the race is over. John said that he felt confident that he would recover enough to be ready to start the water safari. The old Polecat thought that was very optimistic because the race was less than three months away. He told John that he would be praying for him to have a successful surgery and a fast recovery when the call ended.

Pavos and the old Polecat showed up a few weeks later to try out the only USCA C-2 racing canoe that John had for rent. John was painfully hobbling around on crutches. He described the boat as being built for the water safari because it is a lot heavier than the newer models because of the extra layers of carbon on the hull. They launched it for a quick training run on the San Marcos river.

The old Polecat was very worried about the low river levels that they were seeing and the long range for cast was calling for more of the same. The thinking was that they were going to need a very durable racing canoe in order to make it to the finish line in Seadrift. Pavos didn't like the extra weight but agreed that the low water levels were going to force them to do things a little differently. They both agreed that this was the best option available going forward. The quick training run ended and they told John that they definitely wanted to rent the boat.

John tried to talk them into buying the boat instead of renting it but the old Polecat wasn't ready to spend that kind of money. This was probably going to be his last race and he didn't need another expensive racing canoe collecting dust on the boat racks back home. The thought of trying to explain the purchase of another racing canoe to Darla scared the heck out of him.

The old Polecat tried to talk John into trading the boat to him in return for several calf's. He had several large calf's that were ready to be sold and John owned a small ranch, so this offer made sense. John didn't seem to be very interested in the offer because of the drought and lack of rain. The rental price was agreed to and the boat was loaded on the truck for the ride back home.

John and the old Polecat were having a good time exchanging old water safari stories when the rental agreement was finalized. That is when John surprisingly confessed that he would be racing against them in the USCA C-2 division and he would be looking forward to the competition. He had recruited a well known canoe racer from Missouri to be his partner.

Pavos knew who he was talking about and commented that Joe had a reputation of doing very well in the Missouri 340 canoe race. This discussion caught the old Polecat by surprise and he agreed with John that he would also be looking forward to the competition. They now had a racing canoe that was ready to go. The bigger problem going forward was if they would be able to get enough training time in together before race day.

The next several weeks went by pretty quickly. Pavos and the old Polecat entered the Texas river marathon canoe race in early May. This sprint race determines the starting positions for the water safari and it is usually a very fast race. The old Polecat is not a sprint racer. The young and talented canoe racers always seem to dominate these shorter races. If you add another 230 miles to the race course then the old Polecat can be competitive. The primary objective in this sprint race is to do the best you can and secure a good starting position for the water safari.

The start of the water safari can be very chaotic and you can usually stay in front of all the crazy stuff with a good starting position. That was the motivation that they had for this race and it would also serve as another good training run opportunity.

Possum Belly called and asked if he could stay at the old Polecat's house on the night before the prelim race. It was good to hear from his old racing partner and he was glad there were no hurt feelings. The Cowboys were able to recruit two more young and talented racers to fill out their six man team and that all ended well. Possum Belly showed up on the Friday night before the race and they had a good time exchanging old racing stories from past years. It turned into an unofficial contest on who could tell the most unbelievable story. Possum Belly can tell funny stories but he still has a long ways to go before he can catch up with the old Polecat. It was getting late and so the laughing and story telling finally had to come to an end because of a scheduled race the next day.

Pavos and the old Polecat filled out the required paperwork and launched their rented racing canoe into the Guadalupe river on that beautiful Saturday morning. After a quick warm up paddle they pulled over to the river bank and started talking to several other racers that Pavos knew. The old Polecat does not know very many of the young racers anymore but they always seem to know who he is. There are very few canoe racers from the 1980's and 90's that are still active in the sport and the old Polecat is one of the few old timers that is still hanging on.

The friendly conversations with the other racers distracted them and the starting horn went off. This caught everyone by surprise. Pavos and the old Polecat started almost dead last because they were more interested in talking to the other racers than they were in paying attention to what was going on around them. One hundred and seven boats jammed in together for a mass start can sometimes be very challenging to get through upright. Sometimes it makes more sense in this environment to hold back at the start and let the field spread out some before sprinting forward.

There were several boats upside down in front of them and the occupants were frantically trying to swim with their submerged canoes over to the nearest bank. Pavos was not very happy with the start of the race but the old Polecat did not see it as a problem. It would be a lot more fun passing the boats in front of them instead of the other way around.

They quickly got up to sixty strokes per minute and started passing the slower boats. They were headed for the famous Polecat rapid just above Floodplain ranch. There were a couple of boats upside down at Polecat rapid when they paddled through the famous area with very few problems. The dry and humid conditions along with the lower river levels were going to make this a long race.

They were passing several teams when they approached Floodplain ranch. The old Polecat could hear his beautiful river dogs howling in excitement. Joseph was standing there with water containers but they did not slow down to do the handoff. The slow start meant that they would have to keep the fast stroke rate going all the way down the race course. Darla was standing on the bank and was able to keep the river dogs from following them down stream. Woody and Jake had followed them down river for seven miles during last years water safari and they did not want to deal with that again. They were very fortunate to find them alive several days later and get them back home.

Pavos and the old Polecat were now back in a group of boats that were moving along at about the same speed that they were. The fast pace picked up even more when they tried to pull in front of this group. There was a young mixed team that was in the USCA C-2 division right in front of them. They tried to pick up the stroke rate and pass them but the young racers were able to stay in front of them. Pavos and the old Polecat tried very hard to pass them in the long open sections of the river. They did not know who this young team was but they were very fast.

This very fast stroke rate continued while they made their way through the Nursery area. Joseph was able to throw a couple of fresh water jugs into the boat when they paddled by him without slowing down. The fast stroke rate and the hot Saturday afternoon temperatures were causing several teams in front of them to slow down. They were able to pass a couple more teams before they paddled by the Victoria riverside park boat ramp. There was only four miles left and the young mixed team that they had been chasing all day was still barely ahead of them. It looked like they were slowly closing in on them when they made the last gradual turn towards the finish line.

That is when they made a critical error and didn't notice that the bow of the boat was being sucked over towards a low hanging tree limb on the left side of the river. The strong current then pulled the boat directly under the very large tree limb and Pavos was dragged out of the canoe. The large limb pinned him down in the boat and then it yanked him out of his seat and into the water. The old Polecat was also pinned down in his seat by the same tree limb and had to slowly crawl out. The water was only about knee deep in this spot and they were both able to stand up in the swift current without getting swept down river.

Another tandem team came flying by at a high rate of speed. They were just about to crash into the pinned canoe when the old Polecat grabbed the stern and pulled it out of their way. They banged into the side of the boat but were able to stay upright and get by the pinned canoe without a wipeout. Pavos grabbed the bow of the pinned canoe and was able to drag it out from under the tree limb. He started dragging it closer to the bank while two more tandem teams came racing by.

Pavos and the old Polecat quickly dumped the water out of the boat and were able to jump back in and sprint across the finish line just a few yards away. The crowd was very entertained by the comedy show and were loudly cheering and applauding when they paddled across the finish line. This unforced error was not a very good ending to a long day of racing and it ultimately cost them three places. Pavos and the old Polecat finished in 36th place overall.

This was not a very impressive performance and the boat pinning incident at the finish line just added salt to the wound. They both had paddled very hard for the entire race. Pavos was probably going to blame the old Polecat for letting the boat get sucked under the low hanging tree limb.

Pavos seemed to be in a good mood while he tried to wipe away all of the blood that was oozing out of the deep scratches and lacerations on his arms and legs. They slowly climbed out of the boat and Joseph helped them carry it up the bank. Most of the canoe racers and spectators that were standing there were talking about the entertaining finish. Polecat tried to explain the incident by saying that they were just trying to make it exciting for everyone at the end.

Darla and the grandkids were there and he quickly had to change gears and start playing with them. Joseph told them that they finished third in the USCA C-2 division and would receive an award at the closing ceremony. The good news was that the main objective in this sprint race had been accomplished. The 36th place finish would probably put them somewhere around the sixth row for the start of the water safari.

The awards ceremony ended and they received a very nice hand made wood cutting board with the Texas river marathon engraved on it.

The old Polecat quickly gave his to Joseph because he had driven all the way down from Houston to be their team captain. Team captains do not get much recognition even though they are a very important part of the team.

Trophies and recognition are not the reasons why the old Polecat still competes in this sport. Darla's blunt comments during the 1988 water safari had forced him to do a reality check and finally understand the real reasons why he was competing in marathon canoe racing. Strengthening his faith and perseverance while pushing himself to his mental and physical limits were the real reasons.

Tom and Paula were at the awards ceremony to watch their son in law Tommy accept the first place trophy. Darla and the old Polecat ventured over to them and started up a conversation. Tom and Paula are good friends that own a campground on the upper San Marcos river. The upper San Marcos river has been taken over with tubers and partiers but Tom and Paula have not bought into that mindset and they continue to use their campground for Christian based groups to gather.

Tom has been dealing with spinal muscular atrophy for several years and it has slowly affected his mobility and his voice. Tom was a mentor to the old Polecat when he was starting out in this sport and he has always appreciated and respected Tom's advice. The old Polecat purchased three racing canoes from him back in the 1980's along with paddles and equipment.

The conversation started out with everyone talking about their families and grandchildren. It soon shifted to old water safari stories. Tom can tell old water safari stories with a lot of humor and the unofficial story telling competition took off. Tom remembered several funny stories about the original Cowboys that the old Polecat had long forgotten about.

Three Dots and the young Polecat were never a serious threat to the top teams but they were fondly remembered by other racers from that time because of the many funny stories that happened to them. Tom is the unofficial historian of the water safari and the old Polecat had several questions about the history of the race that he was able to answer.

The water safari story telling contest seemed to go on for a while before Darla and Paula interrupted and told them that it was time to load up and head for home. Polecat promised to bring them some fresh chicken eggs when he headed up towards the Martindale area for water safari training. It was time to get some rest after a long day of canoe racing.

The next several weeks would be dominated with long training runs on the Guadalupe river and making all the necessary preparations for the water safari. Pavos and the old Polecat would only be able to do one long training run together on the upper San Marcos river before race day. The promised fresh chicken eggs were delivered to Tom and Paula. The river levels were drastically dropping to levels not seen since 2009 and there was no rain in the for cast as race day approached.

The "Texas Water Safari" race week is a very chaotic and busy time that is dominated with making all of the last minute preparations for the hardest thing you will do all year. This race was shaping up to be a lot tougher than usual because of the very low river levels down the entire race course. The weather for cast was calling for 100 degree temperatures on race weekend.

This is not uncommon for the lower sections of the race course near Victoria but this was very unusual for the upper San Marcos river. The reality of the situation was that everyone would be racing down a very low San Marcos river on Saturday in 100 degree temperatures. A young Polecat would have looked at this as an opportunity to level the playing field with the faster teams but the old grey bearded Polecat has slowed down a lot in his advancing age. These extremely hard conditions could possibly slow him down even more.

A reporter from the Victoria advocate newspaper unexpectedly called the old Polecat. The reporter had received his phone number from another canoe racer and he wanted to do a phone interview that could possibly be published in the sports section of the paper on Saturday. The reporter was very interested in the old Polecat's attempt to finish "The Worlds Toughest Boat Race" for the 30th time. The reporter had some basic knowledge of the water safari after doing a phone interview with Allen, the race director.

The old Polecat tried to explain to him in detail just how hard this race was going to be on everyone involved because of the harsh conditions they were facing. The reporter asked some specific questions about his past water safari experiences and the conversation dragged on for a while. The old Polecat told the reporter that the very low river levels were comparable to the 1989 water safari but it was not as low as it was for his first finish in 1984. That could change in a hurry.

Race weekend showed up very quickly and the plan was to ride together to the Friday afternoon check in. Pavos and the old Polecat would then head back home for a good nights rest in their own beds instead of getting expensive motel rooms in San Marcos. This would require a 90 mile drive back up to Aquarena spring lake on Saturday morning but it would end up being a lot easier and less expensive for everyone.

They both chipped in to get Joseph a nice hotel room in San Marcos. Their team captain was going to need a good nights rest before having to follow them down the race course for the next three days. Joseph and Wade had been drafted into the team captain positions for boat number 30. They both had volunteered for the same positions a year earlier and did a great job. They were penciled in for this years race before anyone had the chance to say no. Their names were placed on the official entry list before they were officially asked. It is very hard to find experienced team captains for this marathon canoe race and they had two good ones. It didn't matter whether they wanted to or not.

The 59th "Texas Water Safari" was scheduled to start on the second Saturday in June and it was a very warm and humid morning in San Marcos. Darla was asked to be the designated driver for the team and she agreed to drive them to San Marcos early on that Saturday morning.

There were 138 teams making last minute preparations to their boats and equipment when they arrived at spring lake about an hour and a half before the start of the race. They were both hyped up with excitement and anticipation when they arrived to make the last minute adjustments. Polecat was very busy talking to the other racers that he knew while Pavos did most of the work. Pavos has a tendency to be focused on details that the old Polecat doesn't think are all that important.

The required equipment, big Willy and a backup Cowboy hat were secured on board and everything was good to go as far as he was concerned. Joseph and Wade would be supplying them with food and water along the race course and that had all been planned out in detail ahead of time. The old Polecat was basically going to be on a liquid diet for the next three days. The excitement of race day was here and the old grey bearded Polecat was soaking it all in for the last time.

A young man came up to the old Polecat and introduced himself as a reporter for the Victoria advocate newspaper. This was not the same reporter that he had talked to on the phone earlier. The reporter explained that the first phone interview had generated a lot of on line interest in the story so he was sent to do a second interview before the race started.

Polecat enthusiastically agreed to his request but Pavos was not very excited about the interview offer because he was busy with securing stuff in the boat. The nice young man started asking the old Polecat several specific questions about the race. The excitement of race day was very evident in his funny answers. Joseph was standing there and Polecat tried to get him involved in the interview.

Pavos reluctantly stopped what he was doing for a few minutes in order to answer specific questions that were directed towards him. The interview only lasted for a few minutes because it was getting very close to the time that they needed to get into the lake for a warm up paddle. The interview ended and the old Polecat thanked the reporter for being there.

It was time for the team prayer. The old Polecat took off his well used cowboy hat and lowered his head in humble prayer. "Lord Jesus, thank you for this beautiful day and for the physical ability to be able to compete in the worlds toughest boat race. We pray for the safety of everyone here today. The canoe racers, team captains, volunteers and race officials and all of the spectators that will be following the race down to Seadrift.

We pray that your name will be lifted up and honored during this race. We pray for all of these things in the powerful name of Jesus, Amen".

The old Polecat lifted his head up and put his well used cowboy hat back on. That is when he noticed that several other racers had walked over and joined them in prayer. This race will push everyone involved to their physical and mental limits and having a strong relationship with the Lord is very important. The Lord cares about a personal relationship with you.

Pavos and the old Polecat launched their rented racing canoe into spring lake for a quick warm up before all the chaos started. The advocate reporter followed them over to the lake and took a picture of them while they shoved the boat into the water. All of this undeserved attention was starting to embarrass the old Polecat. A picture of the old grey bearded Polecat shoving his racing canoe into spring lake would be on the front page of the Sunday newspaper. The headline would be "Take me to the river; Thomaston man attempts to complete 30th Texas Water Safari".

The Victoria advocate had not shown this much interest in the water safari for many years. The best way to look at it was that they were helping to promote the race to the crossroads area. It was time for the old Polecat to clear his mind of all this irrelevant stuff and focus on the race.

They did a quick warm up paddle down to the island portage at the end of spring lake and tried to figure out what would be the best route to take. The best route at this portage is usually just taking whatever route is available and not letting yourself get jammed in with other boats. That could mean having to make your own pathway through the dense vegetation that covers the island.

Pavos and the old Polecat made their way back to the starting line and lined up on the sixth row. The brother and sister team that beat them in the prelim race was lined up directly in front of them on row five. This was going to be a lot different race and they were not to worried about them. The team they were more concerned about in their division was Joe and John and they were starting way back in the pack.

John was not able to compete in the prelim race after his knee surgery but had recovered enough to start the water safari. They are both strong paddlers with a lot of experience and would probably end up being the main competition on the lower sections of the race course.

Pavos was very busy talking to his racing friends that were in the multi man teams lined up in front them. The old Polecat was quiet and was staring at the floating dock that was on the left side of the lake. The floating dock is the very same platform where his old friend Ralph the swimming pig would proudly stand guard over the start of the race many years ago. Ralph would be grunting in excitement when the stating gun went off. This was one of the many water safari traditions that had ended over thirty years ago. The old grey bearded Polecat would soon be joining Ralph as just another fading memory in the "Worlds Toughest Boat Race".

It was great to hear Tom's voice when he briefly went over a few last minute race announcements. Tom then asked everyone to bow their heads and he led a beautiful prayer. The old Polecat is thank full that the water safari board still lets him do that. That is the one water safari tradition that he hopes will never be discontinued. The quiet and stillness around him was deafening while all 138 teams and the large crowd that was watching from the bank listened to the prayer. Tom's voice is not what it used to be but he still gets his message across loud and clear to those who are listening.

Several names were mentioned that had just recently passed away. They had a lot of influence on the water safari years earlier. Mr. Daniel was well known to all of the old racers because of his famous log book. He would log everyone's split times on the different sections of the race course while he followed his son Horsefly to the finish line. This was back when split times were logged manually. Donna was one of the early trail blazers who helped put together some very competitive female teams in the late 1980's. This changed the race for the better and forced the board to start a women's division. They were both remembered for their contributions and positive influence on the TWS.

The starting horn suddenly went off and the chaos started. The race horse and the old donkey shot out of the sixth row pretty quickly while trying to avoid the large swells that the multi man teams were creating in front of them. The other problem that you try very hard to avoid during a mass start like this is getting stern hooked from behind. That will usually end up very badly when your canoe gets turned sideways and boats start crashing into you from behind.

Pavos was paddling as hard as he could while the old Polecat tried to keep the boat lined up straight and at a safe distance from the other canoes around them. They made it to the island portage pretty quickly and the route they had planned on taking was jammed full with other racing boats. A quick decision had to be made on an alternate route when they paddled the boat up onto the bank.

Pavos was able to jump directly onto the bank but the old Polecat had to jump into chest deep water. Pavos started dragging the boat up onto the island while the old Polecat had to swim a short distance and then crawl up on the bank. By the time the old Polecat was able to get up on his feet Pavos had already drug the boat halfway through the portage. Polecat had to start jogging with his paddle in his hand in order to catch up with him and help carry the boat through the rest of the thick vegetation. This was not an easy portage. They stumbled through the large rocks and vegetation and were able to get over the island with just a few minor problems. The old Polecat's legs were covered with the weeds and vegetation that grow in the water along the banks of the upper San Marcos river. There was no time allowed to stop and pull it off.

The next hurdle to get through would be Rio Vista dam. This has always been a fan favorite place. The banks are lined with water safari fans who are waiting for the next wipeout to watch. The old Polecat's white water experience and mentality has always tried to lure him into paddling over everything. Rio Vista dam used to be just one big drop and it was manageable to paddle over at certain water levels. They made it into three different drops and it changed everything dramatically.

The first drop is not normally runnable unless you are in a kayak. Experienced water safari racers will portage the first drop and then paddle over the next two drops. The old Polecat wanted to do that but Pavos just wanted to portage around all three drops and not risk taking on large amounts of water and wasting valuable time. The debate was heating up when they paddled up to the first drop and climbed out of the boat. The old Polecat was desperately trying to convince Pavos to put the canoe back in and run the last two drops but he was not listening.

Pavos won the argument and they carried the boat around the three drops. The only good thing about that last minute decision was that two of his beautiful grandchildren were standing on the bank cheering them on when they carried the boat by them. The old Polecat was able to smile and wave at Josie and Augie when they quickly ran by. The portage decision was a good choice because they were able to pass several teams that were slowly trying to paddle over the last two drops.

Pavos and the old Polecat got back into the boat pretty quickly and were headed for the next obstacle. The upper San Marcos river is a never ending series of sharp turns and portages. The USCA C-2 division is at a big disadvantage on this section of the race course because rudders are not allowed on these boats. Racing experience and a lot of training in this type of canoe is required in order to successfully navigate through these hard turns without having to slow down very much. Picking up the stroke rate and working together in sync is very critical during this process.

The unlimited teams with rudders on their boats do not have to deal with these type of problems. Pavos was paddling at a high stroke rate while the old Polecat quickly switched sides and pulled the stern into the direction it needed to go without putting a brace out and slowing the boat down. This can be an energy depleting sequence of events while the hard turns and long portages seem to drag on for several hours down the upper San Marcos river.

Joseph and Wade were waiting at the designated handoff spots with cold water jugs and sport bottles that were filled with the high energy drink mix that they would be depending on for the next three days. They managed to pass several other teams during this process and were moving along at a fast stroke rate with very few problems. The old

Polecat was holding up pretty well to all of the hard paddling but was a lot slower than Pavos at the portages. He can't jump in and out of the canoe with reckless abandon like he used to be able to do in the old days. Pavos would be dragging the boat through the portage before the old Polecat could catch up and help. The beefed up USCA C-2 that they rented from John was holding up well through all of the abuse.

The Old Mill rapid has turned into the most challenging rapid to paddle through on the upper San Marcos river. Pavos and the old Polecat carefully navigated through the three different sections of semi submerged rocks and made it through with just a couple of near misses and several hard scrapes on the bottom of the boat.

Cotton seed rapid was next in line and it has drastically changed over the years. This used to be one of the most dreaded obstacles on the upper river but the memorial day flood of 2015 had washed it out and the rapid was not as difficult as it was back in the good old days. The memories of Three Dots and a young Polecat banging into submerged rocks and severely damaging their racing canoe was putting a big smile on his face when they paddled through the rapid.

There was a big crowd gathered along the bank and the old Polecat could here his grandchildren yelling out, "Go Polecat Go". Their dads used to yell the same thing at the same place thirty years ago. The old grey bearded Polecat was soaking up these great memories. This section of the race course has turned into a tubing paradise and he could not see himself paddling through this area again after his water safari days were over.

There were several fisherman in kayaks along with small groups of tubers floating down the river near the Martindale area when the river started straightening out and opening up. Pavos and the old Polecat picked up the stroke rate a little more to take advantage of the longer and wider sections of the river. The small tubing groups were not slowing them down very much at this point and they were able to carefully paddle around them without banging into anyone.

The low river level was starting to force everyone into the deeper channels and that was going to eventually create bottlenecks. Large groups of tubers were jammed together through some very narrow and swift areas. There seemed to be less and less room to safely pass by but they were managing to get through the tubing jams without running anyone over. That was all about to change when they quickly portaged Staples dam and started heading towards Fentress.

Joseph and Wade were waiting at a gravel bar below the dam to give them fresh water jugs and to hand the old Polecat a couple more sport bottles of drink mix. The meal replacement drink mix was helping to keep his energy level up and he was downing them as fast as he could. The chocolate drink mix was all over the front of his long sleeve racing shirt and it looked like the old Polecat had more of it on him instead of in him.

All five of his beautiful grandchildren were there and were excitedly cheering them on. This race was going pretty well for the horse and the old donkey at this point. They were hoping that all of the chaos was now behind them and that they would be able to focus on a fast stroke rate and boat speed instead of human obstacles in the river.

The tubing groups seemed to be getting much larger and louder when they approached the Fentress bridge. Pavos and the old Polecat were expecting to find a large party group in the river at the campground below Fentress but they had no idea what they were about to paddle into. The land owners down in this section of the river have turned their property into riverside party places with cabanas and bars lined up along the river bank.

This same section of river was populated with cows and wildlife forty five years ago when a young Polecat used to do overnight canoe trips through the area. Times sure have changed a lot and they were now paddling into the middle of the biggest party event that they had ever seen. The tubing groups were much larger and were spread out across the river. Pavos and the old Polecat had to follow the deeper channels in order to keep from running aground.

The partying tubers were blocking the channel and did not seem to be concerned about a canoe trying to paddle around them. This was a race and they did not want to slow down but they had no choice. There were a lot of young children in the groups and they could not paddle through them at racing speed without running over several of them.

Pavos was very busy asking them to please open a route through the masses. Some of the tubers were willing to move out of the way but there were many more who would not even respond to his request. This was very frustrating while they carefully paddled through and around the large party group without running anyone over.

The next large group was directly in front of them and this time wasting procedure had to be repeated over and over again. Pavos was getting very irritated with the situation and he suddenly stopped asking for a clear route through and started making his own. The memories of Lone Wolf and a young Polecat running over all of the kayaks that would not get out of their way in the Ireland canoe race in 1998 were making the old Polecat smile. The Irishmen were cursing and using words that Polecat did not even understand when they ran over them at racing speed. They would not move over and give the Texans with no hats a clear route through.

It looked like this was shaping up to be a similar type situation. Pavos and the old Polecat tried to avoid the young children but anyone else who ignored their warnings were fair game. Several of the partiers had to quickly jump out of their tubes before they were bumped into. There was some limited cursing and finger pointing but nothing like what the old Polecat had witnessed in Ireland.

The tubers in front of all this commotion started to get the message that they were not going to slow down and they needed to get out of the way in a hurry. That is when a clear route started to open up and they were able to get through the next few large groups without bumping into anyone.

This was almost like trying to navigate through a very long and turbulent rapid because of all the back and forth maneuvering that had to be done. The tubing jam lasted for several more miles before it started to ease up a little. The old Polecat had never seen this many people on the San Marcos river before. The campground was next in line and they knew that this was going to be another very difficult place to get through.

They made the final turn towards the campground and could not believe what they were about to paddle into. Hundreds of people sitting in lawn chairs in the river and under cabanas along the bank on both sides of the river for as far as they could see. It looked like a sold out outdoor football stadium that was patiently waiting for the home team to come running out onto the field. This was such an overwhelming sight that Pavos and the old Polecat were speechless.

They were having a good time sitting in the water and partying and they were not gathered there to watch water safari teams come racing by. The race horse and the old donkey showed up at just the right time to add some more excitement to the party. There was a large crowd on both sides of the river and they were blocking most of the river with their lawn chairs, canopies and tubes. The large crowd started clapping and cheering very loudly when they carefully navigated through the massive people jam at racing speed. They did not run anyone over because everyone seemed to understand that they were in a canoe race. Everyone was trying to get out of the way.

This was a very different reaction than what they had just experienced with the large tubing groups upstream. Pavos and the old Polecat thanked them for the support while they cautiously paddled through the narrow open lane for over a half mile. This was one of the craziest experiences that the old Polecat had ever been through on the upper San Marcos river. The race horse and the old donkey had been bumping into several angry tubers and then all of a sudden they paddled through a packed sports stadium that was cheering them on. An unbelievable sequence of events.

Pavos had been very quiet through most of the chaos. The river was opening up and the large groups of tubers were starting to thin out a little when he said, "Can you believe what we just went through"? The old Polecat answered, "No, I have never seen anything like that in all the years I have been around the San Marcos river". The river was still the same but the human activity level had drastically changed over the years and there was no going back to the good old days. The times were different and this was not just a canoeing river any more.

The large groups of tubers and partiers were now behind them and they were able to refocus and get back to racing again. The field was spread out while they made their way towards Luling. They were able to pass a couple more teams. The river straightened out and there were fewer obstacles to deal with. Pavos and the old Polecat carried their boat around the Luling dam portage while Joseph and Wade changed out the water containers.

They were feeling pretty good about the stroke rate and the fact that no one had passed them since early in the race. Joseph and Wade did not tell them what place they were in because that was not very important at this stage of the race. The only thing that mattered was that they were maintaining a fast stroke rate and had not made any critical errors up to this point. This was going to be a very long and hard race and the serious competition would probably not start until they reached the lower sections of the race course.

Darla and the grandkids were at the Luling dam portage cheering them through. Pavos and the old Polecat quickly got back into the boat and headed down river after the difficult portage. The sight of his beautiful grandkids yelling and laughing and having a good time put a big smile on his face. The goal was to reach the Palmetto state park checkpoint before dark and they needed to kick it into a higher gear to accomplish that.

The river below Luling is more wide open and has many long straight away sections. Ottine dam used to be a very difficult portage on this section of river but it was torn down several years ago and now there is one less obstacle to deal with. Ottine dam was a historical site that had been tossed into the scrap heap of history. The old Polecat fondly re-membered all of the pain and suffering he endured through while trying to help carry a very long and heavy multi man racing canoe around the difficult portage. These old water safari memories from years past had been dominating his thinking all day long because this was probably going to be the last time he would paddle down this section.

That is when a very scary image of a very old and wrinkled Polecat floating down the upper San Marcos river on a tube suddenly appeared in his mind and that made him smile because there was no way that would ever happen.

The race horse and the old donkey paddled into the Palmetto state park checkpoint just before dark. The low water bridge was covered with racing fans and team captains and they were very loud and enthusiastic. There was another tandem team stopped there taking on food and water. Joseph and Wade quickly changed out the water containers and threw in several more sport bottles full of high energy drink mix. The old Polecat had been living on these drink mixes all day long and they were helping to keep his energy level up.

It had been a long twelve hours of racing at this point and the reality was that they were just getting started on this marathon journey to Seadrift. Darla and the grandkids had to leave after the Luling checkpoint and head back home to take care of animals and chickens. A long night of canoe racing was in front of them. They portaged over the low water bridge as fast as they could in order to pass the team that was stopped there.

Pavos secured the bow light in front of him and turned it on. They were going to be very dependent on a good bow light because it was a very dark night with no moon. The bow light they were using was a water proof diver's flashlight. It was basically just a high powered flashlight that a diver could use under water. Three sets of spare batteries were stored away in the boat because two long nights on the river were ahead of them. They needed to be prepared for possibly a third night because of the low water levels.

The 100 degree temperatures they had to endure through all day long were now getting back into a more tolerable range after darkness set in. Racing down a very dark river at night can produce even more challenges after a long day of navigating through and around all of the obstacles on the upper river. A dark night will sometimes make familiar areas look very different.

The bow person has a big responsibility at night because they are the eyes and ears of the team. They have to recognize a potential hazard early enough in order to alert the rest of the team and give everyone enough time to react and steer the boat out of harms way.

Pavos is good at this and he also seemed to really enjoy barking out orders to the old Polecat. Sometimes these blunt and rude orders can be very hard to take. The more important thing was that they were in a canoe race and all that really mattered was that there were no self inflicted time consuming mistakes made.

The old Polecat smiled while he watched Pavos squirm and violently swat with his paddle at the hordes of bugs that were attracted to the bow light in front of him. This can be a very stressful thing to put up with as hundreds of bugs come zeroing in on you and the bright light. The constant barking out of orders slowed down considerably while he focused on the bug invasion.

Pavos and the old grey bearded Polecat paddled into the Gonzales dam portage after almost seventeen hours of racing. The very low river level, long portages and all the human activity that had to be paddled through along the race course had turned the first day into a test of patience and endurance. Pavos and the old Polecat held up pretty well to all of the hazards and chaos and felt like they were doing about the best they could do at this point in the race.

They had no idea what place they were in. That was not very important because no one had passed them since very early in the race and they had been constantly passing other teams all day long. Joseph and Wade were waiting for them at the portage around the dam to resupply them with fresh water and meal replacement drink mix. They changed out the water containers and threw in several sport bottles of drink mix while Pavos and the old Polecat carried the boat around the long portage.

The old grey bearded Polecat was stumbling a little at first because of the long day of paddling and sitting in a canoe for over seventeen hours. The leg muscles finally came back to life and started to function again after a few minutes of struggling while trying to keep up with Pavos.

The old Polecat knew that this would probably be his last opportunity to get out of the boat and walk for a few minutes because this was the last major obstacle to get around.

The next 180 miles down the Guadalupe river was basically going to be on an open river with very little human activity to deal with. The low river levels might require them to jump out and do a quick portage over a shallow spot but that would probably not happen very often. The old Polecat was trying very hard to keep up with Pavos while they carried the boat next to the hydro electric dam.

Joseph and Wade were trying very hard to change out the water containers while they kept moving forward. Joseph gave them the good news that they were in the top twenty overall and were leading the USCA C-2 division. That was good news and surprising because they did not remember passing Joshua and Susannah. The young and talented brother and sister team had beaten them in the prelim race and they started directly ahead of them at the chaotic start of the race. They had evidently passed them somewhere on the upper river during one of the many portages.

Joseph also said that they had a good lead on Joe and John. They were going to end up being the main competition in this division and would probably have to be dealt with later. This was all good news. They launched the boat back into the river after the very long portage.

There was another team putting back into the river at the same time. Holly and her teenage son William had been ahead of them all day. Holly is a well known canoe instructor and is an experienced water safari racer with a very impressive record of finishes. This was William's first water safari and he was holding up very well because his experienced mother was serving as his mentor and coach.

Pavos and the old Polecat thanked Joseph and Wade for the water and food and they quickly paddled out of sight. The next section of the race course down to Holcheim is over 30 miles long and they would not see them again for several hours. This is a very desolate section of river with only cows and wildlife watching you when you paddle by. It was a very dark night and Pavos was very busy swatting at the bugs that were zeroing in on his body while they tried to pick up the stroke rate.

Holly and William were in a very fast unlimited tandem boat and they were able to pull up along side them. Pavos and Holly know each other from previous races and they started up a conversation. Talking to someone other than your teammate can sometimes help bring you out of your mental fatigue after a long day of canoe racing. Pavos and the old Polecat do not talk very much to each other during the race and he was enjoying the conversation with Holly.

William was very quiet and was focused on maintaining a fast stroke rate. The old Polecat tried to start up a conversation with William. Holly does not know the old Polecat very well but she knew that he had been doing this race for many years. She interrupted and asked the old Polecat to tell William some old water safari stories from years past. Telling old water safari stories is something that the old Polecat is very passionate about so he enthusiastically accepted the offer.

The story telling started out kind of slow but it soon blossomed into very long and detailed funny stories. The area they were in reminded the old Polecat of all the crazy stories from the late 1980's with Three Dots in the boat. William seemed to enjoy the stories and he laughed while the old Polecat rambled on. The story telling seemed to be helping everyone refocus after a long day of racing and helped to divert attention away from all of the physical and mental fatigue they were experiencing. The old Polecat would have to pause the story telling when the canoes had to separate in order to get through a small rapid or shallow spot in the river.

The stroke rate was fast and steady while they made their way towards Holcheim. The story telling and friendly conversations with Holly and William continued. That is when Holly suddenly said that they were going to pull over for a short break. Pavos and the old Polecat would miss the conversation but there was no way they were going to make an unscheduled pit stop. They had to say goodbye to their new friends.

They knew that Joe and John were probably not that far behind them and they needed to keep it in high gear and keep moving forward.

Tom's good advice of taking a no doze pill and just keep paddling always makes sense when your sleep deprived mind starts to lose focus and go into a fog.

The sun made its glorious appearance on Sunday morning and they still had several more miles to go before reaching the Holcheim checkpoint. The long night was now over and the bright sun was slowly helping to bring them out of their delirious state of mind. They were still moving forward with a good stroke rate and had not made any serious time consuming mistakes. The low water levels had slowed the race down considerably and the field was spread out.

Pavos and the old Polecat had figured that they would have to drag their racing canoe over very shallow gravel bars all night long but thankfully that did not happen. The river level was very low and you had to find the deeper channels to get through the shallow spots. This required a lot of frequent boat maneuvering and that just ended up adding more physical stress to an already over abused body. Pavos was holding up pretty well to all of the physical abuse. The old Polecat was surprisingly holding up and was able to keep up with the fast stroke rate.

The second day of the water safari can be a game changer when you paddle down the long middle sections of the race course after 24 hours of racing. The for cast was calling for over 100 degree temperatures and high humidity. Polecat used to love the second day of the race and would pick up the stroke rate even more in order to put pressure on the competition, but those days were long gone. The old grey bearded Polecat was hanging in there but was feeling the effects of 24 hours of racing on his old and abused body. This race was not even at the halfway point yet.

Pavos and the old Polecat paddled in to the very quiet Holcheim checkpoint around mid morning on that beautiful Sunday morning. Joseph and Wade were patiently waiting there with fresh water and sport bottles of drink mix. It was great to talk to them while they enthusiastically changed out the water containers. Joseph said that they were still in the top twenty and were leading the USCA C-2 division but Joe and John were not very far behind.

Wade handed the old Polecat a hot cup of coffee in a travel mug and he immediately became the best team captain that he ever had. The coffee smelled great and it perked the old Polecat up a little. It didn't really matter if he actually had the opportunity to drink it or not because just the smell of a fresh cup of coffee was good enough. The old days of jalapeno dried sausage, canned peaches and energy bars were now replaced with meal replacement drink mixes and a cup of coffee. The rules and the technology sure have changed a lot over the last forty years. Pavos and the old Polecat started heading down river after the handoff and they thanked their team captains for the support.

It was now time to honor Jesus on this Lord's day with a couple of gospel songs that the old Polecat had practiced singing before the race. There is nothing joy full about the old grey bearded Polecats voice and he can't sing as well as Three Dots can. His heart was into it and he wanted to honor the Lord in song and prayer. "Why me Lord" along with "Ten Thousand Reasons" was loudly being sang and was echoing down river.

Pavos was trying to join in with the the old Polecat while they both sang out as loud as they could. The old Polecat would occasionally miss a few words and there was no background music to sing along with but they were giving it everything they had in honor of the Lord. There were several river owls and birds squawking at them from the large cypress trees along the bank. They were apparently trying to join in with the loud singing.

That is when they noticed a racing canoe about a half mile behind them and it looked like it was slowly closing in. The old Polecat figured it was probably Joe and John. They are both very strong paddlers and it was just a matter of time before they would eventually pick up the pace and close the gap between them. Pavos and the old Polecat had a great first day and a good first night. There were no major time consuming mistakes made and no one had passed them since early in the race.

The competition will usually heat up on the lower sections of the race course when you have a fast team chasing you. They were paddling at a strong stroke rate and had not slowed down very much. Joe and

John had kicked it up a few notches and were now right behind them. Pavos seemed to be a little depressed that their main competition had caught up with them and were closing in for the pass. The old Polecat tried to calm things down some and said that they were not even at the halfway point yet and there was no reason to panic. Pavos and the old Polecat were doing the best they could and there was a long ways to go in this race. Things can change in a hurry is the best way to look at it.

The old Polecat had been on the other side of this situation many times before and he knew what was coming next. Joe and John would pick up the stroke rate even more and they would pass them very quickly. They would try to give the impression that they were much stronger and faster and there was no way to stay up with them. They would be sending a message to their main competition that this race was over.

Joe and John pulled up next to them and the old Polecat tried to start up a conversation. "Where have y'all been, we have been expecting you since yesterday"? This comment caught them by surprise and they both started laughing. John answered that they were very conservative through all of the portages and hazards on the upper San Marcos river because of his leg problems. The race course was wide open now and they were trying to maintain a much faster stroke rate down river.

The old Polecat continued, "The biggest obstacle we had to paddle through yesterday was all of the tubers and partiers that were clogging up the river". They both smiled and agreed with the old Polecat that they had never seen that many people on the river before. The conversation was very friendly and ended on a positive note while they quickly paddled by.

The race horse and the old donkey were moving along at a fast and consistent stroke rate but could not keep up with them and they slowly pulled away. This was going to be a scorching hot second day of racing and things would probably change very quickly. That was the positive attitude that the old Polecat tried to focus on and he did not let himself dwell on the negative stuff. There would be many more physical and mental hurdles to overcome before this race was over.

The second day ended up ranking right up there with some of the hottest days the old Polecat had ever experienced during the water safari. Pavos and the old Polecat pulled in to the Highway 72 bridge checkpoint near Cuero (Peacock bridge) and his Christian brother John Q. was the race official there. It was great to be able to talk to someone different while Joseph changed out the water containers. Pavos and the old Polecat had been focused on the stroke rate and staying in the deeper channels and there was very little conversation going on between them.

The only conversation between them was when Pavos would bark out orders to move the boat in one direction or the other to avoid a shallow spot in the river. The old Polecat suddenly tried to entertain everyone at the checkpoint when he awkwardly started calling the Peacocks. The party bunch was not there anymore to get things started so it was up to the old Polecat to try and call out to their Peacock friends across the river. There was no response back but the crowd seemed to enjoy the comedy show. They were laughing while they tried to figure out what was wrong with that old grey bearded man in boat number 30. Joseph quickly changed out the water jugs and resupplied them with several bottles of high energy drink mix. The race horse and the old donkey headed down river towards Floodplain ranch.

Joseph gave them the good news that there were two tandem teams not very far in front of them. The bad news was that Joe and John had extended their lead on them. They were still moving along at a very strong stroke rate and the old Polecat tried to focus on the two tandem teams that were directly in front of them and not dwell to much on the negative stuff. There was a lot of hard miles to go in this marathon canoe race and things can change in a hurry.

The race horse and the old donkey picked up the stroke rate and were able to pass the two tandem boats that Joseph told them about. The 100 degree temperatures along with the very high humidity will sometimes slow the competition down and they were determined to take advantage of that. They paddled through the famous Polecat rapid upright and Floodplain ranch was just ahead.

The sun was starting to make it's glorious disappearance on the western horizon when they pulled up to the makeshift boat ramp. Three of the old Polecat's beautiful grandchildren were yelling out encouragement to them. Aiden, Landry and Graham were yelling "Go Polecat Go" and their voices were loudly echoing down river. The large pack of river dogs were howling in excitement. Darla was trying very hard to keep them from jumping in and following the boat down river.

Joseph was busy changing out the water containers while Pavos talked to his family. The old Polecat tried to talk to Darla and his canine friends. The enthusiasm and excitement was helping to lift them up out of the physical and mental fatigue they were experiencing after a long second day of racing. This reception was just what they needed to help get motivated for the second night. The race horse and the old donkey started paddling again after the water handoff ended. The yelling and barking continued to echo down river while they paddled out of sight.

The Nursery rapids were next in line and they would be a little harder to paddle through because of the very low water conditions. Several large rocks located at the bottom of the rapids would now be fully exposed because of the low river level. This would require a lot more maneuvering to avoid a violent crash and wipeout. Darkness had set in and this added more drama to the difficulty.

Pavos was yelling out orders to the old Polecat to steer the boat in one direction or the other in order to avoid contact with the large rocks. There were several close calls and a few minor collisions but they made it through the series of rapids with no wipeouts or damage. The bow light was doing a good job lighting up the river directly in front of them after Pavos changed out the batteries. It was a very dark night and they needed all the help they could get to paddle down river at racing speed.

The Victoria riverside park checkpoint was next in line and the hallucinations started to make their ugly appearance. The rapids had forced them to remain focused but they were now in some very long and open sections of the river. This is usually when the weird and unbelievable images start appearing in the trees and along the bank. Fire breathing dragons and funny cartoon characters will suddenly appear in the tree tops. Dams and bridges that do not exist will block the river in front of you. It was over 40 hours into the race and the mental fatigue was starting to take its toll on them.

This is when water safari racing experience can make a big difference. The old Polecat was smiling and laughing at all of the crazy images that suddenly appeared in the trees. Pavos seemed to be amused while the old Polecat tried to describe to him in detail what he was seeing. The stroke rate was hanging in there above fifty strokes per minute while they closed in on mile 200. Take a no doze pill and keep paddling is the best advice the old Polecat ever received from Tom.

The old Polecat pulled out one of the very warm plastic bottles of coke that was stored away under his seat and downed it as fast as he could. A cup of hot coffee would have been much better but you just have to be satisfied with whatever you have.

The race horse and the old donkey pulled in to the very quiet riverside park checkpoint a couple of hours before daylight on Monday. Joseph was patiently waiting to exchange water containers and hand them fresh bottles of high energy meal replacement drink mix. The good news was that they were steadily gaining ground on a tandem boat directly in front of them but the bad news was that Joe and John had increased their lead on them.

They were doing the best they could and there was no reason to get depressed over that news. Pavos and the old Polecat were now refocused on trying to break into the top fifteen. They were not dwelling on the bad news because there was not much they could do about it. Joseph handed the old Polecat a fresh cup of hot coffee in a travel mug and he immediately became the best team captain that he ever had. The smell of fresh coffee was just what the old Polecat needed to help get out of the mental fog he was in. The quick pit stop ended and they paddled off into the darkness.

Pavos told the old Polecat that he needed to stand up for a couple of minutes in order to stretch out some aching lower back and leg muscles. The old Polecat does not like to make unscheduled pit stops but it sounded like Pavos really needed a few minutes to stretch out some aching muscles. They pulled over into some calm water next to the bank and noticed that they were just upstream of the area where the Texas river marathon canoe race had ended five weeks earlier.

They suddenly noticed a bow light directly behind them. Joe and Libby quickly paddled by and didn't say anything. This unexpected pass was surprising and it caused the competitive attitude to return. That is what they needed to get back into racing mode after a long second night of paddling.

The interesting part of that story is that this was the same exact spot where they had passed Pavos and the old Polecat in the Texas river marathon canoe race after they were swept into a low hanging tree limb and were pinned down under the tree. Joe and Libby were probably laughing to themselves about that. It was time to kick it into a higher gear and catch back up with them. The swinging bridge checkpoint and the logjam cuts were next in line. There was still 60 miles to go. The race horse and the old donkey needed to shift into a higher gear and put the peddle to the metal.

The sun started making it's glorious appearance on Monday morning while they headed for the swinging bridge checkpoint. This section of the race course would usually be paddled through at night during a normal year but the very low river levels had slowed the race down considerably.

Pavos and the old Polecat were maintaining a good stroke rate when they passed the 48 hour mark. They finished the race around this same time last year with much higher river levels and a calm bay. The reality of the situation was that there was still a long third day of racing ahead of them. The bright sun was helping to bring the old Polecat out of his sleep deprived mental fog.

It is hard to describe in words how pushing yourself to your physical and mental limits can affect your decision making and thought process. The old Polecat was usually able to get through these extended down periods by shifting his mind into neutral and just keep paddling. Some people would agree that his mind is always in neutral and that is not an unusual condition for him.

There was very little conversation going on between them and the only word being spoken was "hut". That was the signal to switch sides with your paddle after seven strokes. The constant sound of "hut" echoing down river can be very irritating after 50 hours of non stop canoe racing. Pavos would reluctantly have to take over calling out the switch signal because the old Polecat would suddenly lose count and his mind would drift off into neutral.

The best way to describe this condition is when your brain function deteriorates to the point where you can't focus on anything for very long and your mind drifts in and out of la la land. It was time for the old Polecat to splash some warm river water into his face and get back to racing because there was a long day of paddling ahead.

The race horse and the old donkey pulled into the swinging bridge checkpoint when the 100 degree south Texas summertime temperatures started to show up again on Monday afternoon. Darla and her friend Cheryl were yelling out encouragement to them while they watched all of the pain and suffering from under a large shade tree. Joseph was very busy changing out the water containers when he gave them the bad news. The south westerly winds were picking up and it looked like they were going to have to deal with some very rough bay conditions.

The good news was that Joe and John had slowed down some and they had narrowed the lead. That was the good news they needed to hear. The rough bay conditions would affect everybody in a negative way and there was no reason to dwell on that bad news right now. Darla was busy trying to get their attention and warn everyone about an alligator that was swimming in the river next to them.

The old Polecat turned around and noticed the large alligator staring at him from just a few feet away. A big smile came across the old Polecat's face while he stared back. There was no need to panic because the large alligator was staying a safe distance away and was probably just surveying the situation to plan out his next meal . Pavos loudly splashed his paddle into the river as a warning and their new friend disappeared under water. The quick water handoff ended and they headed down stream for the log jam cuts and alligator lake.

The massive log jam was just ahead of them and would be the next major obstacle to get around. They had done a training run through this area five days earlier and they knew exactly which log jam cut was open. This is the old Polecat's favorite section of the race course and he was slowly starting to regain some focus and enthusiasm after 55 hours of non stop canoe racing.

There was one large tree down across the cut and it had to be carefully portaged over but everything else was open. This was a big improvement over last years race when the river and all the cuts were blocked with major log jams. Pavos and the old Polecat were moving along at a good stroke rate and they paddled by the alligator lake entrance. There was no clear way to get through alligator lake because of the very low river levels. This is usually the fastest route to take but it would have to be avoided and bypassed.

The very hot late afternoon temperatures were taking a toll on them but they just had to ignore that and keep paddling. The old Polecat dipped his well used cowboy hat into the river and then quickly placed it back on his over heated head. Splashing water on your teammates back with your paddle is another good thing to do in these terrible conditions.

The race horse and the old donkey paddled in to the salt water barrier checkpoint around the 57 hour mark. The dreaded 60 hour syndrome had been slowly making its ugly appearance and was slowly causing the old grey bearded Polecat to lose focus again. Pavos seemed to be mentally alert and had been trying to keep the old Polecat focused with conversation.

A warm coke and a no doze pill is what the old Polecat needed to get mentally back into the game. The south westerly winds were howling through the trees when they pulled up to the mandatory portage around the salt water barrier dam. Joseph was patiently waiting there to change out the empty water containers and hand them several sport bottles filled with high energy drink mix.

Joseph then gave them the good news. Joe and John were struggling and had taken a long break at the check point. They were not that far ahead of them. Pavos and the old Polecat had an opportunity to catch up with them if they could just keep the fast stroke rate going. This was the good news that they needed to hear and it allowed the competitive attitude to make a comeback.

That good news was quickly followed with the bad news when Joseph reluctantly told them that the bay was very rough and was getting worse. The teams ahead of them were having a very difficult time trying to get across. The old Polecat tried to not let himself think about that in a negative way but looked at it as an opportunity. The rough bay conditions would slow everything down considerably and it could work to their advantage. That would be the best way to react to that news.

The rough bay could very well end up being their demise and cause them to lose several places but the old Polecat would not allow himself to think about it that way. The quick handoff ended and they awkwardly carried the boat around the portage and headed for San Antonio bay.

The race horse and the old donkey were able to pick up the stroke rate after hearing the news that their main competition was back within reach. The enthusiasm and a positive attitude was what they both needed and it brought the old Polecat out of his delirious state of mind. Joseph was going to meet up with them at the old wooden bridge in Seadrift cut and that would be the last handoff before they paddled into a rough San Antonio bay.

The sun was getting much lower on the western horizon on late Monday afternoon when they paddled into Seadrift cut and headed for the old wooden bridge. The numerous and thick patches of water Hyacinth had to be paddled over and carefully maneuvered around but they were able to keep moving forward while maintaining a steady stroke rate. The old wooden bridge had been replaced with a new cement bridge but the old timers still liked to call it by its former name.

Pavos and the old Polecat pulled up to the boat ramp just past the bridge and noticed a five man team standing in the water next to their long multi man racing canoe. They did not look very happy. This was a fast five man team that had been way ahead of them for most of the race. Pavos recognized several of the team members but they were not in a friendly or talkative mood.

Joseph was standing at the boat ramp and started changing out the water containers. The old Polecat could hardly believe that they had just caught up with a very fast multi man team and he started to think that it was just a hallucination. Joseph was talking to Pavos while the old Polecat stared at the long racing canoe that was tied up to the bank.

The decision had already been made before they got there to snap on the spray skirt before proceeding. Darla was standing there and was trying to encourage them while they slowly snapped on the spray skirt. Hands and fingers do not work very well after 59 hours of non stop paddling at a high stroke rate. Trying to snap on a very tight fitting spray skirt can be a difficult task when your hands and fingers are cramping and not functioning properly. The pain and agony could be seen on their faces while they tried to work together and get this done in a timely manner.

One of the five man team members walked over and was watching the comedy show. The old Polecat recognized Edoh and they started a conversation with each other. Edoh said that they had decided to wait it out for a while and were hoping the winds would die down some after dark. He asked the old Polecat if they were going to try and paddle through the five foot waves and 35 mile per hour winds that were waiting on them in San Antonio bay.

The old Polecat smiled and said "yes, we are going to keep moving forward either by paddling or swimming or whatever it takes to get to the finish line". Edoh smiled and said that he would be looking forward to hearing the stories at the finishers banquet. The comedy show finally ended and they slowly squeezed their lower bodies into the small spray skirt openings and back into their seats. The winds were howling and seemed to be getting worse while they headed for the open bay.

Pavos yelled back at the old Polecat that there was another multi man team pulled up on the bank back at the bridge. Joseph told him that the Cowboys were laid out on the bank just out of their view. The loud wind gusts made it very difficult to hear exactly what Pavos was saying.

The old Polecat could not believe what he thought he had just heard him say so he asked Pavos to repeat himself. Pavos repeated himself that they had just passed the Cowboys.

This was an unbelievable sequence of events. Pavos and the old Polecat had just passed two fast multi man teams that were several hours ahead of them. The old Polecat could not help himself when he laughed and a big smile suddenly appeared on his sunburned face. This was by far the highlight of the race. The old Polecat never thought that beating the Cowboys was possible but they were now ahead of them with less than ten miles to go.

Things can change in a hurry in this race and that is why it has earned the name, "The Worlds Toughest Boat Race". The old Polecat started feeling bad for his Cowboy brothers and could only imagine how difficult it must have been while they watched slower boats pass by. The old Polecat had been in situations like that before and he understood how depressing that can be. This is an endurance race and everyone in front of you has a large target on their back. That is the only way you can look at it if you are competitive.

Pavos then yelled out some more good news. Joseph told him that there were several teams camped out at the barge canal point. They were apparently waiting for the 35 to 40 mile per hour wind gusts to die down some before attempting to paddle across the last section of open bay. The old Polecat tried to soak in this very interesting news while they picked up the stroke rate a little more.

Joseph told Pavos that they had a chance to break into the top ten if they could just paddle across San Antonio bay upright and not waste any valuable time swimming. That was going to be a very difficult thing to do because of the four to five foot waves that were waiting on them.

Pavos and the old Polecat were reenergized with all of this good news and were still paddling hard after almost sixty hours of racing. The biggest problem going forward was if they could paddle over these large whitecap waves and keep the boat upright for the next several hours. This was going to be the ultimate test of balance and mobility and white water experience all tied together into one bundle. The old Polecat quietly dwelled on all of this for a few minutes while they made the final turn out of Seadrift cut and headed straight into San Antonio bay.

The old Polecat yelled out to Pavos that they should just go straight across and then try to paddle alongside the barrier island shoreline. Pavos was in agreement with that while they headed straight into the large waves. The old Polecat then yelled out to Pavos that if they were able to make it to the barge canal point upright there was no way he could stop and wait for calmer winds with the other teams. "We will just have to swim across the point and keep moving forward" were the last words that the old Polecat could get out of his mouth before the wild rodeo started.

The four foot waves were crashing into Pavos when they started paddling straight across San Antonio bay. The preferred route would normally be to slowly angle across towards the barge canal point but that was not an option in this environment because of the wind direction and the size of the waves. The wind was intensely blowing out of a south westerly direction and it was forcing them straight across. Pavos and the old Polecat had to quickly get in sync with each other while they tried to maneuver over the large whitecap waves at a 45 degree angle.

Keeping the boat at an angle would help with the stability during the rapid descent down the backside of the wave and would hopefully prevent the bow from completely submerging at the bottom of the wave. This technique would have to be performed over and over again for the next several hours if they wanted to stay upright.

Pavos was doing a good job quickly switching sides with his paddle and keeping the boat stable while paddling over the whitecap at the top of the waves. The old Polecat was trying very hard to keep the boat at the desired angle in order to prevent a bad wipeout at the bottom of the wave. The boat stability and working together was very critical at this point and everything seemed to be working out while they carefully navigated over the waves. The wind was blowing them straight across and all they could do was keep the boat at a 45 degree angle and paddle forward.

This procedure seemed to drag on for a long extended time while the sun started making it's glorious disappearance on the western horizon behind them. It was a late afternoon skyline that was lit up with amazing colors. Pavos and the old Polecat had to stay focused on the next wave and could not watch the beautiful sunset. They had been sitting in a canoe and paddling at a high stroke rate for over sixty hours. The finish line was only seven miles away and they did not know that this bay crossing adventure was just getting started.

The race horse and the old donkey were able to successfully keep the boat upright over the three to four foot turbulent waves. There were several close calls when the boat almost capsized but they were able to avoid the violent wipeout with a quick paddle brace and then leaning in the opposite direction. The barge canal barrier island was within view when darkness set in and the southwesterly winds seemed to be getting stronger instead of calming down.

The boat grounded to a sudden stop in the shallow water next to the barrier island shoreline. Pavos and the old Polecat struggled to crawl out of the tight fitting spray skirt while the large waves kept slamming into the side of the canoe. The boat suddenly rolled over in the turbulent water while they awkwardly tried to worm their way out of the spray skirt.

The old Polecat was frantically trying to keep his head above water while he struggled to free himself from the semi submerged canoe. He tried to stand up after freeing himself from the submerged canoe but was knocked down by the next wave. The legs were numb and were not functioning properly after 60 hours of canoe racing and it was going to take a few minutes to regain some feeling and mobility again.

Pavos and the old Polecat were very excited and motivated again after successfully getting across the first section of San Antonio bay upright. It was about three miles to the barge canal point from this spot and there was no time to celebrate. There was a golden opportunity within their reach to catch up with several teams if they could just keep moving forward and not waste any valuable time.

They dumped the water out of the boat after standing in the shallow water for a couple of minutes and regaining some mobility. The wind was blowing the large waves right into them and it was obvious that the best plan going forward would be to walk the boat along the shoreline.

The wind would normally be blowing out of the southeast this time of year and the barrier island would usually be a good wind block, but not this year. The race horse and the old donkey stored their paddles away in the boat and started walking along the shoreline with the boat in tow. There was a rope tied to the bow and the stern. Pavos pulled the boat forward in the knee deep water with the bow line while the old Polecat kept the back of the boat off the shoreline and at the right angle with the stern line. This seemed to be working and they were moving in the right direction again.

It was a dark night but they could still see good enough without a light. Pavos was walking along at a fast pace and the old Polecat was able to keep up with him for a while. The waves were getting bigger and were slamming into them and into the side of the boat. The old Polecat was struggling to stand up in the turbulent water and keep pace with Pavos. This became more difficult when they would suddenly get into an area where the bottom was muddy or covered in large rocks and shell.

The old Polecat would occasionally have to let go of the stern rope and let Pavos take complete control when he was in knee deep mud or stumbling over submerged rocks. The old Polecat eventually had to just get up on the shoreline and walk along the bank in order to not slow down the forward progress. Pavos was very motivated to keep moving forward with the boat in tow as fast as he could. The old Polecat would just have to keep up the best way he could manage. Pavos looked like he was going back in time to his high school football days when the coaches made them pull large tractor tires during offseason workouts with a rope tied around their waist.

The boat towing procedure seemed to go on for a long extended time while they carefully made their way towards the barge canal point. There are several long gaps located along the barrier island and these areas are wide open into the barge canal. The open gaps have to carefully be navigated around because if your spot tracker shows that you have ventured into the barge canal there will be a two hour penalty added to your finishing time.

Pavos and the old Polecat avoided these open areas by staying as far away from them as they possibly could. The barge canal point was within their view when they made the last gradual turn along the barrier island. Pavos was plowing ahead with the boat in tow when he suddenly noticed a bow light not to far behind them. This was the wakeup call they needed to get back in the boat and start paddling again before being passed from behind.

Trying to squeeze yourself into a tight fitting spray skirt while large waves are crashing into you can be a very difficult task. Pavos was able to get in and he held the boat stable with his paddle lodged firmly into the muddy bay bottom while the old Polecat slowly crawled into the stern seat. This was a very difficult task and the old Polecat had to just grit his teeth and deal with the pain in his lower body while bending and squirming back into the tight fitting spray skirt. The two mile long walk had loosened up the stiff lower body muscles and had helped him get some mobility back after almost 259 miles of canoe racing.

Pavos and the old Polecat started paddling towards the barge canal point. The south westerly winds seemed to be picking up even more while they slowly tried to maneuver over the large waves at an angle and stay upright. The stroke rate was gradually increasing and they tried to get back to racing speed but this was going to be a slow process because of the wind direction and the turbulent waves. The only positive thing was that if they had a violent wipe out, the shallow water next to the barrier island was not very far away.

They eventually made it to the point upright and noticed a couple of racing boats pulled up on the bank along the shoreline. A couple of bright head lights shined on them when they paddled up to the last turn towards Seadrift. Several water safari teams were camped out on the bank waiting for the wind conditions to improve before proceeding to the finish line.

A loud voice yelled out from the tall grass, "Are you going to try and paddle in to the finish line in these rough conditions"? The old Polecat quickly responded "Yes, we are headed for swan point either by paddling or swimming or whatever it takes to get there". It was very hard to hear because of the howling winds and the short conversation quickly ended.

The race horse and the old donkey made the last turn and the bright lights from Seadrift were lighting up the sky. There was only about four miles left to swan point and they were determined to get there. That is when they noticed Vance and his partner Sam standing on the bank.

Pavos said that they needed to stop and dump water before attempting to paddle across the mouth of the barge canal. The old Polecat agreed and they headed for the shoreline. They pulled up into the shallow water next to the shoreline and awkwardly rolled out of the boat into the water.

The waves at this spot were between four to six foot because of the much deeper water across the mouth of the barge canal. It was pretty obvious that they would have a very difficult time trying to paddle across this area. The old Polecat started up a conversation with Vance and Sam while Pavos tried to drag the half submerged boat into the shoreline. Vance could not believe that they were going to keep moving forward by whatever means necessary.

The old Polecat started telling the story of when he watched Chris and Shannon swim across the deep channel with their boat in tow during very rough bay conditions in the 2018 race. The old Polecat was convinced that they could do the same thing. The only problem would be if the south westerly winds pushed them into the canal and that would cause a two hour penalty.

Vance explained that as long as you started at the point it did not matter if you were forced into the canal by winds or a strong current and there would be no penalty. Vance is a former water safari head judge and the old Polecat trusted his comments. Sam was listening to this loud discussion and jumped in to the conversation. "We need to follow them and do the same thing". "I'm tired of waiting here and we need to make a move". Vance and Sam got into a debate with each other while Pavos and the old Polecat started putting the swimming plan together. Pavos was in agreement that they needed to keep moving forward any way possible. The old Polecat was not going to wait with the other teams for better wind conditions because that may not happen ant time soon.

Pavos and the old Polecat waded out into the deeper water until they could not touch bottom anymore. The old Polecat was leading the swimming adventure and started swimming in front of the boat with the bow line in one hand. Pavos was behind the boat and he would push the boat forward while swimming from behind the stern. They had to hold their breath when the turbulent water crashed over their heads and then start swimming again in between the large waves. It was hard to judge if they were making any progress or not.

The old Polecat glanced over to the shoreline and noticed that they were being swept out into the open bay instead of heading in the direction they wanted to go. It became obvious that the tide was going out and it was pulling them out with it. The only option left was to head for shallow water and regroup. They eventually made it back over into a shallow area and stared at each other in disbelief.

The plan was not working and now they were back to square one. "What do we do now", Pavos yelled out in a very angry tone. The old Polecat responded, "We are going to have to get back in the boat and try to paddle across to the other side". That was the only option left. The old Polecat slowly tried to crawl into the bow seat in the chest deep water but his energy depleted and severely abused body was not cooperating. Pavos was able to carefully push off the bottom and pull himself up into the stern seat. The old Polecat was hanging on to the bow and was gasping for air while the large waves kept rolling over his head and into the side of the boat.

There is no good explanation for it but the old Polecat suddenly had the idea that he could just hang on to the bow and be a stabilizing anchor while Pavos paddled the boat across the deep channel. The old Polecat yelled out to Pavos to start paddling and he would just have to hang on to the bow. Pavos started paddling as hard as he could while the old Polecat tightly wrapped his arms and legs around the bow of the boat and tried to keep his head above water. This comedy scene probably resembled a car with an ugly hood ornament or maybe more like a scary looking character that was mounted on the bow of a historic sailing ship.

Pavos was paddling hard and they were slowly making some progress across the deep channel. The old Polecat was forced to hold his breath for long periods of time and hang on for dear life when the large waves rolled over him. The human anchor strategy seemed to be working because the boat was semi stable and still upright. Four to six foot waves were crashing into them and the 35 to 40 mile per hour wind gusts were pushing them across the channel. The canal crossing adventure seemed to drag on for an extended time before the old Polecat was finally able to ease up a little with his death grip on the bow and he lowered his legs to see how deep it was.

The excitement in his voice was apparent because he was able to touch bottom and stand up. They had just made it across the hardest section of the bay and they could walk it in to the finish line from here if they had to. There was finally a light at the end of the tunnel and things were looking up. Pavos jumped out of the boat and they both started walking it in to the nearest shoreline. The old Polecat was excited and the pain and agony he was feeling just a few minutes earlier had subsided.

The shoreline was within sight and they started to pick up the walking pace in the shallow water. They needed to dump water because the boat was about half full. It was an amazing accomplishment to keep it upright with that much water in the boat. The bilge pump had quit working and they needed to check out what the problem was. The old Polecat was stumbling around in the knee deep water and suddenly heard voices along the shoreline.

It seemed like he was hearing strange things because Pavos was apparently talking to somebody several yards away in the distance. It was a very dark night and the loud wind gusts were causing the voices he heard to sound garbled. The old Polecat dragged the semi submerged race boat closer in to the shoreline and noticed Pavos talking to someone. There was a tandem racing canoe pulled up on the shoreline and it looked like they were in the process of getting back into their boat.

The old Polecat was in the early stages of a complete mental meltdown after 64 hours of paddling, walking and swimming in "The Worlds Toughest Boat Race" and he did not recognize who they were. Pavos was in a discussion with one of them. The old Polecat slowly walked up and listened in.

The other team member was laying on the sandy shoreline and was trying to get up. The old Polecat asked the young man what division they were in. The young man looked at the old Polecat with a confused look before he answered. "I'm Joe, your competition in the C-2 division".

The old Polecat suddenly realized who he was talking to. John was slowly getting up off the sandy beach and was walking towards them but he did not say anything before he climbed back into their boat. The old Polecat apologized for not recognizing them and blamed it on mental fatigue that was caused by the extended bay crossing adventure.

Joe said that they were going to try and paddle across the last section of open bay and head straight in to the finish line. The old Polecat looked at Pavos and excitedly yelled out, "We need to dump this water and get back to racing so we can give these guys some competition". They had been chasing Joe and John for over 140 miles and had finally caught back up with them. The same team that had passed them above Cheapside and then established a big lead were now right beside them. Things can change in a hurry in this race and they were now in a heated battle with their main competition for the USCA C-2 trophy with less than four miles to go.

The race horse and the old donkey dumped the water out of the boat and slowly tried to worm their way back in to the tight fitting spray skirt. The winds were not slowing down and this was shaping up to be an exciting finish if they could just stay focused and keep the boat upright. Joe and John started paddling out into the open water. Pavos and the old Polecat were struggling to get back into their seats. This was an exercise in futility but they were finally able to get back to paddling.

Joe and John were still within view when they tried to get up to racing speed again. The bilge pump was not working and the spray skirt had been severely damaged during all of the chaos in the barge canal crossing. The large waves were crashing over the gunnels and the boat was slowly filling up with water. The old Polecat was able to gauge the water depth in the boat with his feet and legs.

The boat was gradually filling up with bay water and his foot was completely submerged. It was extremely difficult to stay upright over the large whitecap waves and now it was becoming even harder because the boat was filling up with water. The boat was getting very unstable because of the large amount of water that was seeping in and they would soon be swimming.

The old Polecat reluctantly yelled out to Pavos that they would soon be swimming if they didn't head back to the shoreline. The boat was filling up with water and there was nothing they could do but head back to shallow water. Pavos was very quiet when they made the gradual turn back to the shoreline. This was the low point of the race for both of them and they were very depressed.

They had a chance to out sprint their main competition to the finish line and it had abruptly ended. Pavos and the old Polecat were not speaking to each other when they finally made it back into shallow water and were able to climb out of the half submerged boat. There was nothing to say at this point because they both knew that they would have to walk it in to the finish line from here.

This area is kind of like being in a Louisiana marsh. They started walking along the edge of the thick vegetation that dominates this section of the shoreline. Pavos quickly reverted back into his plow horse mindset and started dragging the boat behind him in the knee deep water. The old Polecat was trying hard to keep up and help but was trailing behind.

This was quickly turning into one of the hardest bay crossings that the old Polecat had ever been a part of and there was still over three miles to go before reaching the finish line. There was nothing to discuss and the only thing they could do was just suck it up and keep moving forward.

The bay front park at Seadrift was now within sight. The old finish line at the flagpole was less than a mile ahead of them when they climbed up on top of the seawall. Pavos started walking along the top of the seawall with the bow line in his hand and the boat in tow behind him. The boat stayed in the water and was consistently being pushed into the cement wall when the large waves slammed into it. This seemed to be the best strategy going forward because pulling the boat over water is a lot easier than trying to carry it over dry land.

The old Polecat offered to help any way he could but Pavos seemed to have the situation under control and was making good progress. The boat towing operation was basically a one person job at this point and a second person would just get in the way.

Pavos and the old Polecat were still moving forward when all of a sudden someone appeared out of the darkness and started walking up towards them. Mary had been patiently waiting for the Cowboys to show up when she noticed the old Polecat and Pavos walking by. Mary cautiously walked up out of nowhere and startled the old Polecat. Mary is a good friend and Lone Wolf's better half. The old Polecat perked up a little when he finally recognized Mary but he figured that she was just a hallucination. Mary kept a safe distance away and tried to start up a conversation.

"Mary, is that you"? was the old Polecat's response. Mary explained to him that she was waiting for Lone Wolf and the Cowboys and that they should be showing up any time. They were getting close to the former finish line at the flagpole and it reminded the old Polecat of a story that included Mary.

The old Polecat was in a mental fog and was fading in and out of reality after nearly 66 hours of paddling, swimming and walking. The 1992 water safari came back in focus and the old Polecat started rambling on about one of his favorite stories from thirty years ago. The old Polecat fondly remembered that he and Lone Wolf were running along the seawall with their C-2 racing canoe on their shoulders because there was a boat right behind them. They bumped the bow of the boat into the flagpole and won the USCA C-2 division by ten minutes. Polecat turned around to shake Lone Wolf's hand but he was laying in the grass and was motionless. Polecat could not understand what he was doing because they had just ran for over a half a mile with a racing canoe on their shoulders. Mary emerged out of the crowd and leaned down over Lone Wolf to help him. That is when Polecat understood what he was trying to do. Lone Wolf was just trying to get her undivided attention and that was a great opportunity to cash in.

Mary seemed to enjoy the story and the old Polecat kept rambling on while they walked along the seawall. Pavos did not share her enthusiasm and just kept staring back at the old Polecat with an angry look on his face. Pavos was putting everything he had left into pulling the boat down along the Seawall while the old Polecat was having a good time telling water safari stories.

They were now less than two miles away from the finish line and the old Polecat was more interested in telling stories from thirty years ago than he was in finishing this race. Mary said that she had to head back and that she would be looking forward to seeing them at the finishers banquet. The old Polecat desperately needed to refocus and get his head back into the game.

Pavos was starting to struggle with his balance while he cautiously walked along the top of the seawall with the racing canoe in tow behind him. The boat was constantly being slammed into the cement wall by the large whitecap waves. The only positive takeaway from that bad situation was that it was still upright and floating. The old Polecat kept volunteering to take over the towing operation in order to give Pavos a much needed break but he refused to hand over the bow line.

Joseph and Katie suddenly appeared and started walking towards them. Joseph was all pumped up and excited while he tried to explain that they were still in the top twelve overall and that they just needed to pick up the pace some more in order to stay there. The old Polecat reluctantly asked if Joe and John had made it in to the finish line yet and his response was exactly what they needed to hear.

"They must be swimming somewhere out there because their spot tracker has been stationary for a while", Joseph replied while pointing his hand towards the turbulent open bay. That was the motivating news they desperately needed to hear in order to shift themselves into a higher gear and get back to racing again. Katie was yelling out encouragement to the old Polecat but was staying a safe distance away because of the foul smell and his erratic mobility.

Pavos lost his balance and fell head first into the violent waves that were crashing into the seawall. The old Polecat quickly stumbled over to the edge of the seawall to see if there was anything he could do to help. Pavos was having a hard time trying to stand up in the waist deep water while the waves rolled over him. The bow line was still firmly in his grasp and he would not hand it over.

The old Polecat was able to kneel down on the edge of the seawall and grab his life jacket near the shoulder area with both hands. Pavos was struggling to pull himself back up onto the seawall while the old Polecat tried to help by pulling upward with all the strength he had left. Pavos was finally able to crawl back onto the top of the seawall with the bow line still firmly in his grasp. Joseph and Katie were watching the show from several feet away and could only yell out encouragement. The normal reaction for someone watching this would be just to jump in and start helping but Joseph knows the water safari rules very well because he has been a team captain seven times. They had to stay a safe distance away from all the action and just watch the rescue operation from a distance.

Pavos was back on his feet and he started pulling the boat forward again. The large boat marina was now in front of them and they were going to have to make a hard decision. Portage over dry land and stay close to the shoreline or get back into the boat and paddle the last mile straight across the open water into the finish line? Joseph was giving his advice that they needed to get back into the boat and paddle around the marina and head straight for the finish line.

There were several boats not very far behind them and it was shaping up to be a chaotic finish. Pavos and the old Polecat had a quick team meeting and decided to get the paddles back out and end this thing as fast as they could. They were still in the running for the USCA C-2 win and could possibly even finish in the top twelve. That all depended on if they could just keep the boat upright and manage to paddle across the last mile of a very rough bay to swan point.

The race horse and the old donkey waded back out into the turbulent water and struggled to get back into the tight fitting spray skirt. There was no way the old Polecat could contort his severely abused body and squirm his way back into the small opening anymore. Pavos was able to partially get his lower body back into the spray skirt but the old Polecat could not do it after almost 67 hours of canoeing, swimming and walking with no rest.

The only option left was to unsnap the spray skirt from around the stern seat and then climb back in. There would be no spray skirt protection in the stern of the boat and the bilge pumps had quit working a long time ago. This could possibly end up being a disaster waiting to happen but they were determined to keep moving forward and go down with their "boots" on.

Pavos and the old Polecat started paddling again after walking and swimming and towing the boat for almost five miles. Large waves started crashing into the side of the boat and water was pouring in through the uncovered areas. The only way they were going to stay upright and not go swimming was if they could angle the boat over the top of the waves and avoid taking on large amounts of water.

This maneuver seemed to be helping and the amount of water accumulating in the bottom of the boat slowed down some. The old Polecat noticed a large opening in the marina cement wall and yelled out to Pavos that they needed to head that way and try to find a clear route through. The old Polecat figured that since there was an opening on this side of the boat mooring marina that there should be an opening on the other side. This was a self inflicted mistake that they would regret.

Pavos and the old Polecat paddled into the protected marina and started searching for an exit point. The large marina was crammed full of shrimp and fishing boats that were tied up along the cement walls. The marina has been there for many years and the old Polecat never paid much attention to it before because it was not a factor in the race when the finish line was located at the flagpole. The new finish line at swan point is past the marina and that has made it into a potential hazard during rough bay conditions.

It became obvious to both of them that there was no exit opening on the opposite side of the marina. The next decision they would have to make would be to portage over the cement wall and get back into open water or head back to the entrance and start over. The old Polecat was determined to just portage over the wall and get back into the open water as soon as possible and not backtrack.

Pavos was not on board with this idea and the argument started. Pavos blamed the old Polecat for this poor decision and he could not hold back his angry emotions any longer. Sixty seven hours of canoe racing had taken its toll on him and he was now at the end of his rope. There was no patience left and the bad words started flying out of his mouth at a rapid pace. The old Polecat was very surprised to hear him talk that way because that is very unusual behavior.

This marathon canoe race had taken everything they had both mentally and physically and now the lid had been blown off and the bad emotions were flowing out nonstop. The old Polecat was very quiet at first and did not make any comments in return. Pavos did not let up in his emotional outburst. The old Polecat finally had all he could take and he started responding in a very negative way. This was the lowest point of the race for both of them and they were less than a mile away from the finish line. The bay crossing had turned into one of the hardest things that either one of them had ever experienced before and there was still one mile left before they could end this nightmare.

Pavos started to calm down a little and the verbal abuse finally came to an end. The old Polecat was refocused again after the one sided argument subsided. The fastest way to get to the finish line from there was to portage over the marina cement wall and get back into the open water. That is what the old Polecat focused on and the blame game would have to wait until later.

The argument stopped and they paddled straight over to the cement wall. Pavos stepped out of the boat onto a wooden dock that was submerged several inches below the water line. The old Polecat slowly stepped out of the boat and struggled to stand up again. The top of the cement wall was about six feet above where they were standing and they would have to work together to lift the bow of the boat up to the top. They struggled but were finally able to get the bow up over the top of the wall. There were no steps or ladders located in this area so Pavos started pulling himself up.

The old Polecat was trying to help by pushing upward on his lower body. Pavos made it up to the top of the wall and started dragging the boat while the old Polecat awkwardly tried to pick up the stern and shoved it forward. The portage seemed to be going well but the old Polecat was still at the bottom and had to climb the wall. An old senior citizen trying to climb a six foot cement wall after 67 hours of canoe racing was not going to be a pretty sight. The old Polecat is thankful that no one was there to film the comedy scene.

The old Polecat grabbed the top of the wall and tried to pull himself up with no success. Pavos leaned down and grabbed his life jacket with both hands and pulled upwards with all his might. Thank the Lord that Pavos still had some strength left in his arms and was able to help the old Polecat climb up on top of the marina wall. Valuable time had been wasted during this marina adventure and the blinking light at the finish line was now within view.

The race horse and the old donkey launched the boat back into the open bay and started paddling straight towards the blinking light. The swells were manageable at this point because the marina was acting as a barrier to the large waves. The wind had slowed down some but was still gusting over 30 miles per hour. The bay section they were in now was also partially protected by a small island.

Pavos and the old Polecat tried to pick up the stroke rate and get up to racing speed again but the shoulder and lower back muscles were very stiff and were not cooperating. The waves started getting much bigger and were splashing over the gunnels while they slowly made their way towards the blinking light. The boat was filling up with water again and they would soon be swimming if the water was not dumped out. The old Polecat yelled out to Pavos that they needed to head for shallow water before the boat went completely under.

Pavos was very irritated with the situation they were in and was not saying much when they quickly headed for the shoreline and shallow water. Pavos and the old Polecat were able to step out of the semi submerged racing canoe into knee deep water just before the boat went completely under. The angry emotions combined with the excitement of the finish line being within sight helped give them the energy boost they needed to quickly dump the water out and get back to paddling again.

The bright lights at swan point were less than a half mile away and they were focused on getting there as fast as they could. Large waves were continuously pounding into the side of the canoe and splashing over the gunnels. The boat was quickly filling up again and there was no way they were going to make it without dumping the water out one more time. The old Polecat reluctantly yelled out to Pavos that the boat would soon go under again if they didn't stop and dump water out.

Pavos didn't say a word in response and jumped into the waist deep water. The old Polecat did not have that kind of flexibility anymore and had to slowly climb out of the stern seat into the turbulent bay. The finish line was less than a hundred yards away and several people were waving at them.

The old Polecat suddenly realized that they could probably just walk it in from there and avoid another time wasting water dump pit stop. Pavos was in agreement because he was at his emotional limits and just wanted to get this thing over with. The hardest bay crossing that either one of them had ever endured through was just about over with. They started walking the boat in towards the blinking light that was located just a few yards away.

A bright bow light suddenly appeared in the open water to the right of them. It looked like a racing canoe and they were going to have to run with the boat in tow in order to try and beat the bright light to the finish line. Running in knee deep water while pulling a boat behind you is not an easy task after 67 hours of canoe racing.

Pavos and the old Polecat were giving it everything they had left while the small crowd on the bank was yelling out encouragement. The bad thoughts of the bow light they were seeing possibly being from Joe and John's boat were racing through the old Polecat's mentally deranged mind. The boat they were frantically trying to beat paddled in to the finish line just two minutes ahead of them. Bad thoughts and a deep depression were overwhelming his already severely depleted mental state. They ran the boat in to the finish line with their heads down.

Pavos and the old Polecat finished in the official time of 67 hours and 47 minutes. Brenda and Keifer were the mixed tandem unlimited team that finished two minutes ahead of them. Pavos and the old Polecat had passed them in the Cuero area thirty five hours earlier while they were on the bank repairing their damaged canoe.

The old Polecat was crying when Pavos walked over and hugged him. The old Polecat was stuttering while he tried to talk with tears streaming down his face. "I love you son". "I'm sorry for all the angry and bad words at the end of the race". "I can't thank you enough for being my partner and helping me get to the finish line one more time".

Pavos replied, "This was the hardest race I have ever done and I'm proud that we did it together Dad". The angry emotions were now history and it was time for Pavos and the old Polecat to celebrate with their bank crew. Joseph walked up and joined with them in a threesome hug while they tried to keep their balance and stand up in the muddy knee deep water.

Joseph excitedly gave them the good news that Joe and John had not showed up yet and were about a mile from the finish line according to their spot tracker. They had apparently experienced a bad wipeout and were trying to make it in to shallow water with their boat. Joseph told the crying Polecat that they had finished first in the USCA C-2 division and were in fourteenth place overall.

Pavos and the old Polecat were speechless while they listened to Joseph. They both figured that they had lost several places with all of the wasted time while pulling the boat along the seawall and during the marina adventure. The nearly nine hour bay crossing had taken a heavy toll on them and it was hard to believe that they had actually passed several boats in the process.

Joseph and Pavos started carrying the boat up the cement boat ramp and they left the old Polecat standing by himself in the muddy knee deep water. The old Polecat had slowly sank down to his ankles in the mud and could not pull his legs free. The straining and struggling that was required to pull his legs out of the mud caused the old Polecat to fall backwards into the water. The old Polecat was now floating on his back and the life jacket was keeping him afloat while he stared into the dark sky. "Thank you Lord Jesus for helping us get to the finish line safely". "I pray that you will help those that are struggling to get here". "I owe everything to you". "In the sweet name of Jesus I pray, Amen".

The old Polecat was floating on top of the water with his feet and ankles firmly planted into the mud bottom. There was a big smile across his face because he could not believe that he was standing (floating) at the finish line for the 30th time. Never in his wildest dreams did he ever imagine this would happen. This fascination and interest in "The Worlds Toughest Boat Race" that started fifty years earlier had finally ended with the old Polecat floating on his back and stranded in the mud. "Thank you Jesus".

Joseph eventually walked back out into the water to check on the old Polecat because he was motionless and was not responding to anyone on the bank. Darla was patiently waiting to greet him but the old Polecat was just staring into the dark night and was not talking. Joseph grabbed his life jacket and helped him awkwardly stand up before the old Polecat abruptly lost his balance and fell over again. The self inflicted physical and mental abuse after almost 68 hours of canoe racing had taken a heavy toll.

The old Polecat was having a hard time trying to regain focus and was starting to drift in and out of la la land. Joseph struggled to pull the old Polecat up again and then tried to position himself under his left arm. They both fell over backwards into the knee deep water. Joseph yelled out to Pavos to come back out into the water and help but Pavos did not respond. Pavos was very busy hugging his wife and sons on the bank and he did not want to deal with the old Polecat any more.

The race was over and the old Polecat would have to find someone else to help get him up on the bank. There was a young man standing near by that was watching the comedy show unfold. The young man was there to cheer on another team but felt sorry for the old Polecat. He quickly walked out into the water to help. Joseph got under one arm and the nice young man positioned himself under the opposite arm and they helped the old Polecat safely get up to the shoreline.

The old Polecat thanked them for the help and then reached out and hugged Darla as tightly as he could. The love of his life was there to greet him and the old Polecat was very excited to see her. They embraced each other for a long time and there was no need for words. Darla finally spoke up, "You smell really bad and you need to get out of those rank clothes".

The old Polecat started laughing at her comments and then asked where the nearest shower was located. A temporary shower had been set up at the finish line with a water hose and a spray nozzle. Darla was not going to let the foul smelling old Polecat get into her vehicle until he washed off and changed clothes and that was the final word. The old Polecat had no choice but to listen and obey.

Darla tried to help support the old Polecat while he awkwardly made his way over to the makeshift shower. Very loud laughing was coming out of the shower area while she scrubbed him down with a large brush. She then started hosing him down with cold water out of the spray nozzle. This procedure kind of resembled what it looks like when Darla is washing her vehicle or one of the river dogs. The old Polecat just stood there and hung on to the overhead bar for support while she washed off all the mud and slime that had accumulated on his abused body over the last three days.

The comedy show was finally coming to an end when they suddenly noticed another racing canoe paddling across the finish line. Joshua and Susannah, the young brother and sister team that had started the race one row ahead of them came from way behind and finished in fifteenth place overall. They ended up finishing 25 minutes behind Pavos and the old Polecat and were the second USCA C-2 team to cross the finish line.

The last report Joseph gave on them was that they were several hours behind. If Pavos and the old Polecat had wasted any more time walking in to the finish line, they would have beaten them. Joe and John were still out there swimming and had not showed up yet.

The Texas Water Safari has a long history of teams coming from way behind and finishing strong. The extremely difficult bay crossing had turned everything upside down and had opened the door for a crazy finish. "The Worlds Toughest Boat Race" lived up to its name. Pavos and the old Polecat were very fortunate to be celebrating another USCA C-2 win. They just kept the boat moving forward any way they could across the roughest San Antonio bay that either one of them had ever seen before. That determination paid off at the end.

Darla slowly loaded the old Polecat into her vehicle and headed for the rented river cabin near Tivoli. The skyline was starting to brighten up with the morning sun and the finishers banquet was scheduled to start in five hours. There was not going to be much down time available because the old Polecat had volunteered at the check in four days earlier to lead the prayer before the festivities started at the banquet. This was a great honor and privilege that the old Polecat was looking forward to and it would be the highlight of the week. There was no way the old Polecat would not show up for that.

Darla helped the old Polecat stumble up the stairs and get into bed as the sun made its glorious appearance on Tuesday morning. The old Polecat had been up for almost 75 hours at this point with no sleep and the self inflicted mental and physical abuse had finally come to an end. The old Polecat laid in bed and could not move because the body muscles had stiffened and tightened from all of the abuse. The alarm was set and they would have less than four hours of sleep before having to get up.

Darla was having a very difficult time getting the old Polecat to wake up and start moving after the alarm went off. The old Polecat was not responsive to her marching orders and she was getting frustrated. Darla then mentioned that they would not get to the banquet in time for the opening prayer if they did not start getting ready now. The old Polecat finally understood the urgency of the situation and started to slowly climb out of bed but was still suffering from severe mental fatigue. This condition would hopefully be cured after a hot cup of coffee. Some people would probably agree that the old Polecat has always been mentally challenged and this condition is normal for him.

Darla and the old Polecat loaded up and headed back to the finish line at swan point with very little time to spare. Darla dropped the old Polecat off as close to the stage area as she could get before driving off to find a parking spot. The old Polecat walked up to a very surprised race director and excitedly said, "I made it and I'm ready to lead the prayer". Allen responded, "I have been trying to call you and was very worried that we were going to have to start without you". The old Polecat replied, "I'm here and Thank You for giving me the opportunity to do this".

Allen immediately escorted the old Polecat up on to the stage and introduced him to the small crowd. The old Polecat glanced out over the sparse crowd and could not help but think to himself how different it was compared to last year. There was well over a thousand people gathered at swan point for the finishers banquet in 2021 because of the high number of teams that started and finished the race in moderate water level conditions. That was in stark contrast to what the old Polecat was now looking at. The very low river levels combined with the extremely rough bay conditions last night had significantly lowered the finishing numbers. This was very much like the old days when the number of teams that finished the race in time for the banquet were usually less than 30.

The old Polecat asked the small crowd to please bow their heads and join him in prayer. The old Polecat was still having a hard time staying focused but the Lord helped give him the right words to say at the right time. The prayer started by humbly asking the Lord to please help everyone that was struggling to get to the finish line and then included a big thank you to all of the volunteers, race officials and team captains that had donated so much time and effort into the race. The long prayer finally concluded by asking everyone in attendance to take the time needed to strengthen their personal relationship with the Lord Jesus through prayer and studying his word. The Bible warns against wandering from God and shows everyone the way home. It describes the priceless love of our Savior and the blessings that await all who place their faith in Him. Scripture is a lifeline! Amen

The words were not his and the old Polecat is not a good public speaker but the Lord helped him say what needed to be said and it was well received by the small crowd in attendance. This was the highlight of the the race for the old Polecat and everything else did not seem very important in comparison. The finishers banquet was now officially started and everyone quickly turned their attention to the fried shrimp and all of the food that was waiting to be served.

Pavos, Heather and the old Polecat's beautiful grandchildren had spent the night with Joseph and Katy at a rented house in Port O' Conner. Pavos seemed to be in a much better mood than he was at the finish line just seven hours earlier. The bad feelings between Pavos and the old Polecat were now forgotten after some much needed rest. The awards ceremony started with only 31 teams finishing in time to attend the celebration. Allen kicked things off by asking the team that had just finished to please come up on to the stage and be recognized.

The old Polecat was watching the two safari racers stumble up onto the stage after just getting out of their boat and it brought back some great memories from the 1989 race. Three Dots and a young Polecat finished in fourteenth place overall just when the finishers banquet had started after enduring through a sixteen hour bay crossing. They were escorted straight up on to the stage after getting out of the boat and the small crowd wanted to hear a funny story. Polecat told them about losing focus during the bay crossing and the wasted time they spent putting junk metal art together. Everyone seemed to really enjoy the story. That was 33 years ago and it was kind of weird how closely this race resembled that race in so many ways.

Joe and John finished in 70:56 and were called up on to the stage a few minutes later. They had spent a couple of hours hanging on to their capsized boat while it slowly floated in to shallow water just a mile from the finish line. It was painful to watch John when he hobbled up on to the stage with his injured leg in a brace. The Cowboys finished in 70:15 and were in 19th place overall. The old Polecat walked over to Lone Wolf and Mary before the awards ceremony to say hello. Lone Wolf could hardly talk and could not stand up on his own without Mary's help.

The old Polecat felt badly for his close friend and former racing partner. This ended up being a very hard race on him and Possum Belly and their six man team. One of their teammates had to be transported in to the nearest emergency room because of a medical condition while they were waiting in Seadrift cut for the winds to calm down. That was all happening around the same time Pavos and the old Polecat passed them.

Pavos, the old Polecat and Joseph were called up on to the stage to receive the USCA C-2 trophy and the fourteenth place finishers plaque. Bob unexpectedly announced to the crowd that it was the old Polecat's 30th finish. The crowd cheered and applauded loudly. Pavos and Joseph refused to say anything so it was up to the old Polecat to tell a funny story. This is what the old Polecat has become known for over the years and it was time to live up to that reputation. The old Polecat started talking about all of the walking, swimming and paddling that they had to endure through to get across the roughest San Antonio bay he had ever seen before in the water safari.

These stories were all retold in a funny way in order to entertain the crowd. Pavos and the old Polecat did not think these experiences were very funny at the time. The old Polecat could not help himself and finished the story telling with the one thing that stood out the most during the crazy bay crossing. Passing the Cowboys in Seadrift cut was the event that put the biggest smile on his face. The crowd was laughing at his comments and that is when the old Polecat looked over towards Lone Wolf and noticed that he had his head down. The old Polecat regretted saying this and quickly changed gears. "I love my Cowboy brothers after doing so many races with them over the years, but I have to admit that passing them in Seadrift cut put a big smile on my face". The old Polecat ended the story telling with that clarification and walked off the stage while the crowd applauded.

This undeserved recognition caught the old Polecat by surprise because he had never won the race in 31 attempts and his only claim to fame was putting his name on the USCA C-2 trophy six times and making it to the finish line 30 times. The majority of his old water safari friends and competitors would probably say that is really not that much to brag about after so many races.

The old Polecat learned over the years that this very unique marathon canoe race is not about recognition and awards. This race is more about pushing yourself through all of the self imposed mental and physical barriers that you place on yourself. This race is all about faith and perseverance. "I had a good run". "Thank you Jesus"

The race horse and the old donkey on the upper San Marcos river in
2022

The race horse and the donkey on the San Marcos river in the 2022
TWS

Pavos and Polecat portage over the Luling dam in 2022

Pavos and Polecat paddling through the rapids on the upper San
Marcos river

Pavos and Polecat at the finish line with team captains, Wade and
Joseph

Pavos and Polecat with family and grandkids at the finish line at
Swan point

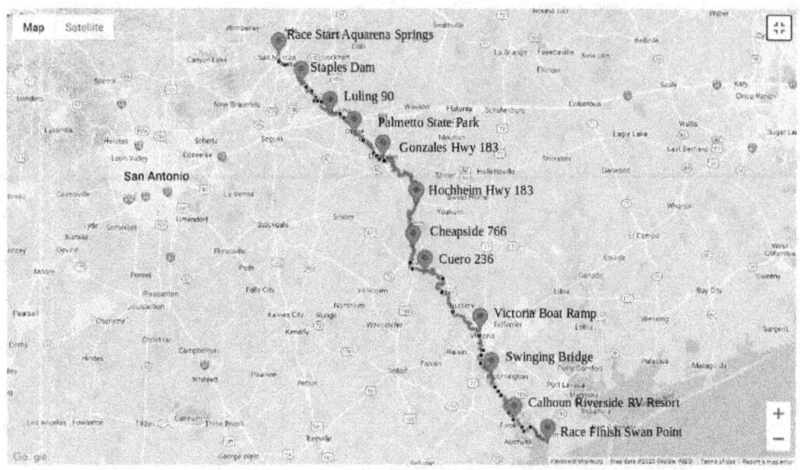

A detailed map of the TWS race course from San Marcos to Seadrift

CHAPTER 24

Summary

The Texas Water Safari has been a big part of my life over the last forty years and it has changed my perspective on how to handle the trials and tribulations that life can sometimes bring. I'm a believer that God is in control of everything but that does not mean that life will be smooth sailing because the Bible tells us that we are all held accountable for our decisions. Several of my water safari friends like to say that "The Worlds Toughest Boat Race" is the hardest thing they will do all year and that makes everything else a lot easier to navigate through.

To some extent, I will agree with that statement because when I didn't think I could go any further and my mental and physical limits had been exceeded I would call out to my Lord for help through prayer and he would always answer in his own time and in unexpected ways. The Lord does not care about what place we are in but he does care about a close personal relationship with all of us that is based on our faith and obedience. Life has its share of whitewater rapids. In one moment it's smooth sailing and then in a second we're paddling like crazy to avoid crashing through the large waves located directly in front of us. These very tense moments can make us keenly aware of our need for a skilled guide and a trusted voice to help us navigate through the very turbulent times we can sometimes find ourselves in.

In Psalm 32, God promises to be that voice: *6Therefore let everyone who is godly offer prayer to you at a time when you may be found; surely in the rush of great waters, they shall not reach him. 7You are a hiding place for me; you preserve me from trouble; you surround me with shouts of deliverance. 8 I will instruct you and teach you in the way you should go; I will counsel you with my eye upon you. 10 Many are the sorrows of the wicked, but steadfast love surrounds the one who trusts in the Lord.*

When we trust him, we can rest assured in his promise to guide us through life's rockiest passages and over the most turbulent rapids we will ever face.

Lord Jesus, thank you for your promise to be my guide in this life. Please help me to seek you out and listen to you as you direct me through the many good and bad times of my life. I pray that you will help me successfully navigate through the whitewater rapids and violent storms that life can sometimes bring. Amen.

CHAPTER 25

Dedication

This book is dedicated to the love of my life, Darla, because she had a big and important part in this life long adventure and I can not thank her enough for all of the love, support and encouragement. All three of my son's have been involved in this race in one way or another and I can not put it adequately into words how much I love them and their families. My precious grandchildren, Aiden, Josie, Landry, Graham and Augie are the lights of my life and they motivate the old grey bearded "Polecat" to stay in decent shape in order to be able to keep up with them. The best thing that ever happened to me was when I accepted the Lord Jesus as my Savior and I owe everything to him. Thank you Jesus for saving a sinner like me.